THE
COMPLETE
INTERNATIONAL
SALAD BOOK

THE

COMPLETE

INTERNATIONAL

SALAD BOOK

Kay Shaw Nelson

STEIN AND DAY/*Publishers*/New York

Library of Congress Cataloging in Publication Data

Nelson, Kay Shaw.
      The complete international salad book.

      Includes index.
      1. Salads. I. Title.
TX740.N39   641.8′3   78-5689
ISBN 0-8128-2502-0

Contents

Contents

Introduction

This book is about salads, their lore, fascination, versatility, and, in particular, their role in cookery. It is a comprehensive and varied selection of the best recipes from around the world, and it also includes valuable background information.

My serious interest in cookery began some twenty-five years ago while I was living in Turkey and Greece where I began collecting material for this book. Exploring food origins and ancient dining customs, I soon realized how important salads have been all through the centuries, even before recorded history.

I have lived and traveled in many countries of the Middle East, North Africa, Europe, the Far East, and the Americas. In the course of that experience I discovered a vast repertoire of salads that has been developed over the years by innovative cooks everywhere. From the homes of friends, noted restaurants, informal eateries, and old cookbooks and manuscripts, I've assembled what I believe is a veritable treasure trove of masterful salad creations.

I've long sought a precise definition of the salad, but after preparing this book, I've concluded that a salad can be made with virtually any food in the world and served at any meal. Since these foods can be combined in any number of ways, categorizing the salads and arranging them according to ingredients would be of little service to the reader. Its place on the menu and its relationship to other dishes will determine which salad should be chosen for a given occasion. That's the way I've presented them, even though some, such as potato salad, are so versatile that several different recipes using some of the same basic ingredients appear in more than one chapter. I have also included a number of so-called exotic salads. Many of these may not seem practical for everyday use. Nevertheless, they are intriguing novelties and certainly make interesting reading. It is also entirely possible that you may find among them unusual creations to highlight special-occasion meals.

Because the home preparation of salads has been sadly neglected in recent years, a great deal of basic information about making salads has been included, in order to insure familiarity with all the principles.

This book is entitled *The Complete International Salad Book.* Obviously, it couldn't be a compilation of every salad ever created—that would take many volumes, to no purpose. This book is, however, a complete and representative collection that will enhance your knowledge of salads, add variety and interest to your menu, and brighten the happy eating experiences of everyone who sits at your table.

THE
COMPLETE
INTERNATIONAL
SALAD BOOK

A Brief
Story of Salads

One of the oldest of culinary creations, the salad has always been an integral part of the diet in virtually every clime. The ancients doubtless dined on whatever roots, seeds, bulbs, stems, pods, leaves, and flowers they could find, perhaps seasoned simply with available herbs or spices. As people grew more civilized, however, so did their taste and manner of preparing food. Evolving cultures all over the world added refinements reflecting their individual preferences. Those efforts have left us a wonderful inheritance—an astounding variety of salad creations.

In the eastern Mediterranean lands, where many of our salad foods originated, the earliest salads were made simply with greens or herbs and dressed with olive or sesame oil and vinegar or lemon juice. Those diners of yesteryear also enjoyed salads made with onions, leeks, beets, cabbage, cucumbers, lettuce, peas, and radishes.

The Bible refers often to salads. After the Hebrews departed from Egypt, they remembered with nostalgia "the cucumbers and the melons and the garlic" that had been so important a part of their fare. In their new homeland they cultivated asparagus, carrots, cabbages, ·peas, and radishes, as well as several kinds of lettuce. The story of Naboth's vineyard reveals that King Ahab wanted the land so that he could grow lettuce, chicory, watercress, onions, and garlic. Herbs were also used for salads in biblical times, as related in II Kings 4:39.

In ancient Greece, according to Homer, salads were regarded as foods of the gods. Cooks vied with each other to create new ideas for salads made with greens, vegetables, and especially mushrooms, which they dressed with "vinegar, or honey and vinegar, or honey, or salt." Their favorite dressing, however, was made with olive oil, which they used liberally to "anoint" salads.

It is to the Romans that we are indebted for the word *salad,* which derives from the Latin *sal,* or salt, which was commonly used as a food preservative. The Romans of imperial times were extremely fond of salads. Lettuce was a great delicacy and was regarded as a sacred plant. Its Latin name derived from *lac,* or milk, presumably because of its rather milky juice. Although sometimes served at the beginning of the meal, it was more customary to have lettuce, perhaps sprinkled with wine, after all the other dishes. Perhaps that was because some Romans thought it induced restful sleep.

Other Roman salads were more exotic. Cucumbers were dressed with pennyroyal, honey, vinegar, and pepper. Vegetables were flavored with dried dates, ginger, pine nuts, coriander seeds, cumin, truffles, mint, chopped leeks, tops of scallions, and chopped olives. Such favorite salad ingredients as cabbage, spinach, melons, wild herbs, chicory, artichokes, and endive were commonly doused with a strong sweet-and-sour fish sauce called *garum,* an all-purpose Roman flavoring that served as the ketchup, soy sauce, or Worcestershire sauce of the time.

By the fourteenth century, European cooks were increasingly utilizing vegetables and salads as supplements to their heavy meat diets. Well established on English menus were salads made with several ingredients, particularly herbs. A recipe for "sallet" from *The Forme of Cury*, a cookbook compiled by the cooks of Richard II of England sometime around 1390, combined parsley, sage, garlic, young onions, onions, leeks, borage, mint, fennel, cresses, rue, rosemary, and purslane, which when washed, cleaned, and torn with the hands, were dressed with oil, vinegar, and salt.

A favorite salad of England's Henry IV was made with diced new potatoes and smoked sardines that were moistened with dressing and flavored with *fines herbes*. Mary, Queen of Scots, liked a specialty salad made with diced boiled celery root and lettuce that was moistened with mustard-flavored cream and garnished with chopped truffles and chervil as well as hard-cooked egg slices.

In Shakespeare's time, salads were called "fountains of youth" and eaten as "tonics" in spring. Marjoram was a particular favorite for salads, about which Shakespeare wrote: "We may pick a thousand salads ere we light on such another herb." Even one of Shakespeare's heroines was complimented by being called "The Sweet Marjoram of the salad bowl."

In Renaissance Italy, as meals became progressively more lavish and refined, a dinner of several courses would begin with a fruit or a salad. Obviously, considerable time and attention was devoted to creating salads. One wedding banquet in 1581 featured a first "service" of "salads decked out with various fantasies such as animals made of citron, castles of turnips, high walls of lemons; and variegated with slices of ham, mullet roe, herrings, tunny, anchovies, capers, olives, caviar, together with candied flowers and other preserves."

Catherine de Medicis, the young Florentine princess who married the future King Henry II of France, introduced novelty salads to France. This probably led to a romantic admiration for salads that even led poets to extol their virtues in verse. A lyrical poem of Ronsard describes the making of a salad that begins with tenderly picking "lamb's lettuce, the daisy with slender leaf .. the sweet-rooted rampion and the buds of the new currant bushes, the first to appear in spring." Then, the poet continues, "they will wash their herbs in the waters of his beautiful fountain, blanche them with salt, sprinkle them with rose vinegar; and anoint them with oil from Provence."

French menus gradually began to include more and more salads as featured dishes in their multicourse meals. The lengthy bill of fare for a banquet of 1571 commenced with a first course of "salads of various kinds." On another elaborate menu, however, a separate course, served after the roasts, comprised "Salads: White-Green-Hop Shoots-Olives-Pickled purslane-Lemon-Pomegranate-lettuces."

The gourmand Louis XIV was a prodigious salad eater. According to royal records, he enjoyed a large plate of salad at each meal and, as he became older and ill, had "All the year round, a great deal of salad at supper." At one of the king's official banquets, a fourth course consisted of "Eight *pâtés* or cold meat and fish dishes and sixteen raw salads, with oil, cream and butter." On one occasion, however, the Sun King received an unwanted salad. While his guests were cavorting at the supper table tossing foods at each other, a lady guest, irritated at being hit with a hard roll, hurled a "fully seasoned salad" at the king.

In the 1600s, European cookbooks listed recipes for complex or grand salads, the origin of what we now call composed or main-dish salads. They were not, however, served as such in those days. One recipe that appeared in *The English House-wife* by Gervase Markham explained that "your compound Sallets, are first the young Buds and Knots of all manner of wholesome Herbs at their springing; as red Sage, Mint, Lettuce, Violets, Marigolds, Spinage, and many other mixed together, and then served up to the Table with Vinegar, Sallet-Oyl, and Sugar."

Other ingredients for Markham's compound salad included blanched almonds, raisins, figs, capers, olives, currants, red sage, spinach, and sugar, dressed with oil and vinegar and adorned with orange and lemon slices, leaves of red cauliflower, olives, cucumber slices, and sliced cabbage leaves. A formidable combination indeed!

The first known published literary work devoted to salads was *Acteria, A Discourse of Sallets,* written by John Evelyn, a noted English diarist and horticulturist, and published in London in 1699. He, and other writers of the time, penned eloquent recipes for the Grand Sallet, much in vogue in Europe and made with a multitude of ingredients. One recipe even suggested seasonal variations for the salad: ". . . . change your Standard; In Summer you ought to resemble a green tree; in Autumn a Castle carved out of Carrots and Turnips; in the Winter, a tree hanged with Snow."

Evelyn's advice on how to flavor a "sallet" is still sound. "Every plant should bear its part without being overpower'd by some Herb of stronger taste, so as to endanger the native Savor and Vertue of the rest; but fall into their places like Notes in Music, in which should be nothing harsh or grating and tho admitting some discords (to distinguish and illustrate the next) striking in the more sprightly and sometimes gentler notes reconcile all dissonances and melt them into an agreeable composition." He also suggested that the greens, after being washed, be placed in a strainer and "swinged and shaken gently."

By the 1700s, salads were increasingly popular in Europe. Court cooks, who set the culinary styles, vied with each other to create exotic and luxurious salads to tempt the royal palate. In a single salad there might be as many as thirty-five ingredients. Flower petals, particularly those of the rose, marigold, nasturtium, and violet, were treasured flavorings. "They say primroses make a capital salad," wrote Disraeli.

Alexandre Dumas, the noted French author and gastronome,

was a celebrated salad maker of the 1800s. He regularly entertained his friends—talented painters, fashionable musicians, and popular singers—at Parisian suppers that consisted of "a pie made from some game, a roast, a fish, and a salad."

Such was the appeal of Dumas' salad that when one of his regular guests could not attend the supper, he sent for his share of the dish "which was taken to him under a great umbrella when it rained so that no foreign matter would spoil it."

Dumas took considerable pride in his ability to make salads and explained his success in words that might well guide the modern cook: "It is because my salad was not just a salad like any other salad. It is the task of the master or mistress of the house, if they are worthy of such priestly duty, to attend personally to the seasoning of all salads."

Dumas was fond of several salads that were made with eggplant, truffles, lamb's lettuce, as well as those featuring beets, which he described as best when combined with glazed white onions, slices of red-skinned potatoes, chunks of artichokes, steamed kidney beans, nasturtium flowers, and cress. He also favored a salad "of great imagination" that had five principal ingredients: "Slices of beet, half-moons of celery, minced truffles, rampion with its leaves, and boiled potatoes."

Other distinguished French gastronomes praised the virtues of salads. Brillat-Savarin declared that salad "freshens without enfeebling and fortifies without irritating . . . and makes us younger." Escoffier's salads, made with romaine, green asparagus, oranges, and celery, were given elegant names. He also created a unique Japanese salad that included pineapple, oranges, tomatoes, lettuce hearts, and fresh cream. It was artistically assembled and garnished.

In the 1900s, the intricate and ornate European salad creations gradually became less fashionable, but every country retained its distinctive and individual taste and recipes, although in some cases there were regional similarities. Europeans still have an excellent repertoire of good and basic salads made with many kinds of food—greens, meat, poultry, fish, shellfish, fruits, and cheese, among others.

Flavorings for European salads have some notable regional distinctions. In northern countries, cooks are partial to sour cream, dill, anchovies, capers, and horseradish. Eastern Europeans favor piquant or sweet-sour dressings. In the Balkans and Greece, yogurt is a common ingredient of salad dressings, and seasonings include garlic, hot peppers, mint, onions, and nuts. The Mediterranean lands favor olive oil, lemon juice, anchovies, capers, and dried or fresh herbs.

Many of the European salads and dressings were eventually brought to America. But the early development of New World salads was quite different from that of Europe.

The Aztecs, Mayas, and Incas prepared interesting salads with such native foods as beans, corn, potatoes, squashes, pumpkins, and manioc, as well as avocados, tomatoes, and other fruits that were well seasoned with lime or lemon juice, oils, hot peppers, and herbs. Most of the early salad creations still survive in Latin America.

North American Indians made simple but nourishing salads with the crisp young roots, stems, and leaves of wild plants, and they gathered greens and flowers that they seasoned with native herbs and other foods.

Early settlers, remembering the "sallets" of their homelands, created new dishes by relying primarily on gourds and root vegetables when wild greens and garden-grown lettuces were not available. Because of the short growing season, Colonial cooks prepared salads for year-round use. These were actually relishes served to enhance the bland basic fare. They were made with beets, onions, cabbage, peppers, beans, corn, and cucumbers, and flavored with spices, seeds, herbs, and vinegar.

The most popular early American salads were wilted lettuces and greens, marinated cucumber slices, pickled beet combinations, salads made with grated carrots, apples, and onions, and coleslaws, originally introduced by the Dutch in New York. Most of them were seasoned with piquant flavorings.

Early American cookbooks had few recipes for salads. Even volumes published in the late 1800s included only coleslaws, watercresses, summer lettuce salads, and potato salads, as well as others made with chicken, lobster, and salmon.

One cookbook author explained that salads were "used chiefly as relishes with other foods," and in general, salads were not favored. Men considered salads as ladies' fare, and they were even rudely dismissed as "rabbit food." Salads were special-occasion rather than everyday dishes that appeared particularly at church or community socials and were served at formal luncheons and weddings.

In the 1890s, two commercial products, powdered gelatin developed by Charles Knox and a sweet, fruit-flavored powdered gelatin called Jell-O, had a great impact on American salads. To sell these products, recipes for molded salads, aspics, and other fancy dishes appeared in great profusion. Before long, every meal worthy of mention featured a colorful gelatin salad.

A decade later, American housewives went even further and began to concoct a fantastic number of outlandish combinations made with all kinds of fresh and canned fruits, marshmallows, cherries, whipped cream, dates, nuts, ginger ale, cola beverages, cream cheese, coconuts, and raisins, among other foods. Called "decorative salads," they were served at luncheons, children's parties, and special-occasion meals. The concoctions were formed to resemble tulips, lilies of the valley, hyacinths, poinsettias, candles, Santa Clauses, Christmas trees, bunnies, or virtually anything else that struck the cook's fancy. The salads were given names to match their design.

Spiral cookbooks published by women's, church, and club groups during the early 1900s included a wide range of frozen, molded, and gelatin salads with such imaginative but precious names as: deep-sea, sweetheart, yum-yum, my favorite, mouth-watering, cool-as-a-cucumber, sunset, millionaire, under-the-sea, green-ribbon, and heavenly. Most of them were drenched and served with very sweet salad dressings peculiar to the United States.

At the same time, nutritionists began to recommend salads, especially those made with greens and fruits, for their food value. Improvements in growing methods and transportation soon made salad ingredients available the year round. Commercial salad dressings came on the market in the 1920s and could be readily purchased in all stores.

Salads became increasingly popular in the United States, so that today Americans have thousands of recipes for salads that can be found nowhere else.

Other countries have a more limited number of salads, generally reflecting national tastes or characteristics.

Africans prepare basic nourishing salads with such native foods as breadfruit, yams, plaintain, seafood, legumes, peanuts, cassava or manioc, palm cabbage, yogurt, and cornmeal, as well as greens and vegetables.

Orientals have long preferred artistic and unusual salads. The Japanese, for example, emphasize visual beauty and cut their salad ingredients into such forms as half-moons, fans, blossoms, quarter-circles, curled shavings, dice, or rectangles, which are then carefully arranged. Even sprouts, leaves, and roots are used for color contrast. Koreans favor salads flavored with hot and spicy seasonings.

The range of Chinese salads extends from tender fresh vegetables with well-seasoned sauces to exotic kinds made with dried jellyfish. Southeast Asians make salads with nutritious, aromatic young shoots and seedlings, raw greens, and their abundance of fresh tropical fruits and vegetables. In Thailand the salads are as delightful to behold as they are to savor. The Thais are masters at combining an almost endless variety of exotic fruits and other foods into lovely works of art, which might include pretty water plants, young tree shoots, and colorful flower blossoms.

The evolution of salads has not gone forward at the same pace in every country. Superstition, fads, availability of ingredients, climate, national characteristics, and even the quirks of royal fancy have had some effect at one time or another. Nevertheless, virtually every country has produced salads that are distinctive and merit an honored place on any menu.

In the past, the unavailability of many necessary ingredients was a prime factor preventing us from exploring and enjoying not only foreign salad creations but many of our own regional favorites as well. Today, however, many hitherto scarce items are readily available all year round. Now you can take advantage of every opportunity to enjoy the world's best examples of the art of salad-making.

Basic Salad Data

TO MAKE A GOOD SALAD

Buying Tips: Choose your salad ingredients with care. A salad is only as good as the foods that go into it, so every ingredient you use should be of prime quality. Select fresh greens that are crisp-looking and free of blemishes and brown-tipped leaves. Head lettuce and cabbage should be firm and heavy for their size.

Select your ingredients imaginatively. Although some salads are made with a number of foods, the secret of many successful cooks is to choose a few ingredients that marry well, complementing each other's color, taste, and texture.

Cleaning and Storing: When they're brought into the kitchen, all greens and lettuces should be washed with care and attention. For tight heads of lettuce and cabbage, cut out the core in a cone shape with a sharp knife. Then hold the head, cut-side up, under running water. The water pushes the leaves apart without bruising. Remove any wilted outer leaves and drain the head very well.

Swish delicate leafy lettuces, such as Boston and garden, up and down in a pan of lukewarm or cold water, changing the rinse, if necessary, to remove all dirt or sand. Carefully inspect each leaf to be sure that it is clean. For other varieties, such as escarole or romaine, cut off the roots or stems and discard any wilted or bruised leaves. Remove the leaves one by one and wash each individually to remove all dirt. For parsley or watercress, separate the sprigs and wash them well.

Leave tiny leaves whole. Large leaves should be torn or broken into bite-size pieces, never cut. Greens and leaves torn with the fingers will combine more easily with the dressing and will be easier to eat with a fork.

Drain all salad greens thoroughly. Pat dry with paper toweling, whirl in a wire basket, or use a mechanical spin dryer.

Wrap greens in a soft towel or plastic wrap or put in foil or a plastic bag. Refrigerate until ready to use. You should chill the greens one hour or more before you use them; that way they will be crisp and dry.

When you're ready to prepare the salad, be sure the greens are free of all moisture. Dry them again if necessary. They must be completely dry so that water won't dilute the dressing. The old adage reminds us that oil and water do not mix; that's certainly true in salads.

Vegetables for salads, whether raw or cooked, should be cleaned and refrigerated or cooked shortly before using because exposure to air detracts from their food value and appearance. Don't peel them unless it's necessary. The greatest concentration of vitamins and minerals is in or near the skin. Don't soak them in water because the nutrient elements are soluble in water. They'll be lost when the liquid is discarded.

Particular care should be accorded the preparation of raw fruits for salads. Some, such as apples, avocados, bananas, and pears, become dark after they're cut, so they must be sprinkled with citrus juice or placed in a dressing immediately afterward.

Salad Dressing: The choice of dressing for a salad is most important and should be given careful consideration. Dressings for salads serve two purposes. In some they bind the ingredients and increase the food value; in others they enhance or develop the flavor. Light oil and vinegar or lemon juice dressings go well with delicate greens. Well-flavored or creamy dressings are good for such greens as iceberg or romaine. Dressings made with mayonnaise, sour cream, or yogurt can be used for seafood, meat, or vegetable salads, whereas there are a number of innovative dressings for fruit salads.

Whatever dressing you choose, keep it simple and properly seasoned. Use only enough to coat the ingredients, since overdressing may ruin a salad. Dressings for salads made with greens and lettuces should be added at the very last minute, and the salad served at once. But the dressing should be added beforehand to salads made with raw or cooked vegetables and other foods as it will blend with and enhance the flavor of the ingredients.

Dressings made from scratch are superior to those bottled or packaged. Additional data about the use and kinds of salad dressings is given in Chapters 2 and 10.

GREENS AND LETTUCES FOR SALADS

Arugala: A pungent salad green with small green leaves, originally from Italy, which has a distinctive bitter flavor. It is an interesting addition to other greens in salads. It is usually sold in Italian or specialty food stores. Also called rocket and garden rocket.

Beet Greens: Young, tender beet greens are excellent additions to mixed salads. They are difficult to find in markets but are accessible to persons who grow beets in their gardens.

Bibb Lettuce: The aristocrat of lettuces, with a small head of tender, soft, deep-green leaves with a delicious mild flavor. It is very crisp and must be carefully cleaned to remove all dirt. Also called limestone lettuce.

Boston Lettuce: A small, soft head of loosely packed, tender leaves of outer green and inner yellow color that have a buttery feel and subtle, sweet flavor. It is very fragile. Also called butterhead lettuce.

Bronze or Red Lettuce: A garden lettuce, similar in texture and taste to leaf lettuce but with a reddish tint to the green leaves.

Cabbage: An ancient vegetable available in several varieties. Early or new cabbage, called green cabbage, has a conical or pointed head; late or winter cabbage has a tight-leaved, silvery-green, compact head; and savory cabbage, tightly crimped, heavily veined, dark leaves forming a head. Red cabbage has a very tight head, deep-purple hue, and stronger flavor than green cabbage.

Chicory: A salad green with very curly, slightly prickly, narrow, thin leaves that shade from dark green at the edges to a pale yellow heart. It has an appealing bitter flavor that enhances mixed green salads, goes especially well with tomatoes and citrus fruits, and may be used as a garnish. Also called curly endive.

Chinese Cabbage: This lettucelike vegetable, native to China, has a large, long, oval, compact shape in a head of pale green to white frilly leaves that are highly prized for their crispness. The flavor is a cross between cabbage and celery. It goes well with other greens. Also called celery cabbage.

Corn Salad: A salad green found wild in America but widely cultivated in Europe. It has small, smooth leaves varying in color from light to dark green with a mild, tangy flavor. It goes particularly well with beets. Also called field salad, lamb's lettuce, lamb's tongue, and, in French, *mâche*.

Cresses: There are a number of peppery herbs or greens that grow wild or are cultivated that are called cresses. They are known by various names, such as winter, garden, or upland cresses. The greens are good additions to mixed salads and are used as garnishes.

Dandelion Greens: The young, crisp, dark-green leaves, gathered wild or grown commercially, have a desirable, slightly bitter flavor and are very nutritious. They are good either alone or with other greens. The leaves should be picked before they flower, as afterward they become too bitter. Good flavorings for dandelion greens are bacon, vinegar, and mustard.

Endive: This small, elongated lettuce has tightly packed, yellowish-white leaves forming a small, pointed head. It is crisp and has an appealing bitter flavor. Most endive is imported from Belgium and is fairly expensive. Also called Belgian endive, French endive, and *witloof*.

Escarole: A green that looks like chicory but has leaves that are broader, less curly, and colored dark-green edging into yellow. It has an appealing bitter flavor and goes well with other greens. Also called broad-leafed endive and chicory escarole.

Fennel or Finocchio: See under Herbs.

Iceberg Lettuce: This most familiar and widely available lettuce has a firm, compact head with tightly packed, light-green leaves. It is crisp and keeps very well but is lacking in flavor. It can be torn, shredded, or cut into wedges. The hearts are particularly tasty. Also called head lettuce.

Leaf Lettuce: Crisp-textured, curly-edged lettuce that grows in leafy bunches of pale- or dark-green colors. Some are red-tipped. It is grown commercially and in home gardens. The leaves are fragile and do not keep well. Because it wilts easily, the lettuce should not be overtossed in mixed salads. The leaves are also commonly used as beds or undergarnishes for some salads. Also called garden lettuce.

Mustard Greens: The small, deep-green, frilly leaves with a peppery flavor come in a number of sizes and shapes. The tender leaves are good additions to mixed green salads.

Oakleaf Lettuce: A popular home garden lettuce that derives its name from deeply notched green or bronze leaves resembling those of oak trees. They have a desirable, delicate flavor.

Rocket: See Arugula.

Romaine: An elongated head with long, heavily ribbed, crisp leaves of green on the outside and whitish-green near the center. It has an appealing, pungent flavor and is popular for mixed green salads. Also called cos lettuce.

Sea Kale: A member of the mustard family that is cultivated for its curly leaves, which have a delicious, nutty flavor and are good in salads, either alone or with greens.

Sorrel: The leaves of sorrel, grown in many varieties both wild and cultivated, have a sour or tart taste. Those used in salads should be young and tender. Also called sour grass and dock.

Spinach: The dark-green, flat, crinkly leaves of spinach, when tender and fresh, are good in salads either alone or mixed with other greens. Spinach has a flavor that's appreciated by many, and it provides a color contrast to paler greens.

Watercress: A member of the mustard family, with small, shiny leaves that have an appealing, peppery taste. It may be served alone or with other greens and is a popular garnish. The leaves are fragile and should be carefully cleaned, washed, and used as soon as possible. The leaves wilt quickly when dressed.

Wild Greens: There are many varieties of wild greens that can be used in salads. They should be picked when young and tender and eaten as soon as possible, since old and tough greens develop a harsh flavor.

HERBS FOR SALADS

The leaves of herbs have long been favorite and widely used flavorings adding subtlety and distinction to salads and salad dressings.

Cooks around the world have a wide and varied selection of herbs to use for salads. Over the years, however, some herbs have become especially popular in certain countries or regions. Dill is highly regarded in Scandinavia. People in the Middle East and North Africa are partial to mint. Coriander is a great favorite in the Orient and Latin America. The French are particularly fond of tarragon, and the Italians frequently use basil and oregano. Parsley is an all-American favorite.

Herbs for salads should be selected and used with care and caution. It's best to use only one herb if it has an outstanding flavor. The amount to be used requires some discretion; begin by adding a little, and increase according to taste.

The other dishes on the menu, and in particular their flavorings, should be considered when you select herbs for salads. For example, a mint-flavored salad is agreeable with a roast of lamb; a basil-flavored tomato salad goes well with poultry or beef.

Some herbs are particularly suitable for certain salads; for example, dill or burnet for fish salads, tarragon for chicken salads, rosemary for meat salads, and mint for fruit salads.

Fresh herbs, particularly those in their prime, will add great flavor and color to mixed green and other salads. But dried herbs are good substitutes and are generally more available to the average cook. Remember, however, that dried herbs are stronger than fresh herbs. As a general rule, ⅓ to ½ teaspoon of dried herbs may be used for each tablespoon of fresh herbs. The flavor of dried herbs deteriorates in storage, so older herbs have less flavor than those recently purchased or dried.

The innovative Shakers, a gifted religious group that flourished primarily in nineteenth-century America, were dedicated herbalists who worked hard to promote the use of herbs in cookery. They learned about growing and using herbs from the Indians, and they imported a wide variety of herbs from Europe.

The Shakers used herbs in their cookery and salads not only as flavorings but to add enchantment to their bland dishes. The words of their manifesto expressed it aptly: "herbs stimulate appetite, give character to food, and add charm and variety to ordinary dishes."

For flavoring salads, the Shakers were particularly fond of basil, dill, mint, parsley, summer savory, tarragon, and thyme, as well as nasturtium and rose petals. Another favorite, borage, with its cucumber flavor, could "awaken in one a new sense of joy that spring is here!"

Here are some of the better-known herbs that are good flavorings for salads.

Anise: A member of the parsley family with a licorice flavor. The leaves impart an unusual, slightly sweet flavor to mixed green, fruit, and vegetable salads. They may also be used as a garnish.

Balm or Lemon Balm: The pointed, lemon-scented, dark-green leaves may be used in mixed green and fruit salads. They are also a good flavoring for mayonnaise.

Basil: The aromatic leaves of a plant of the mint family with a licorice or clovelike flavor. Basil has a special affinity for tomato salads and dressings, but it will also enhance carrot, cauliflower, cucumber, green bean, potato, seafood, and mixed green salads. There are many varieties of basil, such as sweet basil, lemon basil, purple basil, and curly or Italian basil.

Bay Leaf: The dried aromatic green leaves of this evergreen shrub have a strong, pungent flavor that will lend an interesting taste to tomato dressings, seafood, and vegetable salads, and tomato aspics. It is also called laurel leaf.

Borage: The oval, grayish-green leaves with a cucumberlike fragrance and taste are fine additions to mixed green, cabbage, cauliflower, cucumber, green pea, and spinach salads.

Burnet: The young, tender leaves with a distinct and delicate cucumber flavor are good additions to mixed green, beet, cucumber, mushroom, and tomato salads.

Capers: The unopened black or brown flower buds of a vining shrub that are usually cured and have a salty tang. They are good additions to seafood, meat, and tomato salads, and a popular salad garnish.

Celery Leaves: The yellowish-green leaves of celery are good additions to mixed green salads.

Chervil: The delicate green leaves with a parsleylike flavor will enhance mixed green, beet, cucumber, egg, and tomato salads, and are a good garnish.

Chives: The young, slender, tubular leaves with a delicate onion flavor are excellent additions to mixed green, cucumber, and seafood salads, as well as salad dressings.

Coriander Leaves: The aromatic, flat coriander leaves are good additions to mixed green salads and may be used in the same way as parsley, although they have a stronger flavor. They are sold by the bunch in Italian, Latin American, and Oriental markets, and are also called Chinese parsley, *cilantro,* or *culantro.*

Dill: The fresh and dried leaves (dillweed) give an appealing pungent flavor to cottage cheese, cucumber, egg, potato, poultry, and tomato salads. They are also good additions to salad dressings.

Fennel: The fresh leaves and stalks of fennel, a member of the parsley family, have a licorice flavor and are good salad ingredients. They may be used in salads in the same manner as celery. Fennel is also called sweet fennel, *finocchio,* and Italian celery.

Fines Herbes: A French term that means finely minced herbs for seasoning mixed green salads, as well as other dishes. Popular herbs used are basil, chervil, chives, sweet marjoram, parsley, rosemary, tarragon, and thyme. Suggested herb combinations include parsley, chives, and chervil; burnet, parsley, and thyme; and basil, chives, and parsley.

Horseradish: A member of the mustard family with dark-green leaves and a long white root that, when grated or ground, has a pungent or peppery flavor. The young, tender leaves may be added to mixed green salads, while the ground root is used to flavor some meat and vegetable salads and salad dressings.

Hyssop: The sweet-scented, dark-green leaves of hyssop, a member of the mint family, lend an interesting and unusual flavor to fruit and vegetable salads.

Lovage: The pale-green leaves of lovage, a member of the parsley family, have a strong celery flavor and may be used sparingly in mixed green and vegetable salads.

Marigold: The bright, golden, fresh or dried petals of this attractive garden flower will add a subtle flavor to mixed green salads, but it should be used with discretion. The flower is also a good salad garnish. The buds are sometimes pickled and used like capers. Pulverized marigold is sometimes used as a substitute for saffron.

Mint: An herb grown in many varieties, it has an aromatic, sweet, and refreshing flavor and a cool aftertaste. It is a good addition to fruit and vegetable salads and yogurt dressings. Mint is also a popular salad garnish.

Nasturtium: Bright, yellow-red nasturtium leaves and flowers with a delightful fragrance and a peppery, sharp flavor may be added to mixed green and vegetable salads. The young buds and seed pods may be pickled in vinegar.

Oregano: The strong, aromatic leaves of oregano, a member of the mint family, impart an interesting flavor to cheese, egg, potato, seafood, and tomato salads, and are added to some salad dressings. It is also called wild marjoram.

Parsley: A delicate, mild green herb of the carrot family, it is grown in many varieties, of which the two best known are curly and flat-leafed, or Italian, parsley. It is the best known and most widely used of all herbs and goes well with almost all salads. Parsley is also a popular salad garnish.

Purslane: The reddish-green stems and brightly colored leaves of garden purslane or rosemoss are eaten as a salad or added to mixed green salads in Europe and sometimes in America.

Rose Petals: The fragrant and attractive fresh petals of this well-known flower impart a delicate flavor to fruit salads and make good garnishes.

Rosemary: A fragrant, aromatic, strong, sweet herb of an evergreen shrub of the mint family with leaves like pine needles. Rosemary should be used sparingly since a little goes a long way. If used fresh, the leaves should be chopped, and if dried, they should be crushed or crumbled. The herb is a good addition to meat and vegetable salads.

Rue: The bitter, bluish-green leaves of rue impart an unusual flavor to chicken, tuna, veal, and vegetable salads, but should be used sparingly.

Savory: This member of the mint family comes in two varieties: summer savory and winter savory. The latter is more pungent and should be used sparingly. Savory leaves may be added to mixed green, fish, poultry, tomato, and vegetable salads.

Tansy: The aromatic, tender leaves of tansy have an appealing, bitter flavor that will add an unusual touch to mixed green salads and are also a good salad garnish.

Tarragon: A most popular herb for salad. Its pointed, dark-green leaves have a slight licorice flavor and are good additions to mixed green, chicken, egg, mushroom, seafood, and tomato salads. They are also excellent salad garnishes and flavorings for vinegar.

Thyme: A member of the mint family with small, silvery-green leaves that lend an aromatic and slightly pungent flavor to aspic, seafood, tomato, and vegetable salads.

Wild Marjoram: Another name for oregano. See Oregano.

SPICES FOR SALADS

Spices from the barks, roots, buds, seeds, or fruits of aromatic plants grown primarily in the tropics have long been treasured seasonings. Some of them are used to flavor salads and salad dressings. Most are available whole and ground. Because spices lose their flavor quickly, they should be bought in small quantities and kept in tightly sealed jars. Listed below are some of the better-known spices that are good additions to salads.

Allspice: The dried, hard, dark-brown berry of an evergreen tree has a fragrant, pungent flavor that resembles a blend of cloves, cinnamon, and nutmeg—hence its name. Allspice may be used sparingly in fruit, carrot, red cabbage, and tomato salads. Also called Jamaica pepper, pimento, and Jamaica pimento. Available whole and ground.

Cassia: The light-reddish bark of cassia from an evergreen tree has a sweet, pungent flavor similar to cinnamon, and is often called and sold as cinnamon. It may be used to flavor fruit salads. Available in buds, sticks, and ground.

Cayenne: A hot red powder made from the dried ripe fruit of several capsicum peppers. It may be used sparingly in egg, cheese, meat, and seafood salads and some salad dressings.

Cinnamon: The dark-reddish-brown inner bark of an evergreen tree has a strong, sweet flavor. It may be added sparingly to fruit salads. Available in sticks and ground.

Curry Powder: A golden-yellow blend of several spices that can be mild, rather hot, or very hot. It may be used to flavor egg, chicken, meat, rice, some vegetable salads and salad dressings.

Ginger: The pungent, spicy root of the ginger plant has a slightly lemony flavor. It may be used to flavor fruit salads as well as salad dressings. Available ground, cracked, and whole.

Mace: The brownish-orange outer shell of nutmeg has a flavor similar to nutmeg but is more potent and of lighter color. Mace may be used like nutmeg but in lesser quantity. It may be used to flavor fruit salads and vegetable salads made with sweetly flavored vegetables. Available ground.

Nutmeg: The seed of the nutmeg tree has an appealing aromatic and slightly bitter flavor. It may be used to flavor fruit, mushroom, onion, and spinach salads. Available ground or whole, to be freshly grated.

Paprika: The appealing orange-reddish powder made from ground varieties of dried peppers has a slightly sweet taste. The flavor and color depend on the selection of peppers. Hungarian paprika is the most highly regarded. Paprika may be used to flavor egg, fish, potato, and other vegetable salads, and is a popular salad garnish.

Pepper: The world's most widely used spice is available in two varieties. Both derive from the dried berries of an East Indian woody vine. Black pepper, available whole as peppercorns, or ground, is the whole berry. White pepper is the ground, milder inside of the berry. It may be used interchangeably with black pepper but in larger quantity. Its special use is to flavor foods and dishes of light color for which the dotted appearance of black pepper is undesirable.

Turmeric: The aromatic ground root of a plant of the ginger family has a beautiful yellow color and slightly bitter flavor. It is an important ingredient of curry powder and prepared mustard. It may be used to flavor egg, fish, poultry, and meat salads, as well as some salad dressings.

SEEDS FOR SALADS

Since prehistoric times, man has relished the seeds of herbs and spices for flavoring greens and salads and salad dressings. Today's varied and interesting selection from around the world is widely available both ground and whole. This is a list of some of the better-known seeds.

Anise Seed: The greenish-gray seeds have an aromatic, sweet licorice flavor. They are good flavorings for fruit salads as well as some salad dressings.

Caraway Seed: The highly aromatic, tiny brown, dried seeds of the caraway plant. They are good flavorings for beet, cauliflower, cheese, potato, and sauerkraut salads and coleslaws.

Cardamom Seed: The dark-brown, dried seeds of a plant of the ginger family are encased in three-sided, creamy-white, pithy pods. Cardamom has an unusual, pungent aroma. The seeds are good flavorings for fruit salads as well as fruit salad dressings.

Celery Seed: The small, aromatic, light-brown, dried seeds of the celery plant have a celerylike flavor. They are good flavorings for cabbage, cauliflower, fish, fruit, potato, sauerkraut, and tomato salads, as well as aspics and salad dressings.

Coriander Seed: The little, yellowish-brown, dried seeds of the coriander plant have a flavor that is a blend of sage and lemon. The seeds are good flavorings for mixed green, fruit, green pea, lentil, and rice salads, as well as some salad dressings.

Cumin Seed: The tiny, yellowish-brown, dried seeds of the cumin plant have a slightly bitter flavor. They are used to flavor some salad dressings.

Dill Seed: The aromatic, pungent, green, dried seeds of dill have a distinctive, refreshing flavor. They are good flavorings for beet, cabbage, carrot, cauliflower, cucumber, fish, green pea, potato, and turnip salads, as well as some salad dressings.

Fennel Seed: The tiny, sand-colored, dried seeds of the fennel plant have an appealing, light, licorice flavor. They are good flavorings for mixed green, fish, lentil, meat, seafood, and sauerkraut salads, as well as some salad dressings.

Fenugreek: The aromatic, yellowish-brown, dried seeds of the fenugreek plant have a sweetish, bitter flavor. They are used to flavor some salads in the Middle East and Southeast Asia.

Lovage Seed: The fragrant, dried seeds of the lovage plant resemble caraway seeds in appearance but have a sweet, pleasant, celerylike taste. They may be used in any way that celery seeds are used, but only half as much lovage as celery. The seeds are good flavorings for fruit salads.

Mustard Seed: The pungent, light or dark, dried seeds of the mustard plant have an appealing, peppery flavor. They are good flavorings for beet, broccoli, fish, green bean, or potato salads, and coleslaws, as well as some salad dressings.

Poppy Seed: The attractive bluish or white, dried seeds of the poppy plant have an appealing fragrance and walnutlike flavor.

They are good flavorings for fruit salads and salads made with sweetly flavored vegetables.

Sesame Seed: The tiny white and black, dried seeds of the sesame plant have an appealing, rich, nutty flavor similar to that of almonds. They are good additions to fruit, potato, and vegetable salads, as well as some salad dressings.

Star Anise: Star-shaped, brown seeds from an evergreen tree native to China, also called Chinese anise, have a distinctive, sweetish, licorice flavor. They are added to some Oriental salads.

SOME INGREDIENTS AND SEASONINGS FOR SALADS

Salad Oils: It's an old adage that the soul of a salad is a good oil. Certainly the choice of an oil is very important. It should be of prime quality and free of any alien aroma, since the oil carries the flavor in the dressing. The world's oldest oil, made from olives, dates back thousands of years and is still the most frequently used. In many countries olive oil is considered to be the best oil. True olive oil comes from green olives that are pressed in a vat; the best of the many pressings or grades is the lightest, which is called "virgin oil" or "virgin press." It has a light, appealing aroma. If price isn't an important consideration, the choice of epicures is still olive oil imported from France. There are also excellent, but slightly heavier, olive oils from Italy and Spain. Some cooks, for reasons of taste or economy, combine olive oil with salad oils to make blander and less expensive salad dressings.

A number of other oils can add excellent flavor and richness to salads. Among them are those made with almonds, avocados, coconuts, corn, grape seeds, groundnuts or peanuts, mustard seeds, palm nuts, poppy seeds, rape seeds, safflower seeds, sesame seeds, soybeans, sunflower seeds, and walnuts.

In America, bland oils, such as those made from corn, peanuts, cotton seeds, and soybeans, are less expensive than olive oil. There are also imported blends that combine oils such as soy, peanut, walnut, and safflower. Specialty oils from walnuts and avocados are not only very expensive but must be used sparingly and only with specific foods.

A good guideline for choosing salad oils is to select olive oil, or a combination of olive and bland oil, for delicate greens. A blend of oils is best for robust greens or when you're making highly seasoned dressings.

The proportion of oil to vinegar for a salad dressing may vary considerably according to the strength and flavor of both oil and vinegar. It's best to experiment with various kinds of both in order to determine one's personal preferences. A generally accepted formula for a salad dressing is one part vinegar (or lemon juice) to three or four parts oil.

Vinegar: The clear, acid liquid, obtained by the fermentation of fruits, grains, or other foods, has long been used as a preservative, condiment, marinade, and a component of salad dressings. The word *vinegar* derives from the French *vin aigre,* or sour wine, and the first vinegars were made from grapes. Wine vinegars have always been highly regarded and are still among the best. There are many red and white wine vinegars as well as a few made from rosé wines.

In America, cider vinegar, made from apple juice, and white or distilled vinegar, made from cereal grains, are household staples. The English are partial to malt vinegar, whereas Orientals favor red or white rice-wine vinegar.

Vinegars may be plain or flavored with such items as herbs, spices, or flower petals. Among the varieties are basil, chive, dill, mint, tarragon, garlic, chili, rose, date, honey, molasses, banana, orange, peach, pear, pineapple, and raspberry. Ancient French vinegars sold on Parisian streets as "good and beautiful vinegars" were flavored with mustard and garlic.

Vinegars not only come in many flavors but may vary in strength or tartness depending on the amount of acetic acid in them; for example, vinegar that is 5 percent acetic acid will be much stronger than one that is 4 percent.

All vinegars should be clear, of good color, and have a frankly acid taste. They should be used with discretion in salads, as too much vinegar can ruin a salad by overpowering the other ingredients or wilting lettuces or greens.

Flavored vinegars do not appeal to all tastes, but they can provide interesting, sometimes unique, additions to salads. It is best, however, to experiment with them and choose according to personal taste.

Herb vinegars have particular charm for a great many salads and can easily be made. Add 2 cups fresh herb leaves to 1 quart vinegar (wine or cider) in a bottle and let it stand, tightly covered, in a warm place for two weeks, shaking occasionally. Strain, bottle, and seal before using as needed. Or, use 1½ tablespoons dried herbs for 1 quart scalded vinegar and follow the above procedure.

Lemon Juice: The flavorful acid juice of the light-yellow citrus fruit is a treasured addition to many salads. It will point up the flavor of delicate greens and is commonly used to make dressings. It may be used interchangeably with vinegar in salad dressings and is especially desirable with fruit salads and if wine is served with the meal. The juice is also used to prevent cut fruits such as apples and bananas from darkening after they are cut.

Choose firm lemons that are heavy for their size and without any green tinges. Squeeze just before using to prevent loss of flavor and vitamin C content.

Lemon juice is available canned, bottled, and frozen, but the freshly squeezed juice is best in salads.

Mustard: Several varieties of this herb plant are cultivated for their leaves and seeds. Two major kinds (black or brown and yellow or white) are used to make a condiment or seasoning called mustard. The word derives from the old French *moustard,* which came from the Latin *mustum* or *must,* the pulp of grapes or other fruit that was once mixed with ground mustard seeds to make the condiment. Hot, semimild, and mild prepared mustards are each made with different seeds. French and German mustards are made with the more pungent black or brown seeds; American mustards are generally prepared with the milder yellow or white seeds. The ground seeds are mixed with wine, vinegar or water, and spices to make the dark-yellow or light-olive brown mustard. The English and Chinese favor powdered or dry mustard that is hot and pungent.

Mustard has long been treasured as a flavoring for salads. In the seventeenth-century the English writer John Evelyn praised mustard as a seasoning, pointing out that it was "so necessary an Ingredient to all cold and raw Salleting, that it is very rarely, if at all, to be left out."

If used in salads and salad dressings, choose either dry or hot French-style Dijon mustard. Adjust the amount to the type of salad—less for one made with delicate greens and more for one including meats.

Garlic: A member of the lily family, garlic is related to the onion. Its humble bulbous roots are made up of tiny sections, called "cloves," held together by a film of white skin. Garlic has been an important salad seasoning since ancient times. Its strong and pungent flavor and aroma have been both highly prized and disdained since man began eating it.

Dried garlic is sold loose, in strings, or packaged. It should be firm and plump with unbroken outer skin, and small green stems should not have begun to form. To use garlic, break off a clove from the bulb and remove the outer skin. Chop, mince, or put it through a garlic press before you add it to food. Garlic is also available powdered or flaked and in garlic salt and juice.

Whether or not to use garlic in salads is a matter of personal choice. It should be used, whether whole, cut in half, chopped, or crushed, with great care and discretion. A little garlic can be very potent. The dishes preceding, accompanying, or following the salad should also be considered. For example, a garlic-flavored salad is not appropriate before a delicate dessert or with a specially seasoned entrée.

There are a number of ways to add garlic to mixed green or tossed salads. (a) A clove can be cut in half and rubbed over the inside of the salad bowl before using. (b) One or more cloves can be cut into slivers and left in the salad oil to flavor it before the greens are added. (c) The clove can be minced or crushed before adding it to the salad. (d) A garlic clove can be tossed with the dressing and then removed. (e) A garlic clove can be mashed with salt and other seasonings in a salad bowl before adding vinegar and oil. (f) Garlic may be rubbed well on a *chapon,* a piece of stale bread, toast, or crusty French bread that is then tossed with greens and/or other ingredients to flavor them.

ADDITIONAL FOODS AND FLAVORINGS FOR SALADS

Anchovies: Small, flat anchovy fillets, packed in brine or oil, will give an appealing, salty, rich flavor to some salads and salad dressings and are good salad garnishes. Anchovy paste is a good flavoring for some salad dressings.

Bamboo Shoots: The inner white part of young shoots of the bamboo plant have a flavor somewhat like that of artichokes and are good additions to some salads. They are generally available in cans.

Bean Curd: A bland, custardlike soy cheese or soybean curd is a staple nutritious Oriental food that is a good addition to mixed salads. Also called tofu.

Bean Sprouts: Pale, tender soya or mung bean sprouts have a bland flavor but will add crispness to vegetable salads.

Citronella Root: A grasslike plant, somewhat like a scallion, which has a pungent, pleasant odor and distinctive lemon flavor. It is used with discretion to flavor some Southeast Asian salads. It is sold in Oriental stores. Also called lemon grass.

Coconut Milk: A white liquid, called "milk," that is made by grating and squeezing fresh coconut. It is used to flavor some Southeast Asian and Polynesian salads.

Cucumber: The familiar green fruit of a trailing vine of the gourd family is a popular salad ingredient that comes in a number of varieties. Cucumbers are usually eaten raw and may be either peeled or unpeeled, plain or fluted, sliced, cut into strips, or diced. Pickles, called gherkins, made from tiny cucumbers, are also added to salads and used as salad garnishes.

Ginger Root: A gnarled or knobby brown root that, when peeled and sliced, shredded, or grated, will impart an interesting flavor and aroma to many salads and is especially good in fruit salads. It is sold in Oriental stores and some supermarkets.

Mushrooms: Light-tan or white cultivated mushrooms, especially raw slices, are used to make salads and are also added to mixed salads. In some countries, wild mushrooms are also used in salads.

Onions: There are innumerable varieties of onions, such as chives, leeks, scallions, shallots, types of red, white, and yellow onions, and lesser-known varieties such as the Welsh onion and the Egyptian or tree onion, that are commonly used in salads as ingredients and flavorings.

Orange-Flower Water: An aromatic flavoring made from distilled orange blossoms that is used to flavor some North African salads, particularly those made with fruit.

Soy Sauce: A pungent, salty, brown liquid made from fermented soybeans, salt, and other ingredients. It has a special flavor and is used sparingly in Oriental salad dressings. Salt is usually not used with soy sauce due to the latter's salty flavor.

Tomatoes: Tomatoes of many varieties, colors, and shapes are popular salad ingredients and salad garnishes. It is best to cut them into vertical slices so that less juice is lost. Add to salads just before serving, as their juice may dilute or change the salad dressing.

Water Chestnut: An Oriental root vegetable that looks like a chestnut in color and shape on the outside but has a crisp, nutlike inside with a mild, slightly sweet flavor. Chestnuts are good additions to some salads as they provide texture contrast.

Yogurt: The tangy, semisolid cultured milk called yogurt is used to make salad dressings. It is best to use unflavored yogurt. Variations of mayonnaise, sour cream, and other well-known dressings can be made with yogurt as a low-calorie substitute.

SALAD NUTRITIVE FOOD VALUES

Salads are an excellent source of valuable nutrients. Greens contain important minerals and vitamins, especially riboflavin, iron, calcium, and vitamins A and C. Raw vegetables contribute necessary bulk to the diet. Salad oils are good sources of unsaturated fatty acids and some vitamin E. If the salad contains meat, poultry, eggs, cheese, or fish, there will be protein and B vitamins. The amount of nutritive value retained in the greens, vegetables, and fruits depends on how they are handled and prepared. To get the most from your salads, then, take care with the selection of ingredients and the preparation of each dish.

GARNISHES FOR SALADS

Garnishes provide color contrast and add to the appeal of your salad by enhancing its taste as well as its appearance. The garnish you choose should harmonize with the other salad ingredients and colors. In many countries, traditional garnishes include aromatic herbs such as chervil, chives, tarragon, and sometimes parsley and savory; flower blossoms; and croutons of bread rubbed with garlic and seasoned with oil and vinegar.

Other well-known garnishes are flat or rolled anchovies; artichoke bottoms and hearts, whole or sliced; capers; grated horseradish; green and black olives, whole or sliced; paprika; pickled mushrooms, whole or sliced; pimiento slices; gherkins whole, diced, or cut into julienne; and, for those who can afford them, truffles, thinly sliced, chopped, or cut into julienne.

These garnishes require a little preparation:

Asparagus: Cooked tips.

Beets: Raw, boiled, baked; or pickled, sliced, diced; or cut into julienne.

Broccoli: Sliced raw or cooked flowerets.

Carrots: Chopped, sliced, or julienne-cut raw or cooked large carrots; or whole baby carrots. Raw carrot curls (to make, use a vegetable peeler and cut raw carrots into thin strips lengthwise from tip to bottom. Some strips will curl naturally; if not, shape into a curl around a finger and fasten with a toothpick. Put in ice water and refrigerate several hours to crisp.)

Cauliflower: Sliced raw or cooked flowerets.

Celery Fans: To make, cut inner stalks of celery into 1½-inch lengths; make thin slits at one end or both ends and put in ice water to crisp.

Cucumbers: Flute cucumbers, peeled or unpeeled, by drawing a fork lengthwise from one end to the other so the entire surface is scored. Cut into thin slices and crisp in ice water.

Eggs: Chopped, sliced, or quartered hard-cooked eggs.

Green Pepper Rings: To make, slice a firm green pepper crosswise into rings and cut out all inner white portions and seeds. Chill in ice water to crisp.

Mushrooms: Sliced, cleaned raw mushrooms cut crosswise or lengthwise through stems, or small, whole, raw or cooked mushrooms.

Onion Rings: To make, cut Bermuda or Spanish onions crosswise into thin slices and separate into rings. Chill in ice water to crisp.

Radish Roses: To make, cut off roots of red radishes and with a sharp knife make petal-shaped leaves by cutting down sides around radishes from top close to the skin in several places. Chill in ice water until petals open.

EQUIPMENT FOR PREPARING AND SERVING SALADS

An excellent assortment of equipment is readily available to help you prepare and serve your salads. Some utensils are essential; others are helpful but not necessary. Some have to be considered a luxury.

Salad Baskets: There are many different kinds and shapes of baskets in which to wash and dry greens, most of them made of wire mesh. The simplest is a collapsible type that must be spun by hand. Some mechanical baskets can spin and dry the greens in a few minutes. There are also several types of plastic spin driers that quickly dry the greens. A colander or strainer may also be used for washing and draining greens.

Electric Blender: An electric blender or food processor is an excellent time-saver for chopping, grating, and shredding vegetables, herbs, and some other salad ingredients. These machines are marvelous aids when you make salad dressings, homogenize egg sauces such as mayonnaise and Hollandaise, or prepare mixtures for molded salads.

Peppermills: Freshly ground pepper imparts to salads a flavor and aroma that is entirely different from that of commercially ground pepper. Peppermills are available in assorted sizes in woods finished in blond, walnut, rosewood, or mahogany. Some are even made of milk glass, porcelain, pottery, pewter, or sterling silver.

Cruets: Cruets are excellent and attractive accoutrements for serving oil and vinegar. They're available in many shapes and sizes ranging from very small to quite large. Glass, crystal, and china cruets are popular. They're particularly desirable for preparing salads at the table. Then the ingredients can be poured and mixed just before serving.

Salad Bowls: Salad bowls are sold in various sizes. They're made of wood, china, porcelain, silver, crystal, pottery, earthenware, or plastic and are available almost everywhere. The most popular choice is the wooden bowl; most are round, but many come in oval and other shapes. The least expensive are made of inexpensive woods, but those who can afford them often choose handsomely fashioned myrtle, cherry, walnut, teak, or polished mahogany bowls. The ultimate in salad bowls is one carved out of a single piece of olive wood. Good wooden bowls should be of unfinished wood, never varnished or given a shiny treatment. The wood should be porous to absorb some of the good oil and salad dressing. A wooden bowl should be properly seasoned lightly with a salad or specialty oil or according to directions, before it is used and, once used, should be carefully cleaned. Many people maintain that these bowls should never be washed. Some clean their wooden bowls thoroughly with paper towels or wipe them with a damp cloth, but it is best to wash the bowl lightly with lukewarm water and a mild soap to remove any oil that has soaked into the wood and become rancid. Rinse and then dry. Some prefer to dry these bowls in the sun. Whatever you do, never soak a wooden bowl in water or put it in the dishwasher.

Serving Utensils: You'll want a salad serving fork and spoon to mix tossed salads. China, silver, plastic, or wood are nice. They're often made to match the bowl. But some metal and plastic implements may have sharp edges that could bruise or injure the greens thereby causing a discoloration of the salad and a lessening of its vitamin content. Moreover, some metallic implements may themselves be discolored by some dressing ingredients. For these reasons, many people prefer serving utensils made of wood.

Serving Dishes: For salads that are not served in bowls, select plates or platters of china, pottery, or silver that match the dinnerware or are of a color and material that complement the salad ingredients.

Additional Equipment: These salad utensils are necessary or desirable for most home kitchens: cutting knives, vegetable brush, kitchen shears, vegetable parer or peeler, measuring cups and spoons, cutting board, grater and shredder, fruit juicer, food chopper or chopping knife and bowl, food mill or ricer, can and jar opener, kitchen scales, egg slicer, garlic press, grapefruit knife, apple corer, salad molds, small wire whisk, kitchen forks, small skillet and saucepan, large saucepan or kettle, small and large mixing bowls, and glass bottles or jars for salad dressings.

Mixed Green
and Tossed Salads

Salads made with one or more greens or lettuces, simply dressed and mixed, have long been popular. In the course of time, other appealing foods have been added to the basic ingredients, and we now have a veritable galaxy of combination, or tossed, salads that are not only versatile but attractive and nutritious.

Tossed salads are very popular in America and may serve as appetizers, first courses, side dishes, or, if they include hearty foods, entrées. They are favorite attractions at luncheons and buffets, and restaurants feature salad bars where diners may prepare their own tossed salads.

A good mixed green salad, whether simple or complex, should be carefully prepared according to several specific guidelines. That basic data was provided in the previous chapter under the heading "To Make a Good Salad."

The art of making a good salad, however, is so important and often so sadly neglected that some points are worth repeating. Greens and lettuces should be as fresh as possible and free of blemishes. Once picked or purchased, they should be washed and dried carefully. Large leaves should be torn, rather than cut, and chilled until crisp. Before serving, wipe again to remove any moisture.

While iceberg lettuce is very popular, is widely available, has an appealing crispness, and can be shredded or cut, it lacks much flavor. We're fortunate to have a diverse selection of other greens and lettuces in our stores and markets, and available from home gardens.

Consider, for example, such soft and leafy lettuces as Boston, bronze, or oakleaf, as well as escarole, romaine, and curly chicory, or perhaps, dandelion greens, corn salad, Chinese celery or cabbage, or sharp sorrel. Foreign or specialty food stores are good places to find unusual greens.

When combining greens and/or lettuces, strive for harmony in color, texture, and flavor. A delicate lettuce like Bibb should not be overpowered by a hearty green like chicory; the bite of watercress will add to the flavor of romaine. Also, remember that the type of salad must harmonize with other dishes on the menu.

The dressing of the salad is all-important. While a simple vinaigrette may be the best selection for delicate lettuce, robust or hardy greens will be enhanced with the addition of mustard, aromatic herbs, or perhaps Roquefort cheese.

Greens and lettuces wilt quickly at room temperature or after dressing, so they should be mixed or tossed just before serving. The method of doing this varies with the individual salad maker.

Many cooks add some salad oil to the greens before the other ingredients and carefully toss them until the leaves glisten with a coat of oil. The oil helps to keep the leaves fresh by discouraging wilting; the leaves retain more flavor and food value. Follow up with more oil, vinegar, and seasonings. Since vinegar and salt cause the release of juices and lessen vitamin content, they should be added as close to serving time as possible.

Others prefer to prepare the dressing, put it in the bowl, and then add the greens and other ingredients. Still others merely pour the dressing over the salad just before it is tossed.

Whatever the method of preparation, don't use too much dressing—only enough to coat the ingredients. Dressings should accent, not overpower, the ingredients. Overdressed greens or those left too long in a dressing wilt quickly and become soggy. Not only do they become unattractive and tasteless, but, they also lose important food values.

All salad greens should be tossed carefully, preferably with a large wooden fork and spoon, so that the leaves are not bruised, are well coated, and the flavors are evenly distributed.

Before the popularity of ready-made dressings, many cooks combined the dressing ingredients and tossed the salads at the table. It was an event that displayed considerable showmanship. In some homes this is still done. It can be fun, and, with a cruet of fine oil and vinegar, freshly ground salt and grated pepper, and perhaps other flavorings, the salad becomes a first-class presentation.

If you serve wine with the meal, use lemon juice instead of vinegar in the dressing.

Tossed salads, sometimes termed chef's salads or given fancier names in America, may include a diverse selection of foods and usually are most delicious as well as attractive.

Among the most popular additions are green pepper strips or rings, raw cauliflower or broccoli buds, thinly sliced cucumbers, sliced black or stuffed olives, sliced red or yellow onions, onion rings, sliced scallions, sliced or whole radishes, pimiento strips, slivered or sliced carrots, cooked vegetables, tiny whole tomatoes, raisins, crumbled cooked bacon, or croutons.

Some salads call for fruits, such as diced avocados or apples, orange or grapefruit segments, melon balls, seedless grapes, sliced pears, or pineapple chunks.

Heartier salads, often served as main dishes, include some form of protein such as sliced or quartered hard-cooked eggs; strips or cubes of cheese; crumbled Roquefort or blue cheese; diced or flaked cooked fish or shellfish; or julienne-cut strips or cubes of cooked poultry or meat.

It's not always possible to give the exact amount of dressing required for a green or tossed salad because the sizes of heads of lettuce or bunches of greens vary. You'll have to taste and choose proportions according to your personal preference.

French Mixed Green Salad

In France a simple but perfectly prepared mixed green salad, generally made with tender fresh lettuce or wild or cultivated greens in season, is served as a separate course after the entrée. The dressing is generally a simple vinaigrette made with fine oil and vinegar, but it may also include a touch of mustard, chopped shallots or scallions, or fresh or dried herbs. This is one variation.

> *1 shallot or garlic clove, peeled and minced or crushed*
> *Salt to taste*
> *1 to 2 tablespoons wine vinegar*
> *½ teaspoon dry mustard*
> *5 to 6 tablespoons olive oil*
> *Freshly ground pepper*
> *2 quarts mixed salad greens, washed, dried, torn into*
>   *bite-size pieces, and chilled*

Combine shallot or garlic, salt, vinegar, and mustard in a salad bowl. Crush with a pestle or back of a spoon. Gradually add oil; season with pepper; blend with a whisk or fork. Add greens; toss. Serve at once. Serves 6.

Gundel's Hungarian Salad

Karoly Gundel, Hungary's best known restaurateur, created many imaginative dishes that are still served in his country today. This salad is adapted from a recipe in his famous *Hungarian Cookery Book*. Serve as a first course or luncheon entrée.

> *6 medium-sized mushroom caps*
> *6 tablespoons olive or salad oil*
> *1 head leafy lettuce, washed, dried, torn into bite-size pieces, and chilled*
> *1 medium-sized cucumber, peeled and sliced thinly*
> *1 medium-sized green pepper, cleaned and cut into strips*
> *12 cold, cooked asparagus tips*
> *2 tablespoons wine vinegar*
> *Salt, pepper to taste*
> *2 tablespoons chopped fresh dill or parsley*
> *1 large tomato, peeled and cut into wedges*

Clean mushrooms by rinsing quickly under running water or wiping with wet paper toweling to remove all dirt. Wipe dry and slice thinly. Sauté in 1 tablespoon oil for 2 minutes; cool. When ready to serve, put lettuce in a salad bowl. Add remaining 5 tablespoons oil; toss lightly. Add mushrooms and remaining ingredients, except tomatoes; toss. Serve at once garnished with tomatoes. Serves 4 to 6.

Irish Tossed Dandelion Salad

The Irish rely on nutritious greens, particularly dandelions and sorrel, as well as garden lettuces, to make their everyday salads.

Some of them are innovative. Knock Patrick bowl, for example, includes a center of sliced tomatoes that is surrounded with crisp dandelion greens and topped with a small round of Mitchelstown cheese and a black cherry. Serve this salad with ham or pork.

1 pound small, tender dandelion leaves
2 cups chopped celery
½ cup grated raw carrots
1 small onion, peeled and minced
About ⅓ cup sour cream
1 tablespoon fresh lemon juice
Salt, pepper to taste
2 tablespoons chopped fresh dill
1 large tomato, peeled and cut into wedges

Wash and dry dandelion leaves; cut off roots and discard any bruised leaves; tear into 2-inch pieces. Combine with celery, carrots, and onion in a salad bowl; toss. Mix sour cream, lemon juice, salt, and pepper; add to salad; toss. Add dill and tomatoes and toss again. Serve at once. Serves 4.

Israeli Mixed Green–Fruit Salad

A colorful salad to serve as a first course or luncheon entrée.

1 quart mixed salad greens, washed, dried, torn into bite-size pieces, and chilled
2 large navel oranges, peeled and sliced crosswise
1 cup scraped and julienne-cut carrots
½ cup golden or seedless raisins
3 to 4 tablespoons salad oil
2 tablespoons fresh lemon juice

1 tablespoon strained honey
Salt, pepper to taste

Put greens in a salad bowl. Add oranges, carrots, and raisins; toss. Combine remaining ingredients; pour over salad; toss. Serve at once. Serves 4.

Russian Lettuce Salad with Sour Cream

Russians dress many of their salads with their favorite rich, tart *smetana*, sour cream, an excellent flavoring for lettuce and greens. Serve this salad as a first course for luncheon or dinner, or as an accompaniment for poultry or meat.

2 small heads leafy lettuce, washed, dried, torn into bite-
 size pieces, and chilled
1 medium-sized cucumber, peeled and sliced thinly
½ cup sour cream
2 tablespoons wine vinegar
1 teaspoon sugar
2 tablespoons chopped fresh dill
Salt, pepper to taste
2 hard-cooked eggs, shelled and sliced

Combine lettuce and cucumber in a salad bowl; toss. Mix remaining ingredients, except eggs; add to salad; toss. Serve at once, garnished with eggs. Serves 6 to 8.

Provençal Salad Bowl

A good luncheon entrée.

> *2 medium-sized bulbs sweet fennel*
> *1 or 2 garlic cloves, cut into slivers*
> *¼ cup olive oil*
> *1½ quarts mixed salad greens, washed, dried, torn into*
> * bite-size pieces, and chilled*
> *1 to 2 tablespoons fresh lemon juice or wine vinegar*
> *½ teaspoon dried chervil or basil*
> *6 flat anchovies, drained and minced*
> *Salt, pepper to taste*
> *2 hard-cooked eggs, shelled and quartered*
> *2 medium-sized tomatoes, peeled and cut into wedges*
> *8 pitted black olives*

Trim green tops and tough outer stalks of fennel. Cut into wafer-thin slices; chill. Put garlic and oil in a salad bowl; leave 1 hour. When ready to serve, remove and discard garlic. Add fennel and greens to oil; toss lightly. Add lemon juice, chervil or basil, and anchovies. Season with salt and pepper; toss. Serve at once garnished with eggs, tomatoes, and olives. Serves 4 to 6.

Caesar Salad

This celebrated American salad is believed to have been created by Caesar Cardini, the owner of Caesar's Bar and Grill in Tijuana, Mexico, during the 1920s. It is often prepared at the table in front of diners and can include a diverse number of ingredients. This is the original recipe.

1 garlic clove
¾ cup olive oil
2 cups ¼-inch stale bread cubes
2 medium-sized heads romaine lettuce, washed, dried,
  torn into bite-size pieces, and chilled
Salt, pepper to taste
2 eggs°
Juice of 1 large lemon
1 tablespoon Worcestershire
10 to 12 anchovy fillets, drained and minced
½ cup grated Parmesan cheese

Crush garlic clove in a small bowl or jar; add oil; let stand overnight or 8 hours. Remove and discard garlic. Heat ¼ cup garlic-flavored oil in a small skillet; add bread cubes and sauté until golden on all sides. Drain and set aside. When ready to serve, put romaine pieces in a salad bowl. Add remaining ½ cup garlic-flavored oil, salt, and pepper; toss until romaine is well coated with oil. Break eggs into center of salad. Top with lemon juice and toss until romaine is well coated with a creamy dressing. Add Worcestershire and anchovies; toss and taste for seasoning. Add more salt, pepper, and lemon juice, if desired. Sprinkle top with grated Parmesan and add croutons. Serves 10 to 12.

English Lettuce Salad

The English have long been fond of a simple lettuce salad dressed with cream, vinegar, and hard-cooked egg yolks. It is a good accompaniment for meat and poultry, or it can be served as a separate course after an entrée.

° Some recipes call for coddled eggs that have been cooked for 1 minute.

> 2 small heads leafy lettuce, washed, dried, torn into bite-
>   size pieces, and chilled
> ½ cup light cream
> 2 tablespoons malt or cider vinegar
> ½ teaspoon dry mustard
> 1 teaspoon sugar
> 1 hard-cooked egg yolk, sieved
> Salt, pepper to taste
> 2 tablespoons minced chives

Put lettuce in a salad bowl. Combine remaining ingredients, except chives; pour over lettuce; toss. Serve at once garnished with chives. Serves 6.

Portuguese Mixed Green Salad

This colorful salad has a distinctive flavor derived from a Portuguese mixture of crushed garlic, mint, salt, and olive oil. Serve as a first course or as an accompaniment for seafood.

> 1 medium-sized head lettuce
> 1 medium-sized head escarole
> 2 peeled garlic cloves
> 2 tablespoons chopped fresh mint
> ½ teaspoon salt
> ⅓ cup olive oil
> 2 tablespoons fresh lemon juice
> Pepper to taste
> 1 large red onion, peeled, sliced thinly, and separated
>   into rings
> 8 pitted black olives
> 1 large tomato, peeled and cut into wedges
> 2 tablespoons chopped fresh coriander or parsley

Wash and dry lettuce and escarole; tear into bite-size pieces and refrigerate. Crush garlic, mint, and salt in a salad bowl; add oil; mix well; leave 30 minutes. Add greens; toss lightly. Add lemon juice, pepper, and onion rings; toss. Serve at once, garnished with olives, tomatoes, and coriander. Serves 4 to 6.

Green Salad from Gascony

The remote region of Gascony in southwestern France has an imaginative rustic cuisine that relies heavily on game, pork, cornmeal, potatoes, and other vegetables. Most of the characteristic salads are basic types that include one or two ingredients and are well flavored with a garlic oil and vinegar dressing. Serve as an accompaniment for game or meat.

1 medium-sized head chicory
1 medium-sized head escarole
1 2-inch square stale bread moistened with olive oil and
  vinegar
1 peeled garlic clove, cut in half
⅓ cup olive oil
3 cold, cooked, medium-sized potatoes, peeled and sliced
1 medium-sized red onion, peeled and chopped
2 tablespoons wine vinegar
Salt, pepper to taste
2 tablespoons chopped fresh tarragon or 1 teaspoon dried
  tarragon

Wash and dry chicory and escarole; tear into bite-size pieces; refrigerate. When ready to serve, rub bread square well with garlic; put in a salad bowl. Add chicory, escarole, and oil; toss lightly. Remove and discard bread square. Add potatoes and onion; toss. Combine remaining ingredients; add to salad; toss. Serve at once. Serves 6 to 8.

Sicilian Romaine-Tomato Salad

This is a good salad to serve as a first course before an Italian pasta entrée such as spaghetti and meatballs, or as a separate course after an entrée of roast lamb, beef, or pork.

1 or 2 peeled garlic cloves, cut into slivers
⅓ cup olive oil
1 large head romaine, washed, dried, torn into bite-size
  pieces, and chilled
2 tablespoons fresh lemon juice
1 cup croutons
½ teaspoon dried basil or oregano
Salt, pepper to taste
2 medium-sized tomatoes, peeled and cut into wedges
⅓ cup grated Parmesan cheese
4 to 6 flat anchovy fillets, drained and minced

Put garlic slivers and oil in a salad bowl; leave 1 hour. When ready to serve, remove and discard garlic. Add romaine; toss lightly. Add lemon juice, croutons, basil or oregano, salt, and pepper; toss. Mix in tomatoes, cheese, and anchovies; toss. Serves 4 to 6.

Swiss Green Salad with Cheese

The best cheese for this salad is flavorful Emmentaler. Serve the salad as a first course or accompaniment for roast meat or steaks.

1 medium-sized head chicory
1 small head leafy lettuce
½ pound Swiss cheese, cut into cubes or slivers
2 tablespoons drained capers
½ cup sour cream
2 tablespoons wine vinegar
1 to 2 teaspoons sharp prepared mustard
1 teaspoon prepared horseradish
Salt, pepper to taste.

Wash and dry chicory and lettuce; tear into bite-size pieces and refrigerate. When ready to serve, put greens in a salad bowl. Add cheese and capers; toss lightly. Combine remaining ingredients; pour over salad; toss. Serve at once. Serves 4 to 6.

Mexican Vegetable-Green Salad

A colorful salad to serve with roast turkey or broiled chicken.

1 large head lettuce
2 small zucchini, ends trimmed, washed, dried, and
    sliced
2 cups cold, cooked fresh corn or canned whole-kernel
    corn, drained
½ cup diced Jack or Cheddar cheese
2 medium-sized tomatoes, peeled and cut in wedges
½ red onion, peeled and thinly sliced
1 canned green chili, chopped (optional)
⅓ cup salad oil
Juice of 1 lemon
½ teaspoon dried oregano
Salt, pepper to taste

Remove and discard any wilted lettuce leaves. Cut out core. Wash and dry lettuce; tear into bite-size pieces and refrigerate. When ready to serve, put lettuce in a salad bowl. Add zucchini, corn, cheese, tomatoes, onion, and chili; toss lightly. Combine remaining ingredients; pour over salad; toss. Serve at once. Serves 4 to 6.

Ardennes Mimosa Sorrel Salad

Sorrel, sour or acid in flavor, is a highly prized salad green in many countries. Spinach may be substituted for it, but a little lemon juice should be added to the dressing to provide a tart flavor.

> *2 hard-cooked eggs, shelled*
> *4 cups sorrel leaves, washed, trimmed, dried, and chilled*
> *4 scallions, cleaned and sliced, with some tops*
> *3 to 4 tablespoons olive or salad oil*
> *1 tablespoon wine vinegar*
> *Salt, pepper to taste*

Chop egg whites and sieve yolks; combine and set aside. When ready to serve, put sorrel and scallions in a salad bowl; toss lightly. Combine remaining ingredients, except eggs, and pour over salad; toss. Serve at once sprinkled with eggs. Serves 4.

Ensalada Sevillana

This attractive salad from Spain's lovely city of Seville is a good dinner first course or luncheon entrée.

1 medium-sized head escarole
1 small head leafy lettuce
1 chapon (2-inch square stale or crusty French bread
  rubbed with garlic)
⅓ cup olive oil
2 canned pimientos, drained and cut into strips
½ pound cooked ham, cut into julienne strips
2 tablespoons wine vinegar
salt, pepper to taste
12 pitted black olives
2 tablespoons chopped fresh parsley

Wash and dry escarole and lettuce; tear into bite-size pieces and refrigerate. When ready to serve, rub salad bowl with *chapon*. Add salad greens and oil; toss lightly. Remove and discard *chapon*. Add remaining ingredients; toss. Serve at once. Serve 4 to 6.

Luxembourg Lamb's Lettuce Salad

A good salad to serve as a separate course after a hearty meat stew, roast, or other entrée. Spinach may be substituted for the lamb's lettuce, if desired, but the flavor will not be the same. Another name for lamb's lettuce is corn salad.

1 bunch lamb's lettuce or corn salad
1 small head leafy lettuce
⅓ cup olive or salad oil
6 cold, cooked or canned small beets, drained and sliced
  thinly
3 medium-sized stalks celery, cleaned and chopped

3 scallions, cleaned and sliced, with some tops
1 tablespoon wine vinegar
Salt, pepper to taste

Remove any stems from the lamb's lettuce. Wash and dry lettuces; cut into bite-size pieces and refrigerate. When ready to serve, put in a salad bowl; add oil; toss lightly. Add remaining ingredients; toss. Serve at once. Serves 4 to 6.

Venezuelan Spinach-Avocado Salad

A good salad for an outdoor barbecue of grilled meat or poultry.

1 package (10 ounces) fresh spinach
1 large onion, peeled, sliced, and separated into rings
2 hard-cooked eggs, shelled and chopped
1 medium-sized ripe avocado, peeled and cubed
¼ cup olive or salad oil
Juice of ½ lemon
1 tablespoon wine vinegar
1 garlic clove, crushed
Salt, pepper to taste
3 tablespoons chopped fresh coriander or parsley

Wash spinach; cut off tough stems; remove bruised or wilted leaves; dry; tear large leaves into bite-size pieces; refrigerate. When ready to serve, put in a salad bowl. Add onion, eggs, and avocado; toss lightly. Combine remaining ingredients, except coriander or parsley; toss. Serve at once sprinkled with coriander or parsley. Serves 4.

Salade Forestière

Although *forestière* is a French word meaning "of or pertaining to forests," in cookery it refers to dishes that include mushrooms. Once these fungi were found in forests, but today cultivated mushrooms may be purchased in our stores. Serve as a first course or as an accompaniment for poultry or beef.

>*2 small heads leafy lettuce, washed, dried, torn into small pieces, and chilled*
>*½ pound fresh mushrooms, cleaned and sliced*
>*⅓ cup salad oil*
>*1 tablespoon wine vinegar*
>*½ teaspoon dried basil*
>*Salt, pepper to taste*
>*3 tablespoons chopped fresh parsley*

Put lettuce in a salad bowl. Add mushrooms and oil; toss lightly. Add remaining ingredients; toss. Serve at once. Serves 6.

Roman Spinach Salad

Romans are devotees of spinach, which they utilize in a number of interesting dishes such as this salad. Serve as a first course or a separate course after a veal or pork entrée.

>*1 pound fresh spinach leaves*
>*⅓ cup salad oil*
>*6 scallions, cleaned and sliced, with some tops*
>*½ cup sliced radishes*

> *2 cups sliced raw cauliflower flowerets, washed and*
> *dried*
> *2 to 3 tablespoons wine vinegar or fresh lemon juice*
> *1 garlic clove, minced or curshed*
> *6 flat anchovies, drained and minced*
> *Salt, pepper to taste*

Wash spinach; cut off tough stem ends; remove bruised leaves; dry; refrigerate or put in a salad bowl. Add oil; toss lightly. Add remaining ingredients; toss. Serve at once. Serves 4.

Spanish Green Salad with Oranges

A superior salad from Iberia to serve as a first course or accompaniment for seafood.

> *½ garlic clove, split*
> *3 to 4 tablespoons olive oil*
> *2 tablespoons fresh lemon juice*
> *Salt, pepper to taste*
> *1½ quarts mixed salad greens, washed, dried, torn into*
> *bite-size pieces, and chilled*
> *1 large red onion, peeled, sliced thinly, and separated*
> *into rings*
> *2 navel oranges, peeled, white membranes removed, and*
> *sliced crosswise*

Combine garlic, oil, lemon juice, salt, and pepper in a small jar or bowl; leave 1 hour. When ready to serve, put greens, onions, and oranges in a salad bowl; toss. Shake dressing and pour over salad; toss. Remove and discard garlic. Serve at once. Serves 4.

Italian Tossed Salad

This is a good salad for a luncheon or supper entrée, or the ingredients may be doubled and the salad served at a buffet.

1 medium-sized head romaine
1 small head leafy lettuce
2 peeled garlic cloves, cut in slivers
About ½ cup olive oil
1 cup cold, cooked or canned chick-peas, drained
1 cup cold, cut, cooked green beans
½ cup Mozzarella cheese cubes
½ teaspoon dried oregano
Salt, pepper to taste
2 to 3 tablspoons wine vinegar
2 medium-sized tomatoes, peeled and cut into wedges

Wash and dry romaine and lettuce; tear into bite-size pieces and refrigerate. Put garlic and oil in a salad bowl; leave 30 minutes. When ready to serve, remove garlic from oil and discard. Add romaine and lettuce; toss lightly. Add remaining ingredients, except tomatoes; toss. Serve at once, garnished with tomatoes. Serves 6 to 8.

Alsatian Dandelion Salad

A good salad to serve with game, pork, or beef stews.

1 pound young, tender dandelion leaves
4 thin slices bacon, chopped
2 tablespoons wine vinegar

2 shallots or scallions, cleaned and minced
2 garlic cloves, crushed or minced
Salt, pepper to taste
2 tablespoons olive oil

Wash dandelions; cut off roots and any damaged leaves; dry; chill. Fry bacon in a small skillet until crisp; drain on paper toweling. When ready to serve, add vinegar to bacon drippings, and heat. Put dandelions, shallots or scallions, garlic, salt, and pepper in a salad bowl; add oil; toss lightly. Add heated bacon dripping–vinegar mixture; toss. Serve at once, garnished with crisp bacon. Serves 4.

Viennese Red Cabbage Salad

An appealing tossed salad that features red cabbage and is a good accompaniment for pork, game, or poultry.

1 medium-sized head red cabbage
3 tart red apples, cored and sliced
4 scallions, cleaned and sliced, with some tops
About ½ cup sour cream
2 tablespoons fresh lemon juice
1 teaspoon sharp prepared mustard
Salt, pepper to taste

Trim cabbage and cut into halves; remove any wilted leaves; cut out core; shred finely; wash; dry; refrigerate. When ready to serve, combine with apples and scallions in a salad bowl. Mix remaining ingredients; add to salad; toss. Serves 4 to 6.

Arabian Mixed Green Salad

Sesame-seed oil adds a different flavor to this mixed salad.

> *4 cups mixed salad greens, washed, dried, torn into bite-*
> *size pieces, and chilled*
> *1 cup fresh watercress leaves, washed, dried, and chilled*
> *1 cup fresh mint leaves, washed, dried, and chilled*
> *½ cup sliced scallions, with some tops*
> *⅓ cup sesame or salad oil*
> *2 to 3 tablespoons fresh lemon juice*
> *Salt, pepper to taste*
> *¼ cup diced Feta or farmer cheese*
> *2 medium-sized tomatoes, peeled and cut into wedges*

Combine greens, watercress, mint, and scallions in a salad bowl. Mix oil, lemon juice, salt, and pepper; add to salad; toss. Serve topped with cheese and garnished with tomatoes. Serves 4 to 6.

Caribbean Salad Bowl

Serve with seafood or poultry.

> *1 small head leafy lettuce, washed, dried, torn into bite-*
> *size pieces, and chilled*
> *1 medium-sized ripe avocado, peeled and sliced*
> *1 cup grapefruit sections, white membranes removed*
> *1 cup orange sections, white membranes removed*
> *3 to 4 tablespoons salad oil*

1 to 2 tablespoons fresh lime or lemon juice
Dash cayenne or few drops Tabasco
Salt, pepper to taste
2 medium-sized tomatoes, peeled and cut into wedges

Combine lettuce, avocado, grapefruit, and orange sections in a salad bowl; toss. Add remaining ingredients, except tomatoes, and toss. Serve at once, garnished with tomatoes. Serves 4 to 6.

California Green Goddess Salad

The well known Green Goddess salad dressing was created at the San Francisco Palace Hotel in honor of the English actor George Arliss, who was starring in William Archer's play, *The Green Goddess*, in the early 1920s. There are many versions of the salad, which is enhanced by the dressing. This is one of the best.

2 tablespoons minced chives
2 tablespoons minced scallions
¼ cup chopped fresh parsley
4 to 6 flat anchovies, minced
¼ cup tarragon vinegar
2 teaspoons chopped fresh tarragon
1 cup mayonnaise
Salt, pepper to taste
2 quarts bite-size pieces salad greens, washed, dried, and
    chilled
2 medium-sized tomatoes, peeled and cut into wedges

Combine first seven ingredients in a small bowl or jar; season with salt and pepper; mix well. Refrigerate, covered, overnight or for several hours to blend flavors. When ready to serve, put greens in a salad bowl; add as much mayonnaise mixture as desired; toss. Garnish with tomatoes and serve at once. Serves 6 to 8.

Note: Any leftover dressing can be refrigerated. It will keep several days.

Austrian Spinach Salad

A good salad to serve with a casserole, stew, or meat loaf.

1 package (10 ounces) fresh spinach
4 slices thin bacon, chopped
1 cup stale bread cubes
1 garlic clove, crushed
3 tablespoons olive or salad oil
1 tablespoon wine vinegar
Salt, pepper to taste
2 hard-cooked eggs, shelled and finely chopped

Wash and dry spinach; remove tough stem ends and bruised leaves; tear large leaves into small pieces and refrigerate. Fry bacon until crisp; remove with a slotted spoon and drain on absorbent paper. Sprinkle bread cubes with garlic; add to bacon drippings; sauté until golden. Remove cubes with a slotted spoon and drain on absorbent paper. When ready to serve, put spinach in a salad bowl; add oil; toss. Add bacon, bread cubes, and remaining ingredients; toss. Serve at once. Serves 4.

Bulgarian Herbed Mixed Green Salad

In Bulgaria, flavorful sweet green and red peppers are favorite additions to mixed salads such as this one.

> 1 large head romaine, washed, dried, torn into bite-size
>   pieces, and chilled
> 1 large green pepper, cleaned and cut into strips
> 1 large red pepper, cleaned and cut into strips
> 1 medium-sized cucumber, peeled and sliced thinly
> 4 scallions, cleaned and sliced, with some tops
> ½ cup plain yogurt
> 2 tablespoons fresh lemon juice
> 1 garlic clove, crushed
> 2 tablespoons chopped fresh herbs (chervil, dill, parsley,
>   tarragon, or basil)
> Salt, pepper to taste

Combine romaine, peppers, cucumbers, and scallions in a salad bowl. Mix remaining ingredients; add to salad; toss. Serve at once. Serves 6.

Hong Kong Mixed Salad Bowl

A good salad to serve with seafood or pork.

> 2 quarts celery or (Chinese) cabbage, washed, dried, torn
>   into bite-size pieces, and chilled
> 1 cup fresh or canned bean sprouts, washed and dried
> 1 cup sliced white or red radishes
> ½ cup sliced scallions, with some tops
> 1 large carrot, scraped and thinly sliced

⅓ cup peanut or salad oil
2 tablespoons white vinegar
1 tablespoon soy sauce
⅓ cup sliced water chestnuts or bamboo shoots

Put cabbage, bean sprouts, radishes, scallions, and carrots in a salad bowl; toss. Combine remaining ingredients, except water chestnuts; add to salad. Serve at once, garnished with water chestnuts. Serves 4.

Greek Mixed Salad

This is a very attractive salad that can be made with a diverse selection of ingredients. Add also sliced hot peppers, watercress, sliced cooked beets, cubed cooked potatoes, and diced avocados, if desired.

1 medium-sized head romaine, washed, dried, torn into
  bite-size pieces, and chilled
About ⅓ cup olive oil
1 medium-sized cucumber, peeled and thinly sliced
2 medium-sized green peppers, cleaned and cut into
  slivers
1 cup sliced red radishes
3 tablespoons fresh lemon juice
½ teaspoon dried oregano
Salt, pepper to taste
½ cup diced Feta or farmer cheese
8 pitted black olives
2 large tomatoes, peeled and cut into wedges

Put romaine pieces in a salad bowl. Add 2 tablespoons oil and toss lightly to coat romaine. Add cucumber, green peppers, and radishes; toss. Combine remaining oil, lemon juice, oregano, salt, and pepper; toss. Serve at once garnished with cheese, olives, and tomatoes. Serves 6 to 8.

French Watercress Salad

Watercress has long been esteemed as a salad ingredient in France as well as other European countries. Not only does it have an appealing, peppery flavor, but it is also valued for its high vitamin content.

2 bunches watercress
⅓ cup sliced scallions, with some tops
2 hard-cooked eggs, shelled and sliced
3 to 4 tablespoons olive oil
1 tablespoon wine vinegar
Salt, pepper to taste
2 medium-sized tomatoes, peeled and cut into wedges

Wash watercress well; cut leaves from stems, discarding any wilted ones. Wipe dry and refrigerate or combine with scallions and eggs in a salad bowl. Add oil, vinegar, salt, and pepper; toss. Serve at once, garnished with tomatoes. Serves 4.

Appetizer and
First-Course Salads

Over the years, ingenious cooks have created an appealing variety of attractive and delectable salads that may be served as appetizers, at a party, or as a first course at luncheon and dinner.

These appetizer salads vary from a simple bowl of well-dressed mixed greens to an elegant combination of compatible foods. The salad you choose is important to the menu because as a precursor to the main part of the meal, it sets the scene and must attract the eye, whet the appetite, and please the palate.

Since salads have long been favorite fare at pre-meal gatherings everywhere, many countries have creative recipes and traditional serving platters for them.

In Near Eastern and Mediterranean areas, salads made with local vegetables, mushrooms, chick-peas, rice, yogurt, legumes, cracked wheat, seafood, or other foods, bathed in flavorful olive oil and lemon juice or other dressings, are still served as important components of the array of appetizers.

Imaginative salads of vegetables, fruits, seafood, meats, and poultry are also featured in such galaxies of appetizers as the Scandinavian *smorgasbord,* Russian *zakuski,* German *Vorspeisen,* and Italian *antipasti.*

In France, significant elements of the pre-luncheon *hors d'oeuvre* are light salads artfully made with one or more vegetables in season, or a mixture of raw and cooked vegetables, meats, poultry, or seafood bound with a well-seasoned dressing.

Cooks in the Orient utilize such favorite foods as bean sprouts, raw vegetables, and seafood in making appetizers, and those of Southeast Asia make skillful use of native spices and other exotic flavorings. The avocado and other fruits or seafood are popular in Latin American and Caribbean salads; Africans often favor highly seasoned greens, and vegetables, as well as fruit salads.

Salad as a first course has been a popular custom on the West Coast of the United States for some time, and no one seems to know exactly how or why the tradition began. The mystery notwithstanding, Californians continue to make their marvelous fresh fruits and vegetables, seafood, and greens into imaginative and attractive dishes.

In recent years, the first-course salad has gained wide appeal throughout America, particularly in restaurants, where it provides the diner with something good to eat while waiting for the entrée. That eliminates the need for another first course and a later salad course.

The most popular first-course salad is one of mixed greens, with or without other foods, which may range from croutons and cheese to smoked salmon or turkey. Such a salad should be carefully prepared with only the freshest and finest ingredients, and be served attractively. Some of the recipes in the preceding chapter make excellent first-course salads, too.

Here's a round-the-world appetizer salad sampler:

West African Avocado Salad

The tropical avocado, or alligator pear, is a treasured element of salads in many countries, especially in West Africa. Its appealing, delicate, nutty-flavored flesh with a buttery texture may be served unpeeled in halves or peeled in sections, with only salt, lemon or lime juice, or various salad dressings. Very often the halves are stuffed; or the fruit may be combined with other foods. Because the avocado discolors quickly when cut, it must be sprinkled at once with lemon juice or vinegar. This is an appealing salad for a first course at dinner.

> *1 head leafy lettuce, washed, dried, and refrigerated*
> *3 medium-sized ripe avocados, peeled, pits removed, and*
>   *cut into rings*
> *3 hard-cooked eggs, shelled and sliced*
> *3 medium-sized tomatoes, peeled and sliced*
> *1 cup chopped peanuts*
> *⅓ cup peanut or salad oil*
> *Juice of 1 lemon*
> *2 tablespoons wine vinegar*
> *¼ teaspoon cayenne*
> *Salt, pepper to taste*

Arrange lettuce leaves in a salad bowl. Place avocado rings, egg and tomato slices, in circles over lettuce. Sprinkle with chopped peanuts. Combine remaining ingredients in a small jar; shake well and pour over salad. Serve at once. Serves 6 to 8.

Korean Bean Sprout Salad

The pale, tender shoots or sprouts of the soya or mung bean are a staple Oriental food, often used in salads. They not only add crispness but are valued for their rich vitamin C content. Because of their bland flavor, bean sprout salads should be well seasoned. Although canned sprouts are widely available, the fresh variety sold in some supermarkets and Oriental food stores is best. Serve it as a first course for luncheon or supper.

> *1 pound fresh bean sprouts or one 1-pound can bean*
> *   sprouts, drained*
> *2 cups shredded raw carrots*
> *½ cup diced celery*
> *1 cup raw spinach leaves, washed and dried*
> *¼ cup sliced scallions, with some tops*
> *3 tablespoons soy sauce*
> *3 tablespoons sesame or peanut oil*
> *2 garlic cloves, crushed*
> *½ teaspoon sugar*
> *Pepper to taste*
> *Crisp lettuce leaves, washed and dried*

If fresh bean sprouts are used, place in a colander, pour boiling water over them, and drain thoroughly. Canned bean sprouts may merely be drained. Mix with carrots, celery, spinach, and scallions in a large bowl. Combine remaining ingredients, except lettuce, and mix well. Pour over vegetables; toss lightly. To serve, arrange lettuce leaves in a bowl or serving dish and spoon salad over them. Serves 4 to 6.

Aïda Salad

This French salad is an attractive first course for a special luncheon.

>1 head chicory, washed, dried, torn into bite-sized pieces,
>   and chilled
>1 package (9 ounces) frozen artichoke hearts, cooked,
>   chilled, and cut into halves
>1 canned pimiento, drained and cut into strips
>2 hard-cooked egg whites, chopped
>⅓ cup olive or salad oil
>2 tablespoons wine vinegar
>Salt, pepper to taste
>2 medium-sized tomatoes, peeled and sliced

Place chicory in a salad bowl. Top with artichoke hearts, pimiento strips, and chopped egg whites. Combine remaining ingredients, except tomatoes, and pour over salad. Toss lightly. Add tomatoes; toss. Serve at once. Serves 4.

Tunisian Mixed Pepper Salad

North Africans are devotees of salads made with flavorful sweet green peppers and plump red tomatoes that are grilled over charcoal and then peeled and seeded. This traditional dish, called *mechwiga* or *meshwya*, is subject to variation. Garnishes of tuna fish and pickled lemons may be added, if desired. It's a good salad to serve with pre-meal drinks.

6 large green peppers
6 large tomatoes
3 large onions
4 garlic cloves, crushed
About ½ cup olive oil
Juice of 1 large lemon
3 tablespoons chopped fresh coriander or parsley
Salt, pepper to taste
2 hard-cooked eggs, shelled and cut into quarters
6 pitted black olives
6 pitted or stuffed green olives
2 tablespoons drained capers
6 flat anchovies, drained

Broil peppers, tomatoes, and onions until skins blister, turning once or twice while broiling. Peel off skins; remove pepper and tomatoe seeds; cut vegetables into small pieces. Combine vegetables with garlic, oil, lemon juice, coriander or parsley, salt, and pepper; spoon onto a plate, shaping into a mound. Top and surrounded with remaining ingredients. Serve with pieces of pita bread or crusty French bread. Serves 4 to 6.

Rumanian Leek-Mushroom Salad

Rumanians are fond of salads made with cold, cooked vegetables in well-seasoned dressings. These are served with other foods as appetizers, or *mezelicuri.* This salad may be served alone as an appetizer, or with stuffed, hard-cooked eggs and slices of cold spicy sausage as accompaniments.

6 medium-sized leeks
Salt
24 medium-sized fresh mushrooms
12 pitted black or green olives

⅓ to ½ cup olive or salad oil
1 lemon, sliced
¼ teaspoon dried thyme
1 teaspoon fennel seeds
1 bay leaf
Pepper to taste
3 tablespoons chopped fresh parsley

Cut off green leaves of leeks and trim roots. Wash white parts well to remove any sand. Cut into 1½-inch pieces. Cook in a little salted boiling water, covered, until tender, about 12 minutes. Drain and cool. Clean mushrooms by rinsing quickly or wiping with wet paper toweling to remove all dirt. Snip off any tough stem ends. Cook in salted boiling water, covered, 5 minutes. Drain and cool. Combine leeks, mushrooms, and olives with remaining ingredients, except parsley, in a bowl. Refrigerate, covered, 2 to 3 days, stirring occasionally. Remove and discard lemon slices and bay leaf. Sprinkle with parsley. Serves 6.

Portuguese Chick-Pea Salad

Chick-peas, or garbanzos, are widely used in Southern Europe in a variety of interesting ways. They are not only versatile, but are inexpensive and a most nutritious legume. Chick-peas may be marinated in a well-seasoned dressing and served as an appetizer, or combined with a diverse selection of foods and enjoyed as a first course. Serve this colorful dish at an informal luncheon or supper.

2 cups cooked or canned chick-peas, drained
½ cup diced green peppers
½ cup sliced scallions, with some tops
2 garlic cloves, crushed

1 canned pimiento, drained and chopped
3 tablespoons chopped fresh coriander or parsley
⅓ cup olive oil
2 tablespoons wine vinegar or lemon juice
Salt, pepper to taste
Crisp lettuce leaves, washed and dried
1 large tomato, peeled and cut into wedges
8 pitted black olives

Combine chick-peas, peppers, scallions, garlic, pimiento, and coriander or parsley in a large bowl. Mix together oil, vinegar or lemon juice, salt, and pepper; pour over chick-pea mixture and mix well. Refrigerate 1 hour or longer to blend flavors. When ready to serve, line a salad bowl with lettuce leaves; top with chick-pea mixture. Garnish with tomato wedges and olives. Serves 4 to 6.

Russian Vegetable Salad with Sour Cream

In Russia a characteristic appetizer, or *zakusky,* is a salad of cooked and/or raw vegetables combined with a sour-cream dressing and flavored with dill pickles, capers, or fresh or dried dill. Serve with other foods with pre-meal drinks or as a luncheon first course.

1 cup cold, cooked carrots
1 cup cold, diced, cooked beets
2 cups cold diced, cooked potatoes
1 cup cold, cooked green peas
2 gherkins, minced
About 1 cup sour cream
2 tablespoons wine vinegar
2 tablespoons chopped fresh dill or 1 teaspoon dried
*   dillweed*

Salt, pepper to taste
6 large lettuce leaves, washed and dried
1 large tomato, peeled and cut into wedges

Combine vegetables and gherkins in a large bowl. Mix sour cream, vinegar, dill, salt, and pepper; add to vegetables. Refrigerate 1 to 2 hours to blend flavors. When ready to serve, place a lettuce leaf on each of six individual plates and top with a mound of salad. Garnish with tomato wedges. Serves 6.

Madagascar Tomato Rougaille

This is a simple but delicious salad from the island of Madagascar, now called the Malagasy Republic, in the Indian Ocean. Serve as an appetizer.

1 cup diced green peppers
½ cup sliced scallions, with some tops
2 cups chopped, peeled tomatoes
1 to 2 tablespoons water
Few drops Tabasco sauce
Salt to taste

Combine peppers, scallions, and tomatoes in a serving dish. Mix remaining ingredients and spoon over vegetables. Serve with pieces of dark bread. Serves 4.

Andalusian Tuna Salad

In Spain's lovely southern province of Andalusia, a typical appetizer salad is made with tuna fish and colorful garnishes such as olives, tomatoes, and peppers. Serve with pre-meal drinks or as a luncheon first course.

1 can (6½ or 7 ounces) tuna fish
½ cup chopped green peppers
1 medium-sized red onion, peeled, sliced, and separated
    into rings
3 tablespoons olive oil
1 tablespoon wine vinegar
2 tablespoons chopped fresh parsley
Salt, pepper to taste
4 pitted black olives
4 stuffed green olives

Drain tuna fish and separate into chunks. Place on a serving plate. Top with peppers and onion rings. Combine oil, vinegar, parsley, salt, and pepper; pour over salad. Garnish with olives. Serves 4.

Burmese Vegetable Salad

The Burmese are fond of well-seasoned cooked vegetable salads that have colorful garnishes ranging from simple fried onions to seafood. Other vegetables may be used as substitutes for those in this recipe, if desired. Serve as a dinner first course.

1 large onion, peeled and chopped
2 garlic cloves, crushed
¼ cup salad oil
1 teaspoon turmeric powder
½ teaspoon ground red pepper
1 tablespoon anchovy paste

Juice of 1 large lemon
Salt, pepper to taste
2 cups cut-up, cooked green beans
2 cups cut-up, cooked cauliflower
12 shelled, cooked, medium-sized shrimp
2 tablespoons chopped fresh mint or parsley

Sauté onion and garlic in oil in a small skillet until tender. Add turmeric and red pepper; cook 1 minute. Mix in anchovy paste and lemon juice. Season with salt and pepper. Cook 1 more minute. Place beans and cauliflower in a serving dish. Pour onion mixture over them. Top with shrimp, and sprinkle with mint or parsley. Serves 4 to 6.

Salade Port Royal

Serve this colorful French salad as a luncheon first course or, with cold meat or tuna fish, for an informal supper.

2 medium-sized cold, boiled potatoes, peeled and sliced
2 red apples, peeled, cored, and sliced
1½ cups cold, cooked French-cut green beans
About 1 cup mayonnaise
Salt, pepper to taste
2 hard-cooked eggs, shelled and quartered
4 small wedges of lettuce

Combine potatoes, apples, and 1¼ cups green beans in a bowl; bind with mayonnaise. Season with salt and pepper. Spoon onto a serving plate and shape into a mound. Coat exterior of salad mound with a thin layer of mayonnaise. Garnish top with remaining ¼ cup green beans. Surround with egg quarters and lettuce wedges. Serves 4.

Danish Cheese Salad

An innovative salad to serve as a first course for luncheon or dinner.

¾ pound Edam or Gouda cheese, cut into ½-inch cubes
½ cup sliced scallions, with some tops
1 tablespoon prepared horseradish
1 teaspoon dry mustard
3 tablespoons salad oil
1 tablespoon fresh lemon juice
Salt, pepper to taste
4 crisp lettuce leaves, washed and dried
1 large tomato, peeled and cut into wedges
2 gherkins, sliced

Combine cheese and scallions in a medium bowl. Add horseradish, mustard, oil, lemon juice, salt, and pepper. Refrigerate 2 hours to blend flavors. To serve, place lettuce leaves on a serving dish and top with cheese salad. Garnish with tomato wedges and gherkin slices. Serves 4.

Jamaican Fruit-Avocado Salad

This attractive salad of fruit-filled avocados is a good first course for a company dinner.

¼ cup olive or salad oil
Juice of 1 large lime
2 tablespoons fresh lemon juice
2 teaspoons sugar

Salt, pepper to taste
3 medium-sized ripe avocados
2 cups fresh or canned pineapple chunks, drained
1 cup diced bananas
6 crisp lettuce leaves, washed and dried
Grated coconut

Combine oil, lime and lemon juice, sugar, salt, and pepper in a jar; refrigerate. When ready to serve, cut each avocado in half lengthwise and remove pits. Carefully scoop out flesh from each avocado half, leaving a ¼-inch rim, and cut flesh into small cubes. Combine with pineapple chunks and diced bananas in a bowl. Add oil mixture and toss. Heap into avocado shells and place each filled avocado half on a lettuce leaf on individual plates. Garnish tops with grated coconut. Serves 6.

Corsican Artichoke-Fennel Salad

On France's Mediterranean island of Corsica, noted for its rugged beauty and individualistic cookery, characteristic salads are made with flavorful, locally grown vegetables. Two of the best are the globe artichoke, a member of the daisy family and an aristocratic relative of the humble thistle, which has an appealing, nutlike flavor; and aromatic fennel, which has an anise flavor. They combine to make an interesting salad. If available, use fresh instead of frozen artichokes. Serve as a first course for luncheon or dinner.

4 medium-sized bulbs fennel
1 package (9 ounces) frozen artichoke hearts, cooked, chilled, and cut into halves
¼ cup olive oil

2 tablespoons fresh lemon juice
¼ teaspoon dried oregano or thyme
Salt, pepper to taste
1 large tomato, peeled and cut into wedges
12 pitted black olives
6 small sardines or flat anchovies, drained

Trim any green, feathery tops from fennel and remove tough outer stalks. Cut into thin slices. Arrange on a plate with artichokes. Combine oil, lemon juice, oregano or thyme, salt, and pepper; pour over vegetables. Garnish with tomato wedges, olives, and sardines or anchovies. Serves 4 to 6.

Ethiopian Lentil Salad

The lentil, one of man's most ancient foods and grown in many varieties, has long been used in Europe and Africa to make flavorful salads. Extremely nutritious and inexpensive, lentils are generally well seasoned with piquant flavorings. Some Ethiopians prefer yogurt instead of oil and vinegar as a dressing for lentil salad. Serve as a first course for a luncheon or supper.

2 cups dried lentils
1 teaspoon salt
3 garlic cloves, peeled
2 hot red peppers, seeded and chopped, or 1 teaspoon
* ground red pepper*
⅓ cup olive or salad oil
3 tablespoons wine vinegar
½ cup sliced scallions, with some tops
3 tablespoons chopped fresh parsley

Pepper to taste
Crisp lettuce leaves, washed and dried
2 hard-cooked eggs, shelled and sliced

Wash lentils and boil 2 minutes in water to cover. Remove from heat and let stand, covered, for 1 hour. Add salt, garlic, peppers or ground pepper; mix well. Bring to a boil; lower heat and simmer, covered, until lentils are tender, about 25 minutes. Do not overcook. Add more water during cooking, if needed. Remove from heat; drain. Remove and discard garlic cloves. Put in a bowl; add oil and cool. When cold add vinegar, scallions, and parsley. Season with salt and pepper. Refrigerate 2 hours or longer to blend flavors. Serve on lettuce leaves, garnished with egg slices. Serves 4 to 6.

French Celeriac Rémoulade

An ancient vegetable called celery root, celery knob, or celeriac is a variety of celery developed for its enlarged root rather than for stalks and leaves. It is highly prized in Europe either raw or cooked. The vegetable deserves to be better known in America, as it is nutritious and has an appealing flavor. In this recipe for a classic French pre-luncheon *hors d'oeuvre*, the raw celery root is marinated in a flavorful rémoulade sauce.

1 celery root or celeriac, about 1¼ pounds
2 tablespoons olive or salad oil
2 teaspoons wine vinegar
⅛ teaspoon dry mustard
Salt, white pepper to taste
About 1 cup mayonnaise
1 tablespoon drained capers

    1 garlic clove, crushed
    ¼ teaspoon dried tarragon
    ¼ teaspoon dried chervil

Cut off tops and roots of celery root and cut into slivers. Put in a bowl and add oil, vinegar, mustard, salt, and pepper. Marinate at room temperature or refrigerate 2 hours to blend flavors. Drain and combine with remaining ingredients in a serving dish. Serves 4.

Bohemian Cauliflower Salad

The attractive cauliflower, a variety of cabbage developed centuries ago in the eastern Mediterranean, is an excellent vegetable to serve raw or cooked in salads. Its leaves, if tender, are good salad greens. The nutritious vegetable is highly prized by the Bohemian cooks of Czechoslovakia, who use it to make a number of interesting dishes, including this salad. Serve with pre-meal drinks.

    1 whole, medium-sized cauliflower
    Salt
    1 tablespoon fresh lemon juice
    3 tablespoons salad oil
    1 tablespoon wine vinegar
    Pepper to taste
    1 cup sour cream
    1 cup chopped, cooked ham
    ¼ cup chopped fresh dill or parsley
    1 tablespoon drained capers
    1 large tomato, peeled and cut into wedges

Cut tough base and outer leaves from cauliflower and separate into flowerets; wash well. Put about 1 inch water in a large saucepan. Bring to a boil; add 1½ teaspoons salt, lemon juice, and flowerets. Cook, uncovered, until tender, about 6 minutes. Drain and put in a large bowl. Add oil, vinegar, salt, and pepper; mix well. Refrigerate 2 hours to blend flavors. When ready to serve, combine sour cream, ham, and dill or parsley, and spoon over cauliflower; mix well. Sprinkle with capers and garnish with tomato wedges. Serves 6 to 8.

Raw Mushroom Salad Italiano

Raw mushrooms are excellent in salads. They may be added to mixed green salads, marinated in sour cream or well-seasoned dressings. or, as in this Italian favorite, served with a flavorful herb vinaigrette dressing. Serve as a luncheon first course, or with olives, raw vegetables, hard-cooked egg wedges, and salami slices as an antipasto.

1 pound fresh mushrooms
⅓ cup olive oil
Juice of 2 lemons
2 garlic cloves, minced or crushed
Salt, pepper to taste
3 tablespoons chopped fresh herbs (basil, tarragon, parsley, or dill)
2 medium-sized tomatoes, peeled and cut into wedges
3 tablespoons chopped chives or scallions
4 flat anchovy fillets, drained and chopped

Clean mushrooms by rinsing quickly or wiping with wet paper toweling to remove all dirt. Cut off any tough stem ends. Wipe dry and slice lengthwise. Place in a serving dish and add oil, lemon juice, garlic, salt, and pepper. Leave to marinate at room temperature 1 hour. Serve sprinkled with herbs and garnished with tomato wedges sprinkled with chopped chives and anchovies. Serves 4 to 6.

Lebanese Tabbouleh

This traditional Lebanese and Syrian salad, or appetizer dip, is made with nutty-flavored cracked wheat (bulgur), which is sold in packages or in bulk in some supermarkets and specialty food stores. The salad is best in summer when garden-fresh vegetables are in season.

1 cup fine or medium cracked wheat (bulgur)
2 cups sliced scallions, with some tops
2 cups chopped fresh parsley
¼ cup chopped fresh mint or dill
2 cups peeled, diced tomatoes
Salt, pepper to taste
½ cup fresh lemon juice
⅓ cup olive oil

Soak cracked wheat in water to cover in a medium bowl for 30 minutes. Squeeze dry by pressing between palms of hands. Combine with remaining ingredients in a large bowl. Mix well and refrigerate 2 hours or longer. Serve in a bowl or on a plate shaped into a mound. Surround with romaine leaves or pieces of pita bread. Serves about 10.

Genoese Condijun

This colorful salad from the Italian port of Genoa is served traditionally as a pre-luncheon appetizer.

6 large tomatoes, peeled and sliced
1 medium-sized cucumber, washed and thinly sliced
1 medium-sized green pepper, cleaned and cut into thin
 strips
1 medium-sized onion, peeled and chopped
2 garlic cloves, crushed
8 flat anchovy fillets, drained and chopped
12 pitted black olives
⅓ cup olive oil
½ teaspoon dried basil
¼ cup chopped fresh parsley
Salt, pepper to taste

Combine tomato and cucumber slices, pepper strips, chopped onions, and garlic in a serving dish. Top with chopped anchovies and olives. Combine remaining ingredients and pour over salad. Mix well. Serves 6 to 8.

Mexican Guacamole

This appealing Mexican specialty, which is now popular throughout the United States, is served as a salad, appetizer, and sauce. There are many versions of guacamole. All are based on well-seasoned mashed or puréed avocados and generally include green chilis, and sometimes tomatoes and finely chopped onions. Other nontraditional additions are chopped, hard-cooked eggs;

crumbled, crisp bacon; chopped nuts; cucumbers; sour cream; mayonnaise; or cottage cheese. It may be served by itself or added to salads made with seafood, chicken, or vegetables. This is a basic recipe for guacamole.

>*2 medium-sized ripe avocados, seeded and mashed*
>*2 tablespoons fresh lime or lemon juice*
>*¼ cup minced canned green chili peppers*
>*2 tablespoons finely chopped onions*
>*Salt to taste*

Combine ingredients in a bowl. Cover with plastic wrap and refrigerate until ready to use. Makes about 1½ cups.

Balkan Cold White Bean Salad

In Europe's southeastern Balkan countries, dried white beans have long been treasured as an inexpensive and nutritious staple food. Although used in many dishes, the beans have particular appeal in salads, which can be prepared beforehand and served at room temperature, or may be served cold as appetizers, for buffets, or as accompaniments to roast, skewered, or grilled meats or fish. The bland beans should be well seasoned with olive oil, garlic, onions, and/or herbs. This salad is a good appetizer for a summer outdoor meal or an informal supper.

>*1 pound dried white beans, pea or navy*
>*3 to 4 garlic cloves, crushed*
>*2 medium-sized onions, peeled and minced*
>*2 medium-sized carrots, scraped and diced*
>*2 medium-sized stalks celery, cleaned and diced*
>*½ cup olive oil*

Salt to taste
2 tablespoons cider or wine vinegar
1 teaspoons sugar
¼ cup chopped fresh parsley

Wash and pick over beans; cover with water; bring to a boil; boil 2 minutes. Remove from heat and let stand, covered, for 1 hour. Drain and add fresh water, enough to cover beans. Bring to a boil; lower heat and cook slowly, covered, 45 minutes, adding more water, if needed. Add garlic, onions, carrots, celery, oil, and salt. Continue to cook slowly until beans are just tender, about 30 minutes. Stir in vinegar and sugar. Cook another 5 minutes. Remove from heat and cool. Mix in parsley. Serve at room temperature or refrigerate until ready to serve. Serves 8 to 10.

Crab Louis

This favorite American West Coast salad, created by a San Francisco chef, is made traditionally with Dungeness crab. Sometimes the dressing is prepared with a combination of mayonnaise and heavy cream rather than mayonnaise alone. Serve as a first course for a company dinner.

1 small head lettuce, washed, dried, and shredded
1 pound crabmeat
3 hard-cooked eggs, shelled and sliced
3 medium-sized tomatoes, peeled and sliced
1 cup mayonnaise
3 tablespoons chili sauce
2 tablespoons chopped sweet pickle
1 tablespoon fresh lemon juice
Salt, pepper to taste
2 tablespoons minced chives

Place shredded lettuce in a salad bowl. Remove any shell or cartilage from crabmeat and place over lettuce. Arrange egg and tomato slices around crabmeat. Combine remaining ingredients, except chives, and spoon over crabmeat. Sprinkle with chives. Serves 4.

Finnish Herring Salad

Northern Europeans are fond of colorful combination salads made with vegetables, fruit, game, fish, meat, or poultry, with well-seasoned dressings, which are eaten as appetizers. This one, called *sillisalaati,* is typical but may also include chopped or julienne-cut cold, cooked meat, if desired. Serve with pre-meal drinks.

> *1 jar (8 ounces) pickled herring, skinned and diced*
> *1½ cups cold, diced, cooked potatoes*
> *1 cup cold, diced, cooked beets*
> *1 cup cold, diced, cooked carrots*
> *1 tart apple, peeled, cored, and diced*
> *2 gherkins, diced*
> *½ cup heavy cream*
> *2 tablespoons cider vinegar*
> *2 teaspoons prepared sharp mustard*
> *1 teaspoon sugar*
> *Salt, pepper to taste*

Combine herring, potatoes, beets, carrots, apple, and gherkins in a medium bowl. Mix remaining ingredients and add to herring-vegetable mixture. Refrigerate 2 hours to blend flavors. To serve, shape into a mound on a large plate. Garnish with hard-cooked egg slices or tomato wedges, if desired. Serves 4 to 6.

Greek Tarama Salata

This traditional Greek salad is made with a favorite delicacy, the roe of red mullet, which is caught in abundance in the Aegean Sea. The light-pink salad, served as a dip, is best made with the imported Greek *tarama* sold in jars in some supermarkets and Middle Eastern food stores.

> *1 jar (8 ounces) red caviar or tarama*
> *1 medium-sized onion, peeled and minced*
> *Juice of 2 lemons*
> *5 slices white bread, crusts removed*
> *1 cup olive oil*
> *3 tablespoons chopped fresh parsley*

Combine caviar, onion, and lemon juice, and mix well, preferably in an electric blender. Dip bread in hot water. Squeeze dry and break into small pieces. Add to caviar mixture and blend well. Gradually add oil and blend until no trace of oil is left. Spoon onto a plate and shape as a mound. Garnish with parsley. Serve with pieces of pita bread. Serves 8 to 10.

Near Eastern Cucumber-Yogurt Salad

Throughout the Near East, and also in the Balkans, a traditional salad is made with cucumbers and yogurt, to which other ingredients may be added according to local preferences. Most often the salad is flavored with olive oil; lemon juice or vinegar; garlic; and dill, parsley, or mint. Sometimes it includes yellow raisins or chopped nuts. During the summer, ice cubes may be added to the salad just before it is served. Serve as an appetizer or a first course at luncheon.

2 cups diced and seeded, peeled cucumbers
Salt
2 cups plain yogurt
2 garlic cloves, crushed
2 tablespoons olive oil
2 tablespoons wine vinegar
3 tablespoons chopped fresh mint or dill
White pepper to taste

Put diced cucumber in a colander and sprinkle with salt. Allow to drain 30 minutes. Drain off all liquid and spoon cucumbers into a bowl. Add remaining ingredients and mix well. Refrigerate at least 1 hour before serving. Serves 4 to 6.

Sicilian Caponata

On the inviting southern Italian island of Sicily, a traditional sweet-sour appetizer salad called *caponata* is made with a combination of flavorful vegetables and piquant seasonings. It is a good dish for entertaining, as the salad can be made in quantity and kept in a tightly closed container in the refrigerator for several days. It is best to use a garden-fresh eggplant and good olive oil. Serve with pre-meal drinks.

1 large eggplant, about 1½ pounds, washed
Salt
About ¾ cup olive oil
1 large onion, peeled and chopped
2 large stalks celery, cleaned and chopped
3 medium-sized fresh tomatoes or drained canned Italian
  plum tomatoes, chopped
¼ cup tomato paste

3 to 4 anchovy fillets, drained and minced
3 tablespoons drained capers
⅓ cup minced black olives
2 teaspoons sugar
Freshly ground pepper
¼ cup wine vinegar
⅓ cup chopped fresh parsley

Cut unpeeled eggplant into small cubes, about 1 inch each. Put in a colander and sprinkle with salt. Allow to drain 30 minutes. Pat dry with paper toweling and set aside. Heat ⅓ cup oil in a large skillet. Add onion and celery, and sauté until tender. Push aside and add eggplant cubes, several at a time, and cook over brisk heat, stirring often, until tender and golden. Add more oil as needed. Add remaining ingredients, except parsley, and cook slowly, uncovered, until vegetables are tender, about 30 minutes. Remove from heat and mix in parsley. Refrigerate at least 24 hours before serving. Serve with chunks of crusty Italian or French bread. Serves 10 to 12.

Maine Sardine Salad

Many varieties of small salt water fish are called sardines. Although they're usually eaten as snacks, they can be used to make interesting salads.

Crisp lettuce leaves, washed and dried
2 cans (3 ¾ or 4 ounces each) sardines in oil, drained
1 medium-sized red onion, peeled, sliced, and separated
  into rings
1 medium-sized green pepper, cleaned and cut into strips
3 tablespoons salad oil

1 tablespoon cider vinegar or lemon juice
1 or 2 garlic cloves, crushed
2 teaspoons prepared mustard
1 teaspoon prepared horseradish
Salt, pepper to taste

Arrange lettuce leaves on a serving dish. Place sardines, onion rings, and pepper strips over them. Combine remaining ingredients; shake well; pour over salad. Serve at once. Serves 4.

Stuffed Tomatoes

Cold, stuffed tomatoes are attractive and delectable appetizer salads that may be served alone or on a bed of watercress or individual lettuce leaves.

For stuffed tomatoes, choose either small tomatoes or large, beefsteak tomatoes that are firm, uniform in size and shape, brightly colored, and with unspotted skins. Stuffed cherry tomatoes make good cocktail party appetizers, and the larger tomatoes are best for first courses or buffets.

Wash and remove tomato stem cores. Cut a slice off the top of each tomato; carefully spoon out seeds and pulp, being careful not to penetrate the shells. Discard seeds; chop and reserve pulp. Sprinkle inside of each tomato with salt, and invert to drain for 30 minutes.

Among the appropriate fillings for stuffed tomatoes are coleslaw, egg salad, cheese combinations, marinated cooked vegetables, Russian salad, seasoned cottage cheese, marinated raw mushrooms, Waldorf salad, cucumbers and sour cream, herring and beet salad, as well as salads of salmon, tuna fish, shrimp, crabmeat, lobster, or chicken.

Given below are two appealing European recipes for stuffed tomatoes.

Belgian Shrimp-Stuffed Tomatoes

10 firm, small, ripe tomatoes
Salt
2 cans (5 ounces each) small or medium shrimp, drained and deveined
1 cup mayonnaise
2 teaspoons sharp prepared mustard
Freshly ground pepper to taste
About 2 tablespoons minced chives

Cut a slice from the top of each tomato; carefully spoon out pulp and seeds. Sprinkle insides with salt; invert to drain for 30 minutes. Wipe shrimp dry with paper toweling. Set aside 20 shrimp to use as garnishes. Combine mayonnaise and mustard. Season with salt and pepper. Add to remaining shrimp and mix well. Spoon into tomatoe shells. Place 2 shrimp on top of each tomato. Sprinkle tops with chives. Serves 10.

Spanish Ham-Filled Tomatoes

4 medium-sized tomatoes
Salt
1 cup minced cooked ham
¼ cup sliced scallions
½ cup minced peeled and seeded cucumber

1 garlic clove, crushed
About ⅓ cup mayonnaise
Pepper to taste
Crisp lettuce leaves, washed and dried

Cut a slice from the top of each tomato. Carefully spoon out seeds and pulp. Sprinkle insides with salt; invert to drain for 30 minutes. Combine remaining ingredients, using enough mayonnaise or dressing to moisten them and mix well. Spoon into tomato shells, mounding at the tops. Chill. Serve each stuffed tomato on a lettuce leaf on individual salad plates. Serves 4.

Main-Dish Salads

Salads served as main dishes, or entrées. are excellent for light meals such as luncheons and suppers. While some are suitable in winter, many have particular appeal for indoor or outdoor meals during hot weather.

Most main-dish salads feature poultry, meat, seafood, or cheese, and raw or cooked vegetables. Some are elaborate versions of tossed salads, although others are attractive combinations of more hearty foods.

Nowadays, salads are frequently featured as the principal element of the American meal. They appeal to the modern cook because they are easy to prepare, nutritious, and delectable. Many salads are particularly appealing to the calorie-conscious.

Main-dish salads require particular attention and care. To present them as attractively as possible, garnishes must play an important role. Some can be partially or wholly prepared beforehand.

You already know that mixed salads of several ingredients,

called composed or compound salads, became very popular in Europe during the eighteenth and nineteenth centuries. There are many interesting recipes for them in old English cookbooks, such as the following vegetable salad from Pierre Blot's *What To Eat and How To Cook It* (1863). I've renamed it:

Olde English Compound Salad

Fish (herring, sprats, anchovies, etc.)
Meat (any bits of left-over meat or cold cuts)
Green vegetables (peas, string beans, salad greens,
    asparagus, artichoke hearts, etc., cooked and cold)
Chopped parsley
Sweet oil
Vinegar
Salt and pepper

I've renamed this dish a "Compound Salad" because it is made of a little of everything that can be served in a salad—fish, meat, green vegetables, and the like. When the whole is mixed, you add chopped parsley, sweet oil, vinegar, salt, and pepper; you move till your arms are sore, and you have a salad *macédoine.* Everyone has a right to try it.

This collection of recipes concentrates on innovative or relatively unknown main-dish salads, but it also includes a few old favorites that have perennial appeal.

Thailand Beef Salad

In Thailand this salad may include young, leafy tree shoots or flower blossoms and have a dressing that is flavored with lemon grass and fish sauce. This is a good salad for an informal dinner.

3 cups shredded lettuce or salad greens, washed, dried,
and chilled
1 pound cold, cooked roast beef, cut into bite-size, thin
strips
1 medium-sized cucumber, peeled and thinly sliced
2 cups raw or cold, cooked zucchini slices
⅓ cup lime or lemon juice
2 tablespoons salad oil
1 tablespoon soy sauce
1 teaspoon sugar
2 garlic cloves, crushed
Pepper to taste
2 medium-sized tomatoes, peeled and sliced
12 radish roses
2 tablespoons chopped fresh mint

Put lettuce or greens in a large bowl or on a platter. Arrange
beef strips, cucumber, and zucchini slices over them. Combine
lime or lemon juice, oil, soy sauce, sugar, garlic, and pepper;
shake well; pour over salad. Serve at once, garnished with
tomatoes, radishes, and mint. Serves 4 to 6.

Bagration Salad

This salad takes its name from a Russian general who fought in
the Napoleonic Wars. His name appears frequently on French
dishes because his chef was the celebrated Antonin Carême. It's
a good salad for a summer weekend luncheon.

1¼ cups mayonnaise
⅓ cup tomato sauce
Salt, pepper to taste
3 cups diced cold, cooked chicken

    1 cup diced celery
    6 cold, cooked artichoke hearts, sliced
    ½ cup diced cooked ham
    1 cup cold, cooked elbow macaroni
    2 hard-cooked eggs, shelled and chopped
    3 tablespoons chopped fresh parsley

Combine mayonnaise, tomato sauce, salt, and pepper. Refrigerate 1 hour to blend flavors. When ready to serve, combine chicken, celery, artichoke hearts, ham, and macaroni in a bowl. Add mayonnaise mixture and spoon onto a serving dish, shaping into a mound. Decorate with chopped egges and parsley. Serves 6.

Mexican Turkey-Avocado Salad

This colorful south-of-the-border combination salad is a good entrée for an outdoor evening meal.

    1 medium-sized head leafy lettuce, washed, dried, torn
       into bite-size pieces, and chilled
    ½ cup sliced scallions, with some tops
    ½ pound cold, cooked turkey, cut into thin strips
    ¼ pound Jack or Cheddar cheese, cut into thin strips
    1 medium-sized ripe avocado, peeled and cubed
    1 medium-sized carrot, scraped and thinly sliced
    ⅓ cup salad oil
    2 tablespoons fresh lime or lemon juice
    ½ teaspoon dried oregano
    Dash cayenne
    Salt, pepper to taste
    2 medium-sized tomatoes, peeled and sliced

Combine lettuce and scallions in a salad bowl. Arrange turkey, cheese, avocado, and carrots over them. Combine remaining ingredients, except tomatoes, and pour over salad. Serve at once, garnished with tomatoes. Serves 6.

Viennese Veal-Asparagus Salad

A good salad for a ladies' or weekend luncheon.

3 cups diced cold, cooked veal
1 cup diced celery
½ cup diced cold, cooked or canned beets
1 medium-sized onion, peeled and chopped
⅓ cup minced dill pickle
About ½ cup sour cream
⅓ cup mayonnaise
Salt, pepper to taste
2 cups cut-up cold, cooked asparagus
¼ cup chopped chives
2 hard-cooked eggs, shelled and quartered

Combine veal, celery, beets, onion, and pickle in a large bowl. Mix sour cream mayonnaise, salt and pepper; add to veal mixture. Carefully fold in asparagus and more sour cream, if desired. Spoon into a bowl or serving dish. Sprinkle with chives, and garnish with egg quarters. Serves 6 to 8.

Laotian Chicken-Vegetable Salad

In the small Southeast Asian country of Laos, salads are made quite spicy or hot by the liberal use of chilis or peppers. This is a mildly flavored dish to which ground red pepper may be added, if desired. It's a good salad for a late evening supper.

> 1 medium-sized head celery (Chinese) cabbage, washed, dried, torn into bite-size pieces, and chilled
> 3 cups diced cold, cooked chicken
> ½ cup diced bean curd
> 2 medium-sized carrots, scraped and thinly sliced
> 1 medium-sized cucumber, peeled, seeded, and diced
> 1 medium-sized red or green pepper, cleaned and cut into strips
> 8 scallions, cleaned and sliced, with some tops
> ½ cup peanut or salad oil
> 3 tablespoons fresh lime or lemon juice
> 1 tablespoon anchovy paste
> ¼ cup chopped fresh mint

Combine cabbage, chicken, bean curd, carrots, cucumber, peppers, and scallions in a salad bowl; toss. Mix remaining ingredients, except mint, and pour over salad; toss. Sprinkle with mint and serve. Serves 6.

Canadian Salmon-Potato Salad

This old favorite can be prepared with freshly cooked or canned salmon. It is a fine salad for a summer luncheon or supper.

> 3 cups fresh-cooked or canned salmon
> 2 cups diced cold, cooked potatoes
> 1 cup diced, peeled, and seeded cucumber
> ½ cup diced celery

¼ *cup finely chopped onion*
½ *cup sour cream*
½ *cup mayonnaise*
2 *tablespoons fresh lemon juice*
Salt, pepper to taste
Crisp lettuce leaves, washed and dried
2 *tablespoons drained capers or chopped chives*

Remove skin and bones from salmon and break into chunks. Place with potatoes, cucumber, celery, and onion in a large bowl. Combine sour cream, mayonnaise, lemon juice, salt, and pepper; add to salmon-potato mixture. Place lettuce leaves on a platter and top with salad; garnish with capers or chives. Serves 6.

Hawaiian Fruited Pork-Rice Salad

A good salad for a weekend luncheon or supper, it can be prepared beforehand and served attractively on lettuce leaves.

3 *cups julienne-cut cold, cooked pork or ham*
3 *cups cold, cooked rice*
2 *cups Mandarin orange sections, drained*
2 *cups fresh or canned pineapple chunks, drained*
1 *cup diced green pepper*
¼ *cup minced onion*
About 1¾ cups mayonnaise
1 *tablespoon soy sauce*
3 *to 4 tablespoons pineapple or orange juice*
Salt, pepper to taste
Crisp lettuce leaves, washed and dried
½ *cup chopped Macadamia nuts or blanched almonds*

Combine ingredients, except lettuce and nuts, in a large bowl, using enough mayonnaise to moisten ingredients. Chill 1 hour or longer to blend flavors. To serve, place lettuce leaves on a platter and top with salad. Garnish with nuts. Serves 8.

Australian Macaroni-Lamb Salad

This hearty down-underer is fine for a family luncheon or supper.

> *2 cups cold, cooked elbow macaroni*
> *4 cups diced cold, cooked lamb*
> *1 large onion, peeled and chopped*
> *1 cup diced green pepper*
> *About ¾ cup salad dressing or mayonnaise*
> *1 tablespoon prepared mustard*
> *½ teaspoon dried dillweed*
> *Salt, pepper to taste*
> *2 medium-sized tomatoes, peeled and sliced*
> *1 medium-sized cucumber, peeled and sliced*

Combine macaroni, lamb, onion, and pepper in a large bowl. Mix salad dressing or mayonnaise, mustard, dillweed, salt, and pepper; add to macaroni-lamb mixture. Garnish with tomatoes and cucumbers, and refrigerate until ready to serve, or serve at once. Serves 6 to 8.

Costa Rican Tuna-Vegetable Salad

Here's an inexpensive, easy salad that children will enjoy for luncheon or supper.

2 cups shredded lettuce, washed, dried, and chilled
4 medium-sized cooked potatoes, peeled and cubed
2 cups cold, cooked green peas
1 cup sliced radishes
2 cups cold, cooked or canned whole-kernel corn, drained
1 medium onion, peeled and minced
About 1¼ cups mayonnaise
2 tablespoons fresh lime or lemon juice
Salt, pepper to taste
2 cans (6½ or 7 ounces) tuna, drained and broken into
  chunks
3 tablespoons chopped fresh coriander or parsley
2 medium-sized tomatoes, peeled and cut into wedges

Line a salad bowl with lettuce. Combine potatoes, peas, radishes, corn, and onion in another bowl. Mix together mayonnaise, lime or lemon juice, salt, and pepper; add to vegetable mixture. Spoon over lettuce to form a large mound. Make a deep depression with a spoon in center of mound and fill with tuna chunks. Sprinkle with coriander or parsley. Garnish with tomatoes. Refrigerate or serve at once. Serves 6 to 8.

Norwegian Brigitte Salad

An attractive fish-vegetable salad that is enhanced with fruit, this is a good salad for a family luncheon.

1 pound cold, cooked white-fleshed fish (cod, flounder,
  halibut, haddock)
2 cups cold, cooked green peas
2 cups shredded raw carrots
1 apple, peeled, cored, and diced
1 navel orange, peeled, sectioned, and diced

2 gherkins, diced
⅓ cup salad oil
2 tablespoons cider vinegar
1 to 2 teaspoons sugar
Salt, pepper to taste
Crisp lettuce leaves, washed and dried

Pick over fish to be sure any bones are removed, and break into bite-size pieces. Toss lightly in a large bowl with peas, carrots, apple, orange, and gherkins. Combine remaining ingredients, except lettuce; add to salad and mix well. Arrange lettuce leaves on a platter and top with salad. Serves 4 to 6.

Dutch Hussar's Salad

This inviting salad from Holland is excellent for a winter luncheon or supper.

2 cups diced cold, cooked beef, veal, or pork
2 cups diced cold, cooked potatoes
1 cup cold, cooked green peas
1 medium-sized onion, peeled and diced
2 tablespoons sweet relish
2 hard-cooked eggs, shelled and chopped
1 medium-sized apple, cored and diced
¼ cup salad oil
2 tablespoons wine vinegar
1½ tablespoons chopped fresh dill or ½ teaspoon dried
    dillweed
Salt, pepper to taste
Crisp lettuce leaves, washed and dried

About ¾ cup mayonnaise
1 medium-sized tomato, peeled and sliced
3 tablespoons chopped fresh parsley

Combine meat, potatoes, peas, onion, relish, eggs, and apple in a large bowl. Mix oil, vinegar, dill, salt, and pepper. Add to meat-vegetable mixture and refrigerate 2 hours to blend flavors. When ready to serve, arrange lettuce leaves on a serving dish. Top with salad, shaping into a mound. Cover with a thin coating of mayonnaise. Garnish with tomatoes and parsley. Serves 4 to 6.

New Zealand Fish-Vegetable Salad

An attractive salad for a company luncheon in spring, it is best prepared with fresh asparagus.

2 cups cold, cooked asparagus tips
¼ cup sliced scallions, with some tops
3 tablespoons vinaigrette dressing
4 cups cubed cold, cooked white-fleshed fish (cod,
*   flounder, halibut, haddock)*
1 cup mayonnaise or salad dressing
2 tablespoons fresh lemon juice
1 tablespoon prepared sharp mustard
2 tablespoons chopped fresh parsley
Salt, pepper to taste
2 cups cut-up cold, cooked green beans
⅓ cup chopped blanched almonds

Combine asparagus tips, scallions, and vinaigrette dressing. Spoon into center of a round platter or large plate. Mix fish, mayonnaise or salad dressing, lemon juice, mustard, parsley, salt, and pepper. Spoon to form a ring around asparagus mixture. Surround with green beans and sprinkle them with almonds. Serves 6.

West Indies Curried Chicken-Fruit Salad

Curried chicken salads enhanced with fruit are traditional luncheon fare in the West Indies. They're prepared in many versions. This is one of the best.

> *3 cups diced cold, cooked chicken (white meat)*
> *1 cup diced fresh or canned pineapple, drained*
> *3 tablespoons fresh lime juice*
> *1 to 2 tablespoons curry powder.*
> *About ¾ cup mayonnaise*
> *Salt, pepper to taste*
> *3 medium-sized ripe avocados, halved and pitted*
> *6 teaspoons chutney*
> *6 teaspoons seedless raisins*
> *6 teaspoons shredded coconut*
> *6 crisp lettuce leaves, washed and dried*

Combine chicken, pineapple, lime juice, and curry powder in a large bowl. Refrigerate 1 hour to blend flavors. Add mayonnaise (enough to bind ingredients), salt, and pepper. Peel avocados; cut in half and remove pits. Spoon chicken mixture into avocado halves, shaping into mounds. Top each mound with a spoonful of chutney, raisins, and coconut. Place on lettuce leaves and serve at once. Serves 6.

Hot Frankfurter-Macaroni Salad

Try this salad for an informal company or family supper.

4 thin slices bacon, chopped
1 medium-sized onion, peeled and chopped
1 medium-sized green pepper, cleaned and chopped
About 3 tablespoons salad oil
1 pound frankfurters, cut into 1-inch slices
1 can (1 pound) sauerkraut, drained
3 cups cold, cooked macaroni
¼ cup cider vinegar
3 tablespoons minced dill pickle
1 teaspoon sugar
Salt, pepper to taste

Fry bacon in a large skillet until crisp and fat is rendered.
Remove bacon and drain. Add onion and green pepper to bacon
fat; sauté until tender. Add 1 tablespoon oil and frankfurters; fry
5 minutes, turning once or twice. Add sauerkraut and cooked
macaroni; sauté until heated, 1 or 2 minutes. Add remaining oil,
as much as desired, and remaining ingredients. Leave on the
stove long enough to blend flavors, about 5 minutes. Remove
from heat and serve hot. Serves 6.

English Salmagundi

The recipe for this very old English salad with the peculiar
name of salmagundi, sallad magundy, solomon grundy, or other
variations, is believed to have been first published in *Royal
Cookery* or *The Compleat Court Book* (1710), written by Patrick

Lambe, who cooked for several English monarchs. The word derives from the old French for a mixture, *salmigondis*. It is a festive salad with colorful ingredients artfully arranged on a bed of greens. Serve it for a company weekend luncheon.

> *1 cup salad oil*
> *⅓ cup wine or tarragon vinegar*
> *2 to 3 teaspoons sugar*
> *½ teaspoon dry mustard*
> *¼ teaspoon paprika*
> *2 teaspoons prepared horseradish*
> *Salt, pepper to taste*
> *2 quarts salad greens (Boston, romaine, endive, leafy lettuce), washed, dried, torn into bite-size pieces, and chilled*
> *1 bunch watercress, cleaned, washed, and dried*
> *1 pound cooked white meat of chicken or turkey, cut into thin strips*
> *1 pound cooked dark meat of chicken or turkey, ham or beef, cut into thin strips*
> *¾ pound Swiss chesse, cut into thin strips*
> *4 hard-cooked eggs, shelled and sliced*
> *6 gherkins, cut in halves*
> *1 can (2 ounces) flat anchovies, drained and chopped*
> *8 pitted black olives*

Combine oil, vinegar, sugar, mustard, paprika, horseradish, salt, and pepper in a small bowl or jar. Refrigerate. When ready to serve, arrange greens and watercress to form a mound or pyramid in center of a salad bowl. Surround with strips of white meat of chicken or turkey, dark meat of chicken or turkey, and ham or beef, with cheese placed between them. Interlard or garnish with remaining ingredients to make an attractive salad.

Shake dressing and serve with salad. Prepare beforehand and refrigerate until ready to serve, if desired. Serves 8.

Ligurian Tuna Salad

The cooks of Italy's northwest Ligurian coastal region have created imaginative dishes featuring their bountiful supply of fish and shellfish. This cold specialty is flavored with typical native flavorings—anchovies, olive oil, olives, and basil. It's good for an outdoor luncheon.

2 garlic cloves, cut in halves
4 large tomatoes, peeled and sliced
2 large green peppers, cleaned and cut into strips
1 large red onion, peeled and thinly sliced
1 medium-sized cucumber, peeled and sliced
2 cans (6½ or 7 ounces) tuna, drained and broken into
  chunks
6 flat anchovy fillets, drained and minced
3 hard-cooked eggs, shelled and quartered
12 pitted black olives
⅓ cup olive oil
2 to 3 tablespoons wine vinegar
½ teaspoon dried basil
Salt, pepper to taste

Rub a salad bowl with garlic halves. Place tomatoes, peppers, onion, and cucumbers in the bowl. Put tuna chunks in the center. Top with anchovies, eggs, and olives. Combine remaining ingredients and pour over salad. Serve at once. Serves 6 to 8.

Bavarian Sausage-Potato Salad

Serve this hearty salad for an informal supper, a mens' get-together, or a weekend luncehon.

> *6 cooked frankfurters or bratwurst sausages, cut into 1-inch slices*
> *4 medium-sized cold, cooked potatoes, peeled and cubed*
> *1 medium-sized onion, peeled and chopped*
> *1 medium-sized green pepper, cleaned and chopped*
> *½ cup diced celery*
> *¼ cup diced dill pickles*
> *½ cup sour cream*
> *½ cup mayonnaise*
> *Salt,pepper to taste*
> *2 hard-cooked eggs, shelled and sliced*
> *2 tablespoons chopped fresh dill*

Combine franfurter or bratwurst slices, potatoes, onion, green pepper, celery, and pickles in a large bowl. Mix sour cream, mayonnaise, salt, and pepper; add to sausage-vegetable mixture. Garnish with egg slices and dill. Serves 8 to 10.

California Crab Salad

A good salad for a ladies' luncheon.

> *2 cups flaked fresh, cooked or canned crabmeat*
> *½ cup diced, peeled, and seeded cucumber*
> *1 cup diced celery*
> *¼ cup minced onion*

3 hard-cooked eggs, shelled and chopped
Salt, pepper to taste
About ½ cup mayonnaise
2 tablespoons fresh lemon juice
6 thick avocado or tomato slices
6 leaves Bibb or Boston lettuce, washed and dried
Paprika

Combine crabmeat, cucumber, celery, onion, and eggs in a medium bowl. Season with salt and pepper. Mix mayonnaise and lemon juice; add to crabmeat mixture. Chill 1 hour or longer to blend flavors. When ready to serve, place an avocado or tomato slice on lettuce leaves on 6 individual salad plates. Top each with a mound of crabmeat salad and sprinkle with paprika. Serves 6.

Salade Parisienne

This well-known salad is made in many variations. At one time all of its recipes called for the addition of lobster and truffles. In recent years, however, the salad has generally been made with cold, cooked beef or veal and vegetables. This dish will be well received at an informal dinner.

6 medium-sized potatoes, washed
½ cup dry white wine
1 tablespoon wine vinegar
3 tablespoons salad oil
1 teaspoon dried tarragon
Salt, pepper to taste
2 pounds cold, cooked beef or veal, cut into bite-size,
thin strips
3 tablespoons minced shallots or scallions

3 medium-sized tomatoes, peeled and cut into wedges
2 hard-cooked eggs, shelled and sliced
Crisp lettuce leaves, washed and dried
1 medium-sized red onion, peeled, thinly sliced, and
    separated into rings
3 tablespoons chopped fresh parsley

Cook potatoes in their jackets in a little salted boiling water until tender, about 25 minutes. Drain; peel; and while still warm, slice into a large bowl. Add wine, vinegar, oil, tarragon, salt, and pepper. Toss lightly. Add beef or veal, shallots, tomatoes, and eggs; toss. Line a salad bowl with onion rings and parsley. Serves 6.

Russian Chicken-Vegetable Salad

This winter-luncheon salad, called vinaigrette in Russia, is an attractive and delectable creation made with chicken, raw and/ or cooked vegetables, and piquant flavorings.

2 cups diced cold, cooked chicken
1 cup diced cold, cooked potatoes
1 cup diced raw zucchini or cut-up cold, cooked green
    beans
½ cup diced radishes
½ cup diced raw mushrooms
½ cup diced peeled cucumbers
1 cup mayonnaise
2 tablespoons fresh lemon juice
2 tablespoons chopped fresh dill or 1 teaspoon dried
    dillweed

Salt, pepper to taste
3 tablespoons chopped fresh parsley
12 cooked or canned beet slices
12 stuffed or pitted black olives

Combine chicken and vegetables in a medium bowl. Mix mayonnaise, lemon juice, dill, salt, and pepper. Add to chicken-vegetable mixture. Refrigerate 1 hour or longer to blend flavors. Spoon into a serving dish, shaping into a mound. Garnish top with parsley and surround with beets and olives. Serves 6.

Scandinavian Shrimp-Cauliflower Salad

This is an attractive and unusual dish for a ladies' summer luncheon.

1 bunch watercress
1 whole cauliflower
Salt
1 tablespoon fresh lemon juice
2 cups shelled, cooked medium shrimp
2 hard-cooked eggs, shelled and chopped
1 cup mayonnaise
1 tablespoon sharp prepared mustard
3 tablespoons chopped fresh dill or 1 teaspoon dried
*   dillweed*
Pepper to taste
2 medium-sized tomatoes, peeled and cut into wedges

Wash watercress well and cut off leaves, discarding any wilted leaves and stems; refrigerate. Cut off base and tough outer leaves of cauliflower. Wash in cold running water, holding upside down. Put about 1 inch water in a large kettle and add salt to taste and lemon juice. Add whole cauliflower and cook, uncovered, 5 minutes. Cover and cook until just tender, about 20 minutes. Drain thoroughly; cool; and refrigerate. When ready to serve, arrange watercress on a platter or in a serving dish and top with cauliflower. Combine shrimp and eggs in a medium bowl. Mix mayonnaise, mustard, and dill; season with salt and pepper. Add to shrimp mixture and refrigerate. When ready to serve, arrange watercress on a platter; place cauliflower over it; top with shrimp mixture. Garnish with tomatoes and serve at once. Serves 4.

Vegetarian Bean Salad

This is an inexpensive and nutritious salad to serve for luncheon or supper.

> 2 cups cold, cooked or canned kidney beans
> 2 cups cold, cooked or canned white beans
> 2 cups cold, cut-up, cooked green beans
> 8 scallions, cleaned and sliced
> 4 stalks celery, cleaned and chopped
> 1 navel orange, peeled, sectioned, and cut up
> About 1 cup plain yogurt
> 2 tablespoons cider vinegar
> 1 tablespoon Worcestershire sauce
> Salt, pepper to taste
> ½ cup chopped walnuts
> ¼ cup golden or seedless raisins

Combine kidney, white, and green beans in a large bowl. Add scallions, celery, and orange; mix well. Combine yogurt, vinegar,

Worcestershire sauce, salt, and pepper; add to salad. To serve, sprinkle the top with walnuts and raisins. Serves 6.

Baltic Fish-Vegetable Salad

In the Northern European Baltic countries, salads, such as this fish-vegetable combination are traditionally seasoned with piquant flavorings and are good main dishes for winter luncheons or suppers.

> 2 cups flaked cooked, cold, white-fleshed fish (cod, flounder, halibut, perch)
> ½ cup diced raw carrots
> ½ cup sliced radishes
> ½ cup diced, peeled, and seeded cucumbers
> 2 medium-sized tomatoes, peeled and cut into quarters
> ¼ cup minced gherkins
> About ⅔ cup mayonnaise or sour cream
> 2 teaspoons prepared sharp mustard
> Salt, pepper to taste
> Crisp lettuce leaves, washed and dried
> 3 tablespoons chopped fresh dill
> 3 hard-cooked eggs, shelled and cut into quarters

Combine fish, vegetables, and gherkins in a large bowl. Mix mayonnaise or sour cream, mustard, salt, and pepper; add to fish combination. Refrigerate 1 hour or longer to blend flavors. Serve on lettuce leaves, garnished with dill and egg quarters. Serves 6.

Belgian Duck Salad

Try this unusual salad for a company winter luncheon or late evening supper.

 2 cups cubed cold, cooked duck or duckling
 2 cups diced cold, cooked potatoes
 1½ cups diced peeled apples
 1½ cups diced cooked beets
 ½ cup diced celery
 ⅓ cup salad oil
 2 tablespoons wine vinegar
 1 tablespoon prepared sharp mustard
 1 tablespoon prepared horseradish
 Salt, pepper to taste
 Crisp lettuce leaves, washed and dried
 3 gherkins, sliced

Combine first five ingredients in a large bowl. Mix oil, vinegar, mustard, horseradish, salt, and pepper; add to duck mixture. Refrigerate 1 hour or longer to blend flavors. Serve on lettuce leaves, garnished with gherkin slices. Serves 6 to 8.

Scottish Finnan Haddie Salad

Smoked haddock, a Scottish national dish, derived its name from the village of Findon in Scotland, and is commonly called by a corruption of the name, finnan haddie. The salad is a good supper dish.

1½ pounds frozen boneless finnan haddie
4 cups diced and peeled cold, cooked potatoes
1 large onion, peeled and diced
1½ cups chopped celery
2 hard-cooked eggs, shelled and chopped
⅓ cup salad oil
3 to 4 tablespoons vinegar
¾ teaspoon sugar
Salt, pepper to taste
1 small head leafy lettuce, washed, dried, and chilled

Put finnan haddie in a large skillet; cover with cold water; let stand 30 minutes; drain. Add fresh water to cover; bring to a boil; lower heat and cook slowly, covered, 10 minutes or until tender. Drain; flake; and put in a medium bowl to cool. Add potatoes, onion, celery, and eggs; mix well. Combine oil, vinegar, sugar, salt, and pepper; add to salad; mix well. Line a salad bowl with lettuce leaves, and spoon fish mixture over them. Serves 6.

Chicken Salads

There are many recipes for chicken salads that have long been popular in Europe, Latin America, and North America. The salads are particular favorites for summer meals but appear on home and restaurant tables the year round. A good chicken salad should be made with freshly cooked chicken that is moist, lean, and free of any gristle, fat, skin, or bones. It is generally cubed or diced and may come from either a whole stewing chicken that was cooked in a well-flavored broth or boiled chicken breasts.

What is called a basic classic chicken salad is made with white meat of chicken, diced celery, mayonnaise, salt, and pepper. Variations of this dish might include such additional ingredients as chopped nuts, onions, radishes, olives, grapes, apples, hard-cooked eggs, tomatoes, cucumbers, pineapple, green peppers, bananas, meats, or vegetables, and might be seasoned with mustard, scallions, chives, herbs, capers, or spices. Besides mayonnaise, sour cream, yogurt, *crème fraîche,* and oil-and-vinegar combinations are also popular dressings.

Chicken salad may be served by itself, over lettuce leaves, or in tomato, avocado, or other fruit shells, and may be simply or elaborately garnished.

Here are a few outstanding recipes for chicken salads.

Old-Fashioned Chicken Salad

2 cups diced cooked white meat of chicken
1 cup diced celery
About ½ cup mayonnaise or salad dressing
Salt, pepper to taste
Boston lettuce leaves, washed and dried
Garnishes: Capers, tomato wedges, sliced hard-cooked
*   eggs, and/or sliced stuffed olives*

Combine chicken, celery, mayonnaise or salad dressing, using as much as desired. Season with salt and pepper. Serve on lettuce leaves decorated with one or more garnishes. Serves 4.

Swedish Chicken Salad

This curry-flavored chicken salad, called *honssallad,* is a Swedish *smorgasbord* specialty, but it may also be served as a luncheon entrée.

3 cups diced cold, cooked chicken
½ cup mayonnaise
⅓ cup sour cream
2 to 3 teaspoons curry powder
Salt, pepper to taste
Crisp lettuce leaves, washed and dried
2 hard-cooked eggs, shelled and cut into wedges
6 stuffed olives, sliced
2 tablespoons capers, drained
3 tablespoons finely chopped dill pickles

Combine chicken with mayonnaise, sour cream, and curry powder. Season with salt and pepper and mix well. Refrigerate 1 hour or longer to blend flavors. When ready to serve, arrange lettuce leaves on a platter and spoon salad over them. Decorate with remaining ingredients. Serves 4 to 6.

Easy Chicken Salad

½ cup mayonnaise
⅔ cup sour cream
2 tablespoons fresh lemon juice
1 tablespoon grated or minced onion
½ teaspoon Tabasco sauce
1 to 2 teaspoons curry powder
1 tablespoon drained capers
3 cups diced cold, cooked chicken
1 cup diced celery
Salt, pepper to taste

Combine first seven ingredients in a large bowl; mix well. Add chicken and celery. Season with salt and pepper. Refrigerate 1 hour or longer to blend flavors. Serve plain or over lettuce leaves, if desired. Serves 4 to 6.

Ladies' Luncheon Chicken Salad

This delectable chicken salad recipe was given to me by my friend and neighbor, Mary Mulligan, who serves the specialty at luncheons during the summer.

> *3 whole chicken breasts*
> *Salt, pepper to taste*
> *About ⅔ cup mayonnaise or ⅓ cup mayonnaise and ⅓*
> *   cup sour cream*
> *2 tablespoons grated lemon rind*
> *½ pound seedless white grapes, cut in halves*
> *3 ounces almond slivers, toasted*

Remove skin from chicken breasts and sprinkle with salt and pepper. Put in a large skillet or saucepan with about 1 inch water. Bring to a boil. Lower heat and cook slowly, covered, about 25 minutes, or until tender. Take from skillet and cool. Remove meat from breasts. Discard bones and remove any gristle from meat. Cut meat into bite-size pieces and put in a large bowl. Add remaining ingredients and mix well. Season with salt and pepper. Serve over lettuce leaves, sliced tomatoes, or avocados, if desired. Serves 6 to 8.

Chef's Salad

This great American salad is a perennial favorite for luncheons and suppers.

> *2 quarts mixed salad greens, washed, dried, torn into*
> *   bite-size pieces, and chilled*
> *½ cup sliced scallions, with some tops*

3 cups slivered cold, cooked ham (about ¾ pound)
2 cups slivered cold, cooked chicken or turkey (about ¾ pound)
½ pound Swiss or American cheese, slivered
2 medium-sized tomatoes, peeled and cut into wedges
1 medium-sized cucumber, peeled and thinly sliced
3 hard-cooked eggs, shelled and cut into wedges
6 radish roses
1 cup vinaigrette or French dressing

Arrange salad greens in a salad bowl. Place scallions, ham, chicken or turkey, and cheese over greens. Top with tomatoes, cucumber, eggs, and radish roses. Serve dressing with the salad. Serves 6.

Side-Dish Salads

The traditional role for salads in many countries has been as a side dish, or accompaniment, for meats, poultry, or seafood. When served in this manner, the salad should be carefully chosen and prepared so that it will be an agreeable companion for the entrée and other dishes of the menu.

The type and purpose of the side-dish salad may vary considerably. Hearty salads made with rice and vegetables such as potatoes may take the place of more customary starch and vegetable dishes. In India and Pakistan, cooling yogurt-vegetable salads are served as a contrast to hot curries.

Austrians have long served a thinly sliced cucumber salad with their traditional dishes. In Scandinavian countries, piquant beet salads appear at many meals. Orientals, however, prefer pickled salads or relishes as adjuncts to their native dishes. Some variety of coleslaw is a traditional side-dish salad in America.

When choosing a salad to serve with a particular entrée,

consider its main ingredient, flavor, texture, and sometimes color, in relation to those of the foods to be served with it. While some salads, such as those made with cucumbers and tomatoes, seem to be agreeable accompaniments for almost any entrée, this is by no means true of all. Do not serve tomatoes if a tomato soup or sauce is on the menu. Sauerkraut goes well with pork and game but not with a delicate poultry entrée.

Generally speaking, with intricate main courses, it is desirable to serve a salad that is flavored or dressed simply. Serve creamy or well-seasoned salads with a bland entrée or with a roast or steak.

Some tossed green salads are particularly popular in America as accompaniments for entrées. Recipes for these salads were given in a previous chapter.

With each of the following salad recipes there is a suggestion as to the entrée it might accompany, but these are only guidelines. The entire menu of a luncheon, dinner, or supper must be taken into consideration.

Nigerian Yam Salad

In West African countries, the yam is an important staple food. It is grown in over fifty varieties and is used to make a large number of dishes ranging from appetizers to salads. Yams are very high in protein and can be either quite small or exceedingly large. Use sweet potatoes as a substitute, if desired. Serve with barbecued or roast chicken or pork.

4 cold, cooked or canned medium-sized yams or sweet
  potatoes, sliced
3 hard-cooked eggs, shelled and sliced
1 medium-sized onion, peeled and chopped

2 medium-sized tomatoes, peeled and cut into wedges
¼ cup peanut oil
2 tablespoons fresh lemon juice
Salt, pepper to taste

Arrange sliced yams in a serving dish. Top with egg slices and chopped onion. Surround with tomato wedges. Combine remaining ingredients and pour over salad. Serves 4.

Scottish Syboe Salad

A favorite Scottish salad, it is made with tomatoes and scallions and served as an accompaniment to cold roast meat or poultry.

4 large tomatoes, peeled and sliced
1 cup sliced scallions, with some tops
3 tablespoons salad oil
1 tablespoon cider vinegar
1 teaspoon sugar
Salt, pepper to taste

Arrange tomato slices, overlapping, in a serving dish. Sprinkle with scallions. Combine remaining ingredients and spoon over tomatoes. Let stand at room temperature 30 minutes before serving. Serves 4 to 6.

Japanese Daikon-Cucumber Salad

In Japan, a characteristic side-dish salad is called *sunomono,* meaning tart foods, usually raw vegetables, in a vinegar dressing. One of the most commonly used vegetables is a long, tapered white radish called by the Japanese a *daikon.* It resembles a

Western radish or white turnip in flavor but is less sharp. This radish is sold in some supermarkets and Oriental food stores. Serve with seafood or beef.

1 pound white radishes (daikon), washed and sliced
2 cups thinly sliced peeled cucumbers
2 tablespoons white vinegar
1 to 2 tablespoons soy sauce
1 teaspoon sugar
¼ cup toasted sesame seeds °
White pepper to taste

Combine radishes and cucumbers in a bowl. Mix remaining ingredients and add to vegetables. Mix well. Refrigerate until ready to serve. Serves 4.

Indian Tomato-Yogurt Salad

A refreshing combination of yogurt and vegetables with seasonings is called *rayta* or *raita* in India. It is traditionally served with curries but also goes well with roast meats and grilled poultry. Other vegetables, raw or cooked, may be substituted for the tomatoes, if desired.

2 cups plain yogurt
½ cup minced onions
1 cup diced peeled tomatoes
¼ cup minced green peppers
1 teaspoon ground cumin
Salt, peppr to taste
¼ cup chopped fresh coriander or parsley

° To toast sesame seeds, spread in a pan and toast in a preheated 350°F. oven until golden brown, about 12 minutes.

Combine ingredients in a bowl and refrigerate 1 hour or longer to blend flavors. Serve in the bowl or in individual small dishes. Serves 4 to 6.

Midwestern Hot Green Bean Salad

This favorite old-fashioned American salad is good with hamburgers, frankfurters, meat loaf, or grilled chicken.

> *¾ pound fresh green beans, washed, stemmed, and cut*
>   *into 1-inch pieces*
> *Salt*
> *4 thin slices bacon, chopped*
> *1 medium-sized onion, peeled and chopped*
> *2 tablespoons cider vinegar*
> *1 teaspoon sugar*
> *Pepper to taste*

Cook beans in a little salted boiling water in a medium saucepan until just tender, about 15 minutes, and drain. Fry bacon in a medium skillet until crisp and the fat is rendered. Remove bacon and drain on absorbent paper. Add onion to bacon fat and sauté until tender. Mix in vinegar and sugar. Season with salt and pepper. Add beans and sauté over low heat until beans are hot. Serve warm topped with bacon. Serves 4.

Venetian Green Pea–Rice Salad

Two favorite foods of Venice, tender green peas and rice, are combined with seasonings in this salad, which is an excellent accompaniment for grilled seafood, poultry, or game.

1 cup cold, cooked green peas
2 cups cold, cooked rice
⅓ cup sliced scallions, with some tops
¼ teaspoon dried basil
Salt, pepper to taste
¼ cup olive oil
2 tablespoons fresh lemon juice
3 tablespoons grated Parmesan cheese

Combine ingredients in a medium bowl. Refrigerate 1 hour to blend flavors. Serves 4 to 6.

Ceylonese Curried Vegetable Salad

In the Southeast Asian country best known as Ceylon, but now called Sri Lanka, highly seasoned vegetable salads such as this one are served as accompaniments for grilled seafood, meats, and poultry.

½ pound fresh mushrooms, cleaned and sliced
½ pound fresh green beans, stemmed and cut up
½ pound fresh broccoli, cut up
1 large onion, peeled and sliced
2 garlic cloves, crushed
⅓ cup peanut or salad oil
1 tablespoon turmeric powder
1 teaspoon ground cumin
½ teaspoon ground red pepper
Salt, pepper to taste
Juice of 1 large lime or lemon

Wash and dry mushrooms, green beans, and broccoli, Sauté onion and garlic in oil in a medium skillet until tender. Add turmeric, cumin, red pepper, salt, and pepper; cool 1 minute. Add vegetables and cook slowly, covered, until just tender and preferably a little crisp, about 10 minutes. Remove from heat; cool. Add lime or lemon juice and mix well. Serves 4 to 6.

Polish Sauerkraut Salad

Sauerkraut, a healthful dish rich in vitamins, phosphorous, calcium, and iron, is an excellent addition to vegetable salads that are favorite accompaniments for sausages, frankfurters, ham, or pork.

1 pound bulk or canned sauerkraut, drained and
  chopped
1 cup grated raw carrots
1 cup diced cold, cooked or canned beets
¼ cup chopped celery
2 cups diced cold, cooked potatoes
2 tablespoons minced gherkins
About ⅓ cup salad oil
2 tablespoons cider vinegar
2 teaspoons prepared sharp mustard
Salt, pepper to taste
3 tablespoons chopped fresh parsley

Combine sauerkraut with vegetables and gherkins in a large bowl. Mix oil, vinegar, mustard, salt, and pepper and pour over salad. Mix well. Refrigerate 2 hours to blend flavors. Serve sprinkled with parsley. Serves 6 to 8.

Italian Tomato-Bread Salad

An innovative salad to serve with veal or beef dishes.

8 tablespoons olive oil
3 tablespoons butter or margarine
1½ cups stale bread cubes
4 large tomatoes, peeled and sliced
1½ tablespoons wine vinegar
½ teaspoon dried basil
Salt, pepper to taste
2 tablespoons drained capers
2 tablespoons chopped fresh parsley

Heat 3 tablespoons oil and the butter or margarine in a medium skillet. Add bread cubes and sauté until golden brown. Put in a preheated 275°F. oven for 25 minutes. Drain on absorbent paper. Arrange in layers with tomato slices in a salad bowl. Combine remaining oil, the vinegar, basil, salt, and pepper; spoon over tomato-bread mixture. Sprinkle with capers and parsley. Serve at once. Serves 4.

Korean Spinach Salad

In Korea a *namool*, or salad, made with well-seasoned vegetables is a traditional accompaniment for barbecued meat or grilled fish.

1 pound fresh spinach leaves
¼ cup sliced scallions, with some tops
1 or 2 garlic cloves, crushed

½ teaspoon sugar
1 tablespoon soy sauce
1 tablespoon peanut or salad oil
Pepper to taste
2 teaspoons sesame seeds

Wash spinach and cut off any thick stems and wilted leaves. Cook only in the water that remains on the leaves, covered, until just tender, about 5 minutes. Drain well and cool. Chop and press out any liquid. Combine with remaining ingredients, except sesame seeds, in a bowl. Serve sprinkled with sesame seeds. Serves 4 to 6.

Austrian Cucumber Salad

Austria's classic salad is *Gurkensalat,* cucumber salad, which is prepared in several variations. This is a basic recipe. Vinegar may be replaced with lemon juice. Omit sugar, if desired. Add garlic; garnish with paprika; or add sour cream. In Austria, this salad is served with schnitzels or other veal dishes, pork, and poultry.

2 medium-sized cucumbers
Salt
3 tablespoons white vinegar
3 tablespoons salad oil
1 teaspoon sugar
Freshly ground white pepper
2 tablespoons minced chives, fresh dill, or parsley

Peel cucumbers, cut off ends, score lengthwise with a fork, and slice thinly. Put in a colander and sprinkle with salt. Allow to stand 30 minutes; drain well. Turn into a serving dish. Add vinegar, oil, and sugar. Season with salt and pepper. Refrigerate 2 hours. Serve garnished with chives, dill, or parsley. Serves 4 to 6.

Georgian Carrot-Peanut Salad

Americans have long been fond of salads made with grated raw carrots and raisins. This interesting version is an attractive accompaniment for baked ham or roast turkey.

> *3 cups grated raw carrots*
> *1 cup chopped peanuts*
> *½ cup seedless raisins*
> *1 cup mayonnaise*
> *3 tablespoons orange juice*
> *6 navel orange slices*
> *6 crisp lettuce leaves, washed and dried*

Combine first five ingredients in a bowl and refrigerate 1 hour or longer to blend flavors. When ready to serve, place each orange slice on a lettuce leaf on an individual serving plate. Top with a mound of carrot mixture on each orange slice. Serves 6.

Spanish Rice-Mushroom Salad

A colorful salad to serve with barbecued chicken, roast turkey, or grilled seafood for a outdoor or summer meal.

> *1 cup diced fresh or canned mushrooms*
> *¼ cup olive or salad oil*
> *2 tablespoons fresh lemon juice*

Salt, pepper to taste
2 cups cold, cooked rice
1 cup cold, cooked green peas
½ cup chopped celery
½ cup chopped canned pimiento
3 tablespoons chopped fresh parsley

Sauté mushrooms in oil and lemon juice in a small skillet for 4 minutes if fresh, or 2 minutes if canned. Season with salt and pepper. Remove from heat and cool. Combine with remaining ingredients in a large bowl and refrigerate 1 to 2 hours to blend flavors. Serves 4 to 6.

Danish Pickled Beet Salad

The Danes are fond of piquant beet salads, which are served with meats and game.

2 cups sliced cooked or canned beets, drained
3 tablespoons sugar
½ cup cider vinegar
1 teaspoon caraway seeds
Salt, pepper to taste

Put beets in a bowl. Combine remaining ingredients in a small saucepan and bring to a boil. Reduce heat and simmer, uncovered, 5 minutes. Pour over beets and cool. Refrigerate several hours or overnight. Serves 4 to 6.

Bulgarian Mixed Pepper Salad

This traditional Bulgarian salad is called *shopska salata,* a name that is derived from the village of Shopka on the outskirts of Sofia. Serve with grilled or skewered lamb or pork.

4 medium-sized green or red peppers, cleaned and cut
    into strips
1 medium-sized cucumber, peeled and thinly sliced
4 large tomatoes, peeled and thinly sliced
2 medium-sized onions, peeled and thinly sliced
⅓ cup olive oil
2 tablespoons lemon juice or vinegar
3 tablespoons mixed fresh herbs (dill, parsley, or basil)
Salt, pepper to taste
½ cup diced white Feta or farmer cheese

Place peppers, cucumber, tomatoes, and onions in circles, overlapping each other, on a large plate. Combine remaining ingredients, except cheese, and pour over vegetables. Sprinkle with cheese. Serve at once. Serves 4 to 6.

Iowa Corn Salad

Serve with meat loaf, hamburgers, or frankfurters.

2 cups cooked fresh corn or canned whole-kernel corn,
    drained
¾ cup diced, peeled, seeded cucumber
½ cup diced green pepper
2 tablespoons grated onion

3 tablespoons cider vinegar
1 tablespoon sugar
2 teaspoons celery seed
Salt, pepper to taste

Combine first four ingredients in a medium bowl. Put remaining ingredients in a small saucepan. Bring to a boil and pour over vegetables. Cool. Serves 4.

Hungarian Carrot-Pepper Salad

A super salad to serve with baked ham, roast pork, or seafood.

1 pound (about 8 medium-sized) carrots
2 tablespoons salad oil
2 large green peppers, cleaned and cut in thin strips
¾ cup sour cream
1 teaspoon sugar
1 teaspoon prepared mustard
1 tablespoon prepared horseradish
Salt, pepper to taste
2 tablespoons minced chives

Scrape carrots and cut into julienne strips. Braise slowly in oil in a medium skillet until just tender, about 3 minutes. Remove with a slotted spoon to a bowl and cool. Mix with green peppers. Combine remaining ingredients, except chives and spoon over vegetables. Serve sprinkled with chives. Serves 6.

American Coleslaws

One of America's most popular salads is cabbage coleslaw which is made in an amazing number of variations. All are easy to prepare and always in season. Although generally made with shredded green cabbage, coleslaw can be prepared with red cabbage or a combination of red and green cabbage.

Minced green pepper, pimientos, or carrots are used in traditional slaw recipes. Others might call for the addition of apples, pineapples, pears, cucumbers, celery, grapes, blanched almonds, pecans, hard-cooked eggs, or cheese.

Probably the most elaborate slaw is one called "heavenly slaw" or "Virginia City slaw," which includes, besides the cabbage, pineapple tidbits, miniature marshmallows, and slivered blanched almonds, and is topped with a snow dressing made primarily of beaten egg whites.

Slaws may be hot or cold, crisp or wilted, moistened with French dressing, mayonnaise, salad dressing, boiled dressing, sweet or sour cream, buttermilk, chili sauce, or catsup, and seasoned with pickles, crisp bacon, Worcestershire sauce, dry or prepared mustard, soy sauce, onions, horseradish, curry powder, ginger, aniseed, chives, lemon juice, vinegar, dillweed or dill seeds, parsley, celery, caraway, or mustard seeds.

To make a good slaw, choose cabbage of the best quality that is firm, crisp, and of good color. Shred or grate coarsely. What to do next is a matter of preference. Some cooks wash, drain, and dry the cabbage and put it in the refrigerator until ready to moisten with a dressing if a crisp slaw is desired. Some chill the cabbage in ice water, with or without lemon juice, 30 minutes or longer, to crisp. If so, dry well and refrigerate. Just before serving, moisten and add seasonings.

For a wilted slaw, mix dry, grated cabbage with a dressing and any other ingredients and let stand in the refrigerator until ready to serve. For a hot slaw, combine hot dressing with cabbage and serve at once.

For extra flavor, make coleslaw a day ahead of time so the dressing and cabbage blend well. Keep the slaw covered in the refrigerator; it improves as it mellows.

Included below are some traditional American coleslaw recipes. Other recipes for coleslaw appear elsewhere in the book.

Easy Coleslaw

> *4 cups finely shredded green cabbage*
> *1 tablespoon cider vinegar or lemon juice*
> *½ cup mayonnaise or ¼ cup mayonnaise and ¼ cup sour cream*
> *1 tablespoon sugar*
> *Salt, pepper to taste*

Combine ingredients in a bowl and refrigerate, covered, at least 2 hours. Toss before serving. Serves 4 to 6.

Note: Add 1 tablespoon grated onion, ½ teaspoon celery seed, and/or ⅓ cup minced green pepper, if desired.

Country Coleslaw

> *4 slices thin bacon, diced*
> *¼ cup cider vinegar*
> *Salt to taste*
> *1 cup sour cream at room temperature*
> *4 cups shredded green cabbage*
> *½ cup minced green pepper*
> *1 small onion, peeled and minced*

Fry bacon in a small skillet until crisp and the fat is rendered. Remove bacon with a slotted spoon and drain on absorbent paper. Add vinegar and salt to hot bacon fat and heat. Mix with other ingredients in a medium bowl. Refrigerate, covered, 1 hour or longer to blend flavors. Serve garnished with bacon. Serves 4 to 6.

Old-Fashioned Coleslaw

2 tablespoons all-purpose flour
1½ tablespoons sugar
Salt to taste
1 teaspoon dry mustard
Few grains cayenne
1 egg, beaten
¾ cup light cream or milk
1½ tablespoons melted butter or margarine
¼ cup cider vinegar
4 cups finely shredded green cabbage

Combine flour, sugar, salt, mustard, and cayenne in the top of a double boiler. Mix together egg, cream or milk, and butter or margarine. Gradually add to the dry ingredients, stirring as adding, and cook slowly over simmering water, stirring constantly, until thickened and smooth. Remove from heat, stir in vinegar, and cool. Mix with cabbage and refrigerate a few hours to mellow before serving. Serves 4 to 6.

Pakistani Eggplant-Yogurt Salad

In Pakistan, this characteristic salad is served with grilled meat, especially lamb and chicken.

> *1 medium eggplant, about 1¼ pounds, washed*
> *Salt*
> *About ¾ cup olive or salad oil*
> *1 to 2 teaspoons chili powder*
> *2 garlic cloves, crushed*
> *Salt, pepper to taste*
> *1 cup plain yogurt*
> *2 tablespoons chopped fresh mint*

Cut unpeeled eggplant into 1-inch cubes and put in a colander. Sprinkle with salt and allow to drain for 30 minutes. Wipe dry with paper toweling. Sauté cubes, several at a time, in heated oil in a large skillet until tender and golden brown. Add more oil as needed. When all eggplant cubes are cooked, spoon into a large bowl and cool. Add chili powder, garlic, salt, pepper, and yogurt; mix well. Serve at room temperature or refrigerate until ready to serve. Serve sprinkled with mint. Serves 4 to 6.

Chinese Fresh Broccoli Salad

Broccoli, a dark-green vegetable related to cauliflower and very rich in vitamin C, is used in China for making a number of superb dishes, including interesting salads. It should be cooked until just tender and still crisp. Serve with roast meat, game, or poultry.

1 bunch fresh broccoli
Salt
2 tablespoons soy sauce
1 tablespoon wine vinegar
3 tablespoons peanut oil
2 garlic cloves, crushed
1 teaspoon sugar
Pepper to taste
⅓ cup chopped walnuts or almonds

Cut off and discard large leaves and tough parts of broccoli stalks. Wash and dry. Cut into diagonal slices. Parboil in a little salted boiling water until just tender, about 6 minutes. Rinse quickly with cold water. Drain and cool. Spoon into a bowl. Combine remaining ingredients, except nuts, and pour over broccoli. Serve sprinkled with nuts. Serves 4.

German Vegetable Salad

A good salad to serve with pork or game.

1 package (10 ounces) frozen cauliflower
1½ cups cold, cooked green peas
½ pound fresh mushrooms, cleaned and sliced
¾ cup sour cream
1 tablespoon fresh lemon juice
2 tablespoons chopped fresh dill or parsley
Salt, pepper to taste

Cook cauliflower according to package directions until just tender. Drain and cut into bite-size pieces. Combine with peas and mushrooms in a salad bowl. Mix remaining ingredients and add to vegetables. Refrigerate 1 to 2 hours to blend flavors. Serves 4.

Persian Spinach Borani

In Persia, or Iran, a traditional salad called *borani* is served with meat or poultry. Cooked eggplant or mushrooms, or raw cucumbers, may be substituted for the spinach, if desired.

> *2 packages (10 ounces each) frozen chopped spinach*
> *1 large onion, peeled and minced*
> *2 garlic cloves, crushed*
> *2 tablespoons peanut or salad oil*
> *1 cup plain yogurt*
> *½ teaspoon ground nutmeg or cinnamon*
> *Salt, pepper to taste*
> *2 tablespoons chopped fresh mint or coriander*

Cook spinach according to package directions until tender; drain well; press out all liquid; spoon into a bowl. Combine with remaining ingredients, except mint, and refrigerate 1 to 2 hours before serving. Serve sprinkled with mint. Serves 4 to 6.

Belgian Salade à la Liègeoise

This salad is from the Belgian city of Liège, long noted for its gaiety and superb gastronomy. Serve with pork, beef, or game.

> *¾ pound fresh green beans or 1 package (9 ounces)*
>   *frozen green beans*
> *Salt*

4 medium-sized potatoes, washed
2 thin slices bacon or 1 small piece salt pork
1 large onion, peeled and chopped
¼ cup cider vinegar
Pepper to taste

Remove stems from fresh green beans and break into small pieces. Cook in a little salted boiling water until just tender, about 15 minutes, and drain. If frozen beans are used, cook according to package directions and drain. Meanwhile, peel and cube potatoes. Cook until tender in a little salted boiling water, about 12 minutes, and drain. Chop bacon or dice pork and cook in a medium skillet to release fat and until bacon or pork is crisp. Add onion and sauté until tender. Mix in vinegar, cooked beans, and potatoes. Season with salt and pepper. Leave over medium heat until hot. Serve at once. Serves 4.

Philippine Achara

This traditional salad or relish called *achara* is made with a diverse selection of foods that might include bitter melon and papaya. This is a simplified version. Serve as an accompaniment for seafood, pork, or poultry.

1 large green pepper, cleaned and minced
1 large sweet red pepper, cleaned and minced
1 medium-sized carrot, scraped and grated
2 cups diced raw cauliflower
1 large onion, peeled and minced
2 tablespoons minced ginger root
⅓ cup sugar
⅓ cup vinegar
Salt, pepper to taste

Put peppers, carrot, cauliflower, and onion in a large bowl. Combine remaining ingredients in a small saucepan; bring to a boil; boil 2 minutes. Pour over vegetables and cool. Refrigerate at least 24 hours before serving. Serves 4.

Swedish Dilled Green Bean Salad

Swedish cooks are very fond of adding aromatic dill, either fresh or dried, or tiny pungent dill seeds, to a number of their dishes. A member of the parsley family, dill imparts a marvelous flavor to salads. Serve with seafood or poultry.

> *1 pound fresh green beans, washed, stemmed, and cut*
> *   into 1-inch pieces*
> *Salt*
> *3 medium-sized tomatoes, peeled and sliced*
> *½ cup sliced scallions, with some tops*
> *1 cup sour cream*
> *2 tablespoons chopped fresh dill*
> *1 teaspoon sugar*
> *1 tablespoon fresh lemon juice*
> *Salt, pepper to taste*

Cook green beans in a little salted boiling water until just tender, about 15 minutes. Drain and cool. Place beans, tomatoes, and scallions in a bowl or serving dish. Combine remaining ingredients and spoon over vegetables. Toss lightly. Serve at once. Serves 4 to 6.

Potato Salads

Potato salads are comparatively new dishes since potatoes were not a commonly accepted food until the late seventeenth century. Nevertheless, wherever potatoes were grown, cooks began making and creating potato salads in such a great number of variations that it would be impossible to list all of them.

Certainly the popularity of potato salads has increased over the years. They are still frequently served as side dishes in the home and in restaurants. Sometimes the salad appears as a simple creation on the supper table, or it may be lavishly prepared and served at an elegant buffet. Potato salad holds a place of honor at picnics and is greatly favored for summer outdoor meals. Americans have long enjoyed these salads at church, community, and fund -raising events where the cooks vie with each other to offer original and praiseworthy specialties.

Every cook seems to have one or more good suggestions for potato salads, but there are some general guidelines to follow. Of primary importance are the potatoes, which should be of top quality and freshly cooked. Never use old or leftover boiled potatoes. In America the best kinds of potatoes are the waxy ones such as small or medium reds, or long whites that have a low starch content and firm texture. After being cooked they will remain firm when cut and will not become mushy; nor will they absorb too much dressing.

Some people peel and cut the potatoes before cooking. Others cook them in their jackets, then peel and cut them. The latter method results in more flavorful potatoes. After cooking, the potatoes may be sliced, diced, mashed, or, more commonly, cut into ½- to 1-inch cubes.

Once cut, the potatoes should be dressed or marinated while still warm so they will absorb the flavors as they cool to room temperature. Some cooks like to serve the salad at room temperature; others prefer to chill it in the refrigerator. Either way, the salads are best if prepared sometime before serving so that the flavors have a chance to blend and penetrate the ingredients. In hot weather, the salad cannot be left unchilled for long or it will spoil.

Besides potatoes, the salads may include a number of other foods. Particular favorites are raw vegetables such as celery, green peppers, cucumbers, carrots, and radishes; virtually any kind of cooked vegetable; hard-cooked eggs; cheeses; nuts; raisins; olives; fruits such as apples, pears, or pineapple; anchovies; sausages or frankfurters; cooked bacon, ham, beef, lamb, or pork; or seafood.

Many seasonings are also employed. Salt and pepper are essential. Most cooks use onions, either minced or grated, chives, or scallions. Other favorites are dry or prepared mustard, sweet or dill pickles, capers, seeds (celery, dill, poppy, mustard, caraway), herbs (fresh or dried dill, parsley, tarragon, and basil), and spices (curry or chili powders, red pepper, paprika). Some salads are sweetened with sugar.

There are lots of dressings for potato salads. Some Europeans bathe the warm potatoes in bacon drippings, white wine, or bouillon before adding other ingredients. Old-time recipes often used sour cream, sweet cream, or evaporated milk; modern recipes often call for yogurt or cottage cheese. Most popular are vinaigrette with three parts olive or salad oil to one part vinegar, old-fashioned boiled dressing, mayonnaise or salad dressing, or a bacon-vinegar dressing.

Whatever dressing is used, it should be carefully added to or mixed with the salad ingredients. Use only enough to bind or flavor the salad so that it does not become too runny or oily. A recipe that calls for the use of six medium-sized potatoes cannot stipulate exactly how much dressing is needed because the size of the potatoes may vary. Each cook, then, should add the dressing with discretion, according to his or her personal taste.

It's too bad this book hasn't room for even more potato salad recipes; there are plenty of really imaginative ones. In France, for example, there's a good salad made with potatoes, puréed chestnuts, and celery; it's served with small birds or game. Americans have a flower-bed salad made of potato salad surrounded with cooked vegetables and served on a bed of lettuce. Cornucopia salad is potato salad served in ham or bologna cornucopias.

Here are four traditional potato salad recipes. You'll find others elsewhere in this book.

Viennese Potato Salad with Sour Cream

4 medium-sized potatoes, washed
Salt
1¼ cups sour cream at room temperature
2 tablespoons wine vinegar
½ teaspoon dried dillweed
Pepper to taste
½ cup diced green pepper
½ cup diced celery
½ cup sliced scallions, with some tops
3 hard-cooked eggs, shelled and chopped
¼ teaspoon paprika
1 large tomato, peeled and cut into wedges

Cook potatoes in their jackets in a little salted boiling water until tender, about 25 minutes. Drain well; peel; and, while still warm, slice or cube into a medium bowl. Add sour cream, vinegar, and dill. Season with salt and pepper. Mix well. Add green pepper, celery, scallions, and eggs; mix well. Cool at room temperature and let stand 1 hour or longer to blend flavors. Serve sprinkled with paprika and garnished with tomato wedges. Serves 6 to 8.

Swedish Potato Salad

6 medium-sized potatoes, washed
1 large onion, peeled and chopped
1 cup diced cold, cooked or canned beets
2 tablespoons drained capers
About 1 cup mayonnaise or salad dressing
Salt, pepper to taste
Crisp lettuce leaves, washed and dried
3 tablespoons chopped fresh dill or parsley

Cook potatoes in their jackets in a little salted boiling water until tender, about 25 minutes. Drain well; peel; and, while still warm, slice into a large bowl. Add onion, beets, capers, and enough mayonnaise to bind ingredients. Season with salt and pepper. Cool at room temperature 1 hour or longer to blend flavors. Serve on lettuce leaves garnished with dill or parsley. Serves 8.

German Potato Salad

Kartoffelsalat, potato salad, is a great German favorite, prepared in several variations and eaten either hot or cold. It is served as a traditional accompaniment for sausages, pork dishes, or game.

6 medium-sized potatoes, washed
Salt
1 large onion, peeled and chopped
⅓ cup salad oil
2 to 3 tablespoons wine vinegar
1 teaspoon sugar
3 tablespoons chopped fresh dill
3 tablespoons chopped fresh parsley
Pepper to taste

Cook potatoes in their jackets in a little salted boiling water until tender, about 25 minutes. Drain well; peel; and, while still warm, slice or cube into a large bowl. Add remaining ingredients and mix well. Cool at room temperature at least 1 hour to blend flavors. Serves 8 to 10.

Old-fashioned Hot Potato Salad

6 medium-sized potatoes, washed
Salt
2 hard-cooked eggs, shelled and chopped
4 thin slices bacon, chopped
1 small onion, peeled and minced
1 egg, beaten
¼ cup cider vinegar
Pepper to taste

Cook potatoes in their jackets in a little salted boiling water until tender, about 25 minutes. Drain; peel; and, while still warm, slice into a medium saucepan. Add chopped egg. Fry bacon and onion in a small skillet until fat is rendered and onion is tender. Strain, reserving fat. Add bacon and onion to potato mixture. Slowly add bacon fat to the beaten egg in a small bowl and beat well. Add with vinegar to the potato mixture and mix well. Season with salt and pepper. Slowly heat potato salad, stirring often, until hot. Serves 8.

Alexandre Dumas' Potato Salad

One of the world's most celebrated potato salads was first described in a play, *Francillon*, written by the noted Alexandre Dumas, *fils*, which was popular in Paris during the late 1800s. Whether Dumas actually created the salad is not certain, but it became the rage of Paris and has appeared on international menus ever since. On October 8, 1896, *Salade Francillon* was on the elaborate menu of a dinner given by the President of France for Tsar Nicholas II of Russia.

Over the years the salad, called either Francillon or Alexandre Dumas potato salad, has appeared in many variations. To my knowledge, this is the first and only salad recipe that was delivered on the stage. The original lines from Act I, Scene 2, described the glorious creation that is still praiseworthy.

Annette: Cook the potatoes in broth, cut them in slices as for an ordinary salad and, while they are still very hot, season them with salt, pepper, a very good fruity olive oil, vinegar. . . .

Henri: Tarragon?

Annette: Orléans is better; but that is not important. The important thing is half a glass of white wine: Château-Yquem, if possible. Plenty of *fines herbes* finely chopped. At the same time cook in court bouillon some very large mussels with a stalk of celery; drain carefully and add to the potatoes.

Henri: Not as many mussels as potatoes?

Annette: A third less. So that, little by little, you smell the mussels. You must not be able to detect it, neither must it be too strong. When the salad is made, toss it lightly; arrange in the shape of a *calotte de savant* [a wise man's skullcap] and cover it with sliced truffles.

Henri: Cooked in champagne?

Annette: Of course. This must all be done two hours before dinner so that the salad is very cold when served.

Henri: The salad bowl could be surrounded with ice.

Annette: No! No! No! You must not hurry it. It is very delicate, and its various aromas must be allowed to blend quietly. Was the salad you ate today good?

Henri: Marvelous!

Annette: Well, follow my recipe, and you will have the same pleasure.

Spring

and Summer Salads

Many people feel that the best seasons for salads are spring and summer, when warm weather enhances the desire for cold food, easy cooking, and outdoor dining. There are plenty of rich and interesting varieties well suited to those seasons.

Since ancient times, man has welcomed spring as "a time of anticipation." This meant new and fresh foods as a welcome relief for winter-weary palates. Spring is still the time to seek out tender fresh asparagus, green peas, and some early herbs. One can also find newly grown beet greens, leafy lettuce, and scallions.

It is a springtime custom in many lands, including some parts of the United States, to pick or purchase wild greens for salads. Among those best known in America are dandelion, chicory, purslane, corn salad, dock, sorrel, burdock, and watercress.

Even though many foods used to make salads can now be enjoyed throughout the year, there is nothing to compare with summer's bounty of fresh vegetables, fruits, greens, and herbs, taken from home gardens or purchased at neighborhood stores or markets.

When these foods are at their peak in quality and quantity is the best time to enjoy them. Ripe, plump tomatoes, cucumbers, tender small carrots, squashes, eggplants, corn, green beans, peppers, and new potatoes, among others, are all superb for making summer salads.

In very hot countries, salads are made with summer vegetables, but there are also those prepared with dried beans, legumes, grains, and fruits. Each is deftly seasoned and attractively presented.

In summer we look for salads to serve as light entrées for relaxing weekend meals, luncheons, informal suppers, cook-outs or barbecues, and picnics, whether at home, at the beach, or in the park. Salads made with seafood, fruits, cold rice, and beans, as well as other vegetables, are excellent for these occasions.

Here's a truly international selection of recipes for delectable spring and summer salads.

Australian Summer Tea Salad

This colorful tomato salad is made in several variations. It is served traditionally with summer afternoon tea in Australia.

6 medium-sized tomatoes, washed
Salt
¼ cup finely chopped fresh or canned pineapple
¼ cup finely chopped walnuts or almonds
¼ cup grated Swiss cheese
⅓ cup mayonnaise
6 crisp lettuce leaves, washed and dried
6 watercress leaves

Cut out stem core of each tomato. Cut a slice from top of each tomato and scoop out pulp and seeds. Sprinkle insides with salt and invert to drain for 30 minutes. Discard seeds; chop tomato pulp and combine with pineapple, nuts, cheese, and mayonnaise. Spoon into tomato shells. To serve, place each tomato over a lettuce leaf on a small plate. Garnish with a watercress leaf. Serves 6.

Caribbean Shrimp-Fruit Salad

This is an attractive salad to serve as an entrée for a summer ladies' or weekend luncheon.

1 small head leafy lettuce
½ cup mayonnaise or salad dressing
2 tablespoons fresh lime juice
2 teaspoons curry powder
2 teaspoons Worcestershire
Salt, pepper to taste
1 cup diced fresh or canned pineapple
½ cup diced papaya
½ cup diced mangoes
1 pound shelled cold, cooked medium shrimp

Wash and dry lettuce leaves; refrigerate. Combine mayonnaise, lime juice, curry powder, Worcestershire, salt, and pepper in a small jar or bowl and mix well; chill. When ready to serve, arrange lettuce leaves in a salad bowl. Top with fruits and place shrimp over them. Serve with mayonnaise dressing. Serves 4.

Arabian Parsley-Sesame Salad

This is a favorite salad during the summer in Arab countries and is served traditionally with skewered or grilled meat.

2 large bunches fresh parsley
2 to 3 garlic cloves, crushed
About ⅓ cup tahini (sesame paste) °
Juice of 2 large lemons
Salt, pepper to taste
2 tablespoons olive oil
½ teaspoon ground red pepper

Wash parsley; remove leaves from stems; dry and chop finely. Combine parsley with garlic, *tahini,* lemon juice, salt, and pepper to make a thick, smooth mixture. Spoon into a shallow bowl and top with oil and red pepper. Serve at room temperature or refrigerate. Serve with chunks of white or dark bread. Serves 2 to 4.

Mexican Green Bean–Corn Salad

Two native American foods, beans and corn, are combined to make a good salad for a summer outdoor barbecue or picnic.

1 pound fresh green beans
Salt
2 cups cold, cooked fresh or canned corn, drained
1 medium-sized green pepper, cleaned and chopped

° *Tahini* is sold in Near Eastern and specialty food stores.

1 medium-sized onion, peeled and chopped
1 canned green chili pepper, seeded and chopped
⅓ cup olive or salad oil
3 tablespoons wine vinegar
1 teaspoon chili powder
½ teaspoon dried oregano
Pepper to taste
1 large tomato, peeled and cut into wedges

Wash beans and trim ends. Break into pieces. Cook in a little salted boiling water until just tender, about 12 minutes. Drain and cool. Mix with remaining ingredients, except tomato, in a serving dish. Refrigerate 1 to 2 hours to blend flavors. Serve garnished with tomato wedges. Serves 4 to 6.

Flemish Fresh Asparagus Salad

In Belgium, favorite salads are prepared with tender, plump, pearl-white asparagus. Use green asparagus as a substitute if white asparagus is not available. Serve with seafood or beef.

2 pounds fresh white or green asparagus
Salt
½ cup olive or salad oil
Juice of 1 large lemon
2 tablespoons wine vinegar
1 tablespoon chopped fresh tarragon or 1 teaspoon dried
*   tarragon*
Salt, pepper to taste
2 hard-cooked eggs shelled and chopped

Wash asparagus in cold running water to remove all sand; cut off tough stem ends; remove any large scales. Put in a large skillet and cover with boiling water. Season with salt. Cook, uncovered, over moderate heat until just tender, about 12 minutes. Carefully remove from water and drain; cool. Cut into pieces. Combine oil, lemon juice, vinegar, tarragon, salt, and pepper, and pour over asparagus; toss. Serve sprinkled with chopped eggs. Serves 4 to 6.

Moroccan Herbed White Bean Salad

A good salad to serve at an outdoor meal with grilled or skewered meat or barbecued chicken.

> *3 cups cold, cooked dried white beans, navy or pea, or*
> *canned beans, drained*
> *½ cup olive oil*
> *3 tablespoons fresh lemon juice*
> *½ cup sliced scallions, with some tops*
> *⅓ cup chopped fresh parsley*
> *2 tablespoons chopped fresh mint*
> *¼ teaspoon ground coriander (optional)*
> *Salt, pepper to taste*
> *2 hard-cooked eggs, shelled and cut into quarters*
> *2 tomatoes, peeled and quartered*
> *4 stuffed olives, sliced*

Combine beans, oil, lemon juice, scallions, parsley, mint, coriander, salt, and pepper in a large bowl. Serve garnished with eggs, tomato quarters, and olives. Serves 4 to 6.

Caucasian Cucumber-Radish Salad

In the Caucasus region of southern Russia, this refreshing salad is served in the summer with skewered meat or broiled chicken.

2 medium-sized cucumbers, peeled and thinly sliced
Salt
12 radishes, cleaned and sliced
1 cup sliced scallions, with some tops
½ to ¾ cup plain yogurt
Pinch of sugar
Salt, pepper to taste
3 tablespoons chopped fresh mint or parsley

Put cucumbers in a colander; sprinkle with salt; allow to drain 30 minutes. Wipe dry and combine with radishes and scallions in a shallow bowl. Mix yogurt, sugar, salt, and pepper; spoon over vegetables; mix well. Refrigerate 1 to 2 hours to blend flavors. Serve sprinkled with mint or parsley. Serves 4.

French Cold Rice-Vegetable Salad

A good salad to serve for a summer outdoor luncheon or supper with cold meats or grilled seafood.

1 cup raw long-grain rice
½ cup sliced scallions, with some tops
1 medium-sized green pepper, cleaned and chopped
1 cup cold, cooked green peas
1 cup diced celery
1 cup sliced radishes

2 canned pimientos, drained and diced
⅓ cup olive oil
2 to 3 tablespoons wine vinegar
½ teaspoon dried tarragon or basil
3 tablespoons chopped fresh parsley
Salt, pepper to taste

Cook rice according to package directions; cool. Combine with next six ingredients in a large bowl. Mix together oil, vinegar, herbs, salt, and pepper; add to salad. Refrigerate until ready to serve. Serves 6 to 8.

English Broccoli Salad

A colorful and delicious salad to serve at a company weekend luncheon with cold roast beef or grilled chicken.

1 bunch fresh broccoli, about 1½ pounds
Salt
2 cups shredded raw carrots
2 large tomatoes, peeled and cut into wedges
⅓ cup salad oil
2 tablespoons fresh lemon juice
2 hard-cooked eggs, shelled and chopped
Pepper to taste

Trim and discard outer leaves of broccoli. Split large stalks lengthwise, then cut into 3-inch-long pieces. Cook in a little salted boiling water in a medium saucepan, covered, until just tender, about 12 minutes. Drain; cool; and chill. Spoon into a serving dish. Top with shredded carrots and surround with tomato wedges. Combine remaining ingredients and spoon over broccoli. Serves 4.

West Coast Crab-Cucumber Salad

A good summer luncheon salad.

1 cup mayonnaise
2 tablespoons chili sauce
1 teaspoon prepared horseradish
2 teaspoons Worcestershire
Salt, pepper to taste
2 cans (6½ ounces each) King crabmeat
1 small head leafy lettuce, washed, dried, and chilled
1 medium-sized cucumber, washed, scored, and sliced
  thinly
2 tomatoes, peeled and sliced
1 ripe avocado, peeled and sliced

Combine mayonnaise, chili sauce, horseradish, Worcestershire, salt, and pepper in a small jar or bowl and refrigerate. Remove membranes from crabmeat, keeping large chunks whole. Refrigerate crabmeat. When ready to serve, arrange lettuce leaves in a shallow oval or round serving dish. Top with flaked and small pieces of crabmeat. Cover with large crabmeat chunks. Surround with cucumber, tomato, and avocado slices. Serve with chilled mayonnaise sauce. Serves 6.

Syrian Bread-Vegetable Salad

This salad, called *fatoosh,* or large salad, is served traditionally for summer meals in Syria. It may be garnished with black olives and/or radishes, if desired.

2 to 3 small rounds pita bread
1 small head leafy lettuce, washed, dried, torn into bite-
    size pieces, and chilled
1 medium-sized cucumber, peeled and chopped
8 scallions, cleaned and sliced
1 cup chopped fresh parsley
1 cup chopped fresh mint
⅓ cup olive oil
Juice of 2 large lemons
1 or 2 garlic cloves, crushed
Salt, pepper to taste

Break bread into small pieces and put in a salad bowl. Add lettuce, cucumber, scallions, parsley, and mint; mix well. Combine oil, lemon juice, garlic, salt, and pepper and pour over salad. Toss lightly and serve. Serves 4.

Norwegian Summer Salad

A good mixed salad to serve at a summer supper with cold meats or seafood.

1 medium-sized cucumber, peeled and sliced
4 medium-sized potatoes, cooked, peeled, and sliced
3 hard-cooked eggs, shelled and chopped
2 small heads leafy lettuce, washed, dried, torn into bite-
    size pieces, and chilled
⅓ cup salad oil
3 tablespoons cider vinegar
2 teaspoons sharp prepared mustard
1 teaspoon sugar
Salt, pepper to taste
2 medium-sized tomatoes, peeled and sliced

Combine cucumber, potatoes, eggs, and lettuce in a salad bowl. Mix oil, vinegar, mustard, sugar, salt, and pepper; pour over salad just before serving; toss. Serve garnished with tomato slices. Serves 4 to 6.

Albanian Minted Romaine Salad

In the small Balkan country of Albania, salads, especially those made with garden-fresh lettuces, are traditionally seasoned with olive oil, lemon juice, mint, and nuts.

> *1 medium-sized head romaine*
> *¼ cup sliced scallions, with some tops*
> *2 hard-cooked eggs, shelled and sliced*
> *½ cup chopped walnuts*
> *2 tablespoons chopped fresh mint*
> *¼ cup olive oil*
> *2 tablespoons fresh lemon juice*
> *Salt, pepper to taste*

Wash romaine; separate leaves; break into bite-size pieces; dry thoroughly; refrigerate. When ready to serve, put romaine pieces in a salad bowl. Add scallions, eggs, walnuts, and mint; toss lightly. Combine remaining ingredients and pour over salad. Toss again and serve at once. Serves 4 to 6.

New England Picnic Potato Salad

Serve with cold meat loaf, hot dogs, or hamburgers as a summer holiday or weekend picnic.

6 medium-sized potatoes, washed
Salt
Juice of 2 large lemons
1 cup diced celery
¾ cup diced peeled and seeded cucumber
⅓ cup diced green pepper
⅓ cup chopped fresh parsley
Pepper to taste
About ¾ cup mayonnaise or salad dressing

Cook potatoes in their jackets in a little salted boiling water until tender, about 25 minutes. Drain; peel; and cut into 1-inch cubes while still warm. Put in a bowl and add lemon juice; mix well. Leave at room temperature for 30 minutes. Add remaining ingredients, except mayonnaise, and mix well. Add enough mayonnaise to bind ingredients. Allow to stand at room temperature to mellow, or refrigerate. Serves 6 to 8.

Israeli Summer Squash Salad

The Israelis grow an assortment of flavorful summer yellow squashes and zucchini that are served with herb-flavored dressings. This salad is good with grilled chicken or cold roast poultry.

2 medium-sized yellow squashes, washed, trimmed, and
   cut into ¼-inch slices
2 medium-sized zucchini, washed, trimmed, and cut into
   ¼-inch slices
Salt
2 large tomatoes, peeled and sliced
2 large green peppers, cleaned and cut into slivers
1 large onion, peeled and chopped

⅓ cup olive oil
3 tablespoons fresh lemon juice
2 garlic cloves, crushed
Pepper to taste
2 tablespoons chopped fresh mint or dill

Cook squashes and zucchini together in a little salted boiling water in a large saucepan, covered, until just tender, about 5 minutes. Drain and spoon into a serving dish; cool. Add tomatoes, peppers, and onion, and mix well. Combine oil, lemon juice, garlic, salt, and pepper, and pour over vegetables. Mix well and refrigerate 1 to 2 hours to blend flavors. Serve sprinkled with mint or dill. Serves 6 to 8.

Salade Niçoise

This well-known salad from southern France is an excellent entrée for a summer luncheon or supper, particularly when served outdoors.

2 large tomatoes, peeled and quartered
3 cold boiled potatoes, peeled and sliced
1 cup cut-up cold, cooked green beans
1 medium-sized red onion, peeled and sliced
1 large green pepper, cleaned and cut into strips
12 pitted black olives
6 anchovy fillets, drained and chopped
3 hard-cooked eggs, shelled and quartered
⅓ cup olive oil
2 tablespoons wine vinegar
1 teaspoon sharp prepared mustard
Salt, pepper to taste

Put first five ingredients in a large bowl. Arrange olives, anchovies, and eggs over vegetables. Combine remaining ingredients in a small jar and mix well. Pour over salad and refrigerate 1 hour before serving. Mix again. Serves 4 to 6.

Chilean Chicken-Corn Salad

An innovative and attractive salad to serve at a summer luncheon.

> *3 cups diced cooked white meat of chicken*
> *2 cups cooked fresh or canned corn, drained*
> *2 medium-sized green peppers, cleaned and chopped*
> *4 medium-sized tomatoes, peeled and chopped*
> *1 medium-sized cucumber, peeled and diced*
> *3 tablespoons chopped fresh coriander or parsley*
> *Salt, pepper to taste*
> *2 cups mayonnaise or salad dressing*
> *Crisp lettuce leaves, washed and dried*
> *Paprika*
> *2 hard-cooked eggs, shelled and quartered*
> *12 radish roses*

Combine first six ingredients in a medium bowl. Season with salt and pepper. Add 1 cup mayonnaise or salad dressing and mix well. Refrigerate 1 hour. When ready to serve, place lettuce leaves on a serving dish and top with chicken-corn mixture, shaping into a mound. Coat with remaining 1 cup mayonnaise or salad dressing. Sprinkle with paprika and garnish with eggs and radishes. Serves 4 to 6.

Neapolitan Zucchini Salad

One of our best and most popular summer vegetables is zucchini, a green-and-yellow-striped variety of summer squash developed in Italy. It is also known as Italian squash or summer marrow.

> *4 medium-sized zucchini, ends trimmed and cut into ¼-inch slices*
> *Salt*
> *1 cup finely chopped onion*
> *1 or 2 garlic cloves, minced*
> *2 tablespoons chopped fresh basil or ¾ teaspoon dried basil*
> *3 to 4 tablespoons olive oil*
> *Pepper to taste*
> *2 tablespoons fresh lemon juice*
> *2 large tomatoes, peeled and chopped*
> *3 tablespoons chopped fresh parsley*

Cook zucchini slices in a little salted boiling water until just tender, about 6 minutes. Drain and cool. Mix with onion, garlic, basil, oil and lemon juice. Season with salt and pepper. Refrigerate 1 hour or longer to blend flavors. When ready to serve, top with chopped tomatoes and sprinkle with parsley. Serves 4 to 6.

Early American Wilted Lettuce

This salad is an old and treasured American favorite. It was relished by pioneer families, who made it with greens and cabbage as well as lettuce. Serve with cold meat loaf or cold cuts at an outdoor meal.

4 slices thin bacon, chopped
¼ cup cider vinegar
2 small heads leafy lettuce, washed, dried, and chilled
½ cup sliced scallions, with some tops
½ teaspoon sugar
Salt, pepper to taste

Fry bacon in a small skillet until crisp. Remove and drain on absorbent paper. Add vinegar to fat and bring to a boil. Put lettuce leaves, scallions, sugar, salt, and pepper in a bowl. Pour hot vinegar-fat mixture over salad and toss. Serve sprinkled with crisp bacon. Serves 4.

Egg Salad

No one knows who first created an egg salad, but cooks in many lands have enhanced the basic recipe of sliced or chopped hard-cooked eggs and simple seasonings. Today we have many interesting combinations of eggs with such foods as celery, green peppers, onions, scallions, crumbled cooked bacon, capers, olives, pimientos, and cooked or pickled beets that are bound with flavorful dressings. Egg salad may be served in lettuce-leaf cups and used to fill tomatoes and avocados. Given below is a basic egg salad recipe.

6 hard-cooked eggs, shelled and chopped
1 cup diced celery
2 tablespoons grated or minced onion
Dash of cayenne

Salt, pepper to taste
About ¾ cup mayonnaise or salad dressing
Crisp lettuce leaves, washed and dried

Combine ingredients, except lettuce, in a medium bowl. Refrigerate 1 hour or longer to blend flavors. Serve in lettuce cups, if desired. Serves 4.

Salade Aixoise

An interesting French salad to serve with steaks or grilled fish fillets at a company summer meal.

1 package (9 ounces) artichoke hearts, cooked, halved,
*   and chilled*
1 cup cut-up cold, cooked green beans
3 medium-sized cold, cooked potatoes, peeled and
*   quartered*
2 large tomatoes, peeled and quartered
2 medium-sized green peppers, cleaned and cut into
*   strips*
6 flat anchovy fillets, chopped
12 pitted black olives
1 tablespoon drained capers
⅓ cup olive oil
3 tablespoons wine vinegar
½ teaspoon dried tarragon
2 tablespoons chopped fresh parsley

Place first five ingredients in a large bowl or serving dish. Top with anchovies, olives, and capers. Combine remaining ingredients and pour over salad. Serve at once. Serves 4.

Luncheon Tomato Flower Salad

An attractive salad for a summer ladies' luncheon.

6 chilled large ripe tomatoes
6 large crisp lettuce leaves, washed and dried
½ cup diced celery
½ cup diced, peeled, seeded cucumber
2 tablespoons minced onion
2 tablespoons minced green pepper
2 hard-cooked eggs, shelled and chopped
About ¼ cup mayonnaise

Remove stem cores from tomatoes. Cut each four times from top almost through to bottom to form eight attached petals. Spread apart and place each tomato on a lettuce leaf on a small salad plate. Combine remaining ingredients and spoon into tomato centers. Refrigerate until ready to serve. Serves 6.

Nova Scotian Scallop Salad

Nova Scotian scallops from Digby, the headquarters of one of the world's largest fleets of scallop ships, are traditionally served deep-fried or in this flavorful salad, which is an excellent entrée for a summer luncheon or supper.

1 pound fresh or frozen sea scallops, cooked and chopped
¼ cup minced onions
½ cup sliced radishes
¾ cup diced, peeled, seeded cucumber
¾ cup diced celery

3 tablespoons chopped fresh parsley
½ cup salad dressing or mayonnaise
Salt, pepper to taste
4 large lettuce leaves, washed and dried
1 large tomato, peeled and cut into wedges

Chill chopped scallops before making salad. Combine with remaining ingredients, except lettuce leaves and tomatoes. Make cups with lettuce leaves and spoon scallop mixture into centers of them. Garnish with tomato wedges. Serves 4.

Dill Coleslaw

A refreshing summer coleslaw to serve with hamburgers or hot dogs, but especially good with cold cooked salmon.

3 cups shredded green cabbage
¼ cup minced onion
1½ teaspoons dill seed
2 teaspoons fresh lemon juice
½ cup sour cream or mayonnaise
Salt, pepper to taste

Combine ingredients and refrigerate 1 to 2 hours to blend flavors. Serves 4 to 6.

Alaskan Summer Salmon Salad

One of the glories of summer dining is a cold salmon salad, preferably made with fresh salmon, a rare treat today. A good summer luncheon entrée.

2 cups flaked cooked fresh salmon or canned salmon,
    drained
1 cup diced celery
2 hard-cooked eggs, shelled and chopped
About ½ cup salad dressing
2 tablespoons chopped sweet pickles
3 tablespoons sliced scallions, with some tops
1 tablespoon fresh lemon juice
Salt, pepper to taste
Crisp lettuce leaves, washed and dried

Combine ingredients, except lettuce leaves, and refrigerate. When ready to serve, arrange lettuce leaves on a platter or individual plates and spoon salad over them. Garnish with capers, if desired. Serves 4 to 6.

Iraqi Tomato Salad

Fresh herbs and cumin give a distinctive flavor to this tomato salad. Serve with hamburgers, grilled meat, or barbecued chicken.

4 large ripe tomatoes
1 medium cucumber, peeled and diced
6 scallions, cleaned and sliced, with some tops
¼ cup olive oil
2 garlic cloves, crushed
3 tablespoons chopped fresh parsley
2 tablespoons chopped fresh mint
½ teaspoon ground cumin
Salt, pepper to taste

Peel and slice tomatoes. Arrange on a serving dish and top with cucumbers and scallions. Combine remaining ingredients and pour over salad. Serve at once. Serves 4 to 6.

Midwestern Three-Bean Salad

This favorite American salad appears in many variations on summer outdoor tables and in restaurant salad bars. It is excellent for an informal summer meal whether served indoors or outside.

> ⅔ *cup cider vinegar*
> ⅔ *cup sugar*
> ⅓ *cup salad oil*
> 2 *cups cut-up cold, cooked green beans*
> 2 *cups cut-up cold, cooked wax beans*
> 2 *cups cooked or canned kidney beans, drained*
> ½ *cup chopped onion*
> ½ *cup chopped celery*
> *Salt to taste*

Combine vinegar, sugar, and oil in a small jar or bowl. Mix remaining ingredients in a large bowl. Add vinegar-oil mixture and refrigerate 1 hour or longer to blend flavors. Serves 8.

Provençal Ratatouille

This well-known summer dish from France's lovely Provence is made with a medley of vegetables and seasonings and can be served as an appetizer or an entrée. It is very good with grilled lamb or fish.

> *1 medium-sized eggplant, about 1¼ pounds*
> *Salt*
> *About 1 cup olive oil*
> *2 medium-sized onions, peeled and chopped*
> *2 medium-sized zucchini, about ½ pound each, washed,*
>   *stemmed, and sliced*
> *2 garlic cloves, crushed*
> *1 large green pepper, cleaned and chopped*
> *3 large tomatoes, peeled and chopped*
> *Freshly ground black pepper*
> *¼ teaspoon dried basil*
> *¼ teaspoon dried thyme or marjoram*
> *Juice of 1 large lemon*

Peel eggplant and cube. Put in a colander and sprinkle with salt. Allow to drain 30 minutes. Wipe dry. Heat ⅓ cup oil in a large skillet and add onions; sauté until tender. Push aside and add eggplant cubes, several at a time; sauté until tender, adding more oil as needed. Remove to a plate when tender. Add zucchini; sauté until tender. Return eggplant cubes to skillet. Add remaining ingredients, except lemon juice, and simmer, covered, until ingredients are tender, about 35 minutes. Add lemon juice and cook, uncovered, 5 minutes. Cool. Serve lukewarm or refrigerate several hours before serving. Serves 4 to 6.

Ozark Sweet-Sour Coleslaw

A good summer salad to serve with grilled fish, barbecued chicken, or hot dogs at an outdoor meal.

2 tablespoons all-purpose flour
1 teaspoon dry mustard
⅓ cup cider vinegar
2 tablespoons sugar
1 egg
Salt, pepper to taste
1 cup milk
3 cups finely shredded green cabbage
1 cup grated raw carrots

Combine flour, mustard, vinegar, sugar, egg, salt, and pepper in a small saucepan. Heat, stirring almost constantly, until thickened and smooth. Gradually add milk and continue cooking slowly, stirring, for 2 minutes. Remove from heat and cool. Mix with cabbage and carrots. Refrigerate 3 to 4 hours to blend flavors. Serves 6.

Tuscan White Bean–Tuna Salad

In the northern Italian province of Tuscany, many traditional dishes include native fat and white beans called *cannellini,* which are sold in cans in America. Dried white beans may be used as a substitute. This salad is good for a summer luncheon or buffet.

4 cups canned cannellini *or other cooked or canned*
   white beans, drained
½ cup chopped onions
½ cup chopped fresh parsley
2 tablespoons fresh lemon juice
Salt, pepper to taste
1 can (6½ or 7 ounces) tuna fish in oil

2 tomatoes, peeled and cut into wedges
6 stuffed olives, sliced

If canned beans are used, rinse quickly in cold water. Put beans in a large bowl and add onions, parsley, lemon juice, salt, and pepper. Break tuna into chunks and place over bean mixture. Sprinkle oil from tuna over the salad, and garnish with tomatoes and olives. Serves 6 to 8.

Gulf Coast Shrimp Salad

An easy-to-prepare salad for a summer weekend luncheon.

1 pound cold, shelled, cooked medium shrimp
1 cup diced celery
3 tablespoons minced onion
3 tablespoons minced sweet pickles
⅓ cup mayonnaise
Salt, pepper to taste
Crisp lettuce leaves, washed and dried
3 tomatoes, peeled and cut into wedges

Combine first five ingredients in a medium bowl. Season with salt and pepper. Refrigerate 1 to 2 hours to blend flavors. To serve, place lettuce leaves on a platter and spoon salad over them. Surround with tomato wedges. Serves 4.

Mediterranean Poor Man's Caviar

A popular summer salad in Mediterranean countries is made with eggplant and various seasonings. It is called by a diverse selection of names, but one of the most popular is poor man's caviar.

> 1 medium-sized eggplant, about 1¼ pounds
> 2 to 3 garlic cloves
> ½ cup chopped scallions, with some tops
> 2 medium-sized green peppers, cleaned and chopped
> 1 large tomato, peeled and chopped
> 3 tablespoons fresh lemon juice
> ⅓ to ½ cup olive oil
> Salt, pepper to taste

Prick eggplant in several places and put on a cookie sheet. Bake in a preheated 400°F. oven until soft, about 50 minutes. Cool until able to handle. Peel off and discard skin. Put pulp in a bowl; chop with a wooden spoon or knife. Pour off all liquid. Add remaining ingredients and mix well. Allow to stand to blend flavors at room temperature or in the refrigerator 1 to 2 hours. Serve with pieces of pita bread or chunks of crusty French bread. Serves 6 to 8.

Tomato Salads

One of the great glories of summer is a salad of sweet and flavorful garden-fresh tomatoes. Although tomato salads can be prepared the year round, they are best when tomatoes are in season. They may be served as appetiziers, first courses, or side dishes.

Wherever tomatoes are grown they are enjoyed in salads, and the varieties are seemingly endless. Although most salads are made with red tomatoes, they can also be prepared with those that are yellow or other colors.

It is essential to use only the best tomatoes for salads. Choose those that are plump and firm, of good color, and without spots. They should feel heavy for their size.

Garden-fresh tomatoes should not be chilled, as their flavor is best at room temperature. Use as quickly as possible after buying or picking.

It is a matter of personal preference whether or not the tomatoes should be peeled. Many people feel that the skins of the tomatoes ruin the salad; others value them for their vitamin content. Tomatoes are easily peeled. Pierce the stem end with a fork and hold over a gas flame until the skin wrinkles. Instead, you may elect to dip the tomato into boiling water for a minute. Then simply slip off or pare the skin with the edge of a knife.

Tomato salads should be prepared just before serving and eating. Cut out the stem-end cores of tomatoes and slice them crosswise or vertically. Ideally, oil and salt should not touch tomatoes until just before eating. That explains why many people all around the world prefer to season at the table with oil from a cruet and freshly ground salt.

Since this is not always possible, however, the salads may be dressed in the kitchen and brought to the table. The simplest dressing is one of olive oil and vinegar, using 3 parts oil to 1 part vinegar, coarsely grated salt, and freshly ground pepper. (Some people eschew vinegar and use only oil.) The salad may also be sprinkled with sliced scallions, chopped chives or shallots, minced garlic, and such fresh or dried herbs as basil, parsley, tarragon, thyme, or oregano.

Other palate-pleasing techniques use lemon or lime juice instead of vinegar; still others top the tomatoes with a spoonful of sour cream or mayonnaise, finely chopped hard-cooked eggs, crumbled crisp bacon, or anchovies.

Given below is a recipe for French tomato salad. You'll find recipes for other tomato salads elsewhere in this book.

Salade De Tomates

A colorful salad made with garden-fresh ripe tomatoes is an excellent first course for luncheon. It may also be served as a side dish.

3 large ripe tomatoes, peeled and thickly sliced
2 to 3 tablespoons olive oil
¼ cup sliced scallions, with some tops
3 tablespoons chopped fresh parsely
½ teaspoon dried basil
1 or 2 garlic cloves, crushed (optional)
Salt, pepper to taste
1 large green pepper, cleaned and cut into slivers

Arrange tomato slices on a plate. Sprinkle with oil, scallions, parsley, basil, and garlic. Season with salt and pepper. Garnish with pepper slivers. Serve at once. Serves 4.

Autumn
and Winter Salads

In America and elsewhere, salads have usually been sadly neglected or given short shrift by cooks during autumn and winter. This is unfortunate because during these months appealing and interesting salads will not only enhance the daily menu but provide necessary vitamins and other nutrients.

When autumn days are still warm and thoughts return to serious cooking, you can take pleasure trips to roadside stands or to well-stocked supermarkets for salad vegetables and greens. It's an excellent time to switch from ordinary tossed salads and to experiment with others. Marvelous salads can be made with cauliflower, for example, and with Brussels sprouts, and hearts of celery.

Winter provides a fine crop of hardy vegetables for the salad fancier. While some of these familiar foods, such as beets, carrots, cauliflower, and members of the cabbage family, are now available all year round, they are in peak supply and at their best during the colder months. Winter is the best time to serve them in colorful salads that go with hearty cold-weather dishes.

This is also the time to look for less familiar vegetables such as celery root or celeriac, kohlrabi, oyster plant, leeks, Jerusalem artichoke, and an old favorite, parsnips. Dried peas, dried beans, lentils, and chick-peas are also good for making nourishing and inexpensive salads.

Cooks in Central and Northern European countries have long served some of their most interesting salads during the coldest months, when these dishes have a daily place of honor in the home.

A recipe for a simple but good winter salad by Thomas Walker appeared in his weekly English magazine, *The Original,* in 1836. He recommended it to his readers, suggesting that the dish should be better known.

"Boil one or two large onions, till soft and perfectly mild. When cold, mix the onion with celery, and sliced beetroot, roasted in the oven, which has more flavor than when boiled. Dress this salad with oil, vinegar, salt, and pepper. The onion and beetroot are very good without celery. Roast beef with this salad and potatoes browned in the dripping-pan, or in the oven, is a dish to delight the constitution of an Englishman in the winter months."

Many of the following recipes are from European countries, but the selections come from other continents, too. Cooks everywhere have long recognized the importance of autumn and winter salads.

Swiss Kohlrabi Salad

Kohlrabi, or cabbage turnip, is a purplish-white vegetable grown primarily for its swollen root, which has a pleasing, nutty flavor. It can be prepared in any of the ways that are suitable for turnips. When cooked and cold, it may be served with an oil-vinegar dressing or mayonnaise. Greatly treasured in Central and Northern Europe, the vegetable goes well with pork and game.

4 medium-sized kohlrabi
Salt
½ cup sliced radishes
⅓ cup salad dressing
2 tablespoons cider vinegar
½ teaspoon dry mustard
1 teaspoon sugar
Salt, pepper to taste
Crisp lettuce leaves, washed and dried
½ cup grated carrots

Cut off tops and pare thick kohlrabi stems. Slice and cook kohlrabi in a little salted boiling water, covered, until just tender, about 15 minutes. Drain and cool. Combine with radishes in a serving dish. Mix salad dressing, vinegar, mustard, and sugar. Season with salt and pepper and add to vegetables. Refrigerate 1 hour or longer to blend flavors. Serve on lettuce leaves, garnished with carrots. Serves 4 to 6.

Italian Onion-Watercress Salad

Italians are very fond of onion salads. Some are simple dishes of sliced onions with one or more garnishes; others contain a mixture of onions and other foods. One old-time recipe for an Italian onion salad called for sliced large onions, scallions, chives, and chibbols (similar to leeks). Serve with meat or game.

1 bunch watercress
2 large red onions, peeled and thinly sliced
2 to 3 tablespoons olive oil

1 tablespoon wine vinegar
½ teaspoon dried oregano or thyme
Salt, pepper to taste
4 flat anchovies, drained and chopped
8 pitted black olives

Wash watercress well to remove all dirt. Remove leaves from stems; discard any wilted leaves. Dry leaves and refrigerate. When ready to serve, place watercress leaves on a plate and top with onion slices. Sprinkle with oil, vinegar, oregano or thyme, salt, and pepper. Top with chopped anchovies and garnish with olives. Serves 4.

Norwegian Raw Vegetable Salad

A good winter salad to serve with meat loaf or a roast.

3 cups shredded green cabbage
1 cup julienne-cut, peeled celery root or celeriac
1 cup grated raw carrots
1 medium-sized onion, peeled and chopped
2 medium-sized apples, cored and chopped
About ⅔ cup mayonnaise or salad dressing
2 tablespoons fresh lemon juice
1 teaspoon sugar
Salt, pepper to taste
2 tablespoons chopped fresh dill or parsley

Combine cabbage, celery root, carrots, onion, and apples in a medium bowl or serving dish. Mix remaining ingredients, except dill or parsley, and combine with vegetables and apples. Serve sprinkled with dill or parsley. Serves 6 to 8.

Georgian Kidney Bean Salad

In the Soviet republic of Georgia, winter salads are often made with dried beans, especially kidney beans, which are flavored with unusual seasonings such as those in this dish. Serve with skewered or grilled meat.

2 cups cold, cooked or canned kidney beans, drained
½ cup sliced scallions, with some tops
3 tablespoons olive or salad oil
2 tablespoons cider vinegar
½ cup finely chopped walnuts
¼ to ½ teaspoon ground red pepper
Salt, pepper to taste
3 tablespoons chopped fresh mint or parsley

Combine ingredients, except mint or parsley, in a medium bowl. Refrigerate 2 to 3 hours to blend flavors. Serve sprinkled with mint or parsley. Serves 4 to 6.

Pennsylvania Dutch Sauerkraut Salad

An old-fashioned salad that is traditionally served during the winter with sausages or other pork dishes.

1 pound bulk or canned sauerkraut, drained and
  chopped
1 medium-sized onion, peeled and chopped
¾ cup chopped green pepper
½ cup diced raw carrots
⅛ teaspoon mustard seeds

⅛ teaspoon celery seeds
3 tablespoons salad oil
3 tablespoons chili sauce
2 teaspoons sugar
Salt, pepper to taste

Combine ingredients in a serving dish. Refrigerate 2 to 3 hours to blend flavors. Serves 4 to 6.

Polish Celery Root Salad

Celery root is highly prized in Poland as a salad ingredient. Its appealing flavor is enhanced by an herb-flavored oil-vinegar or sour cream dressing. This salad is excellent with meat or game.

1 small celery root or celeriac
Salt
¼ cup salad oil
2 tablespoons cider vinegar
1 teaspoon sugar
2 tablespoons chopped onions
2 tablespoons chopped fresh dill
Pepper to taste

Wash celery root well; cut off tops. Peel root and cut into 1-inch cubes. Cook in a little salted boiling water until just tender, about 15 minutes. Drain and cool. Put with remaining ingredients in a medium bowl. Refrigerate 2 to 3 hours to blend flavors. Serves 4.

Chilean Chick-Pea Salad

This flavorful salad, called *ensalada campesina,* or peasant salad, is a nourishing and inexpensive salad to serve with any kind of meat.

2 cups cooked or canned chick-peas, drained
2 medium-sized red onions, peeled and thinly sliced
½ pound Jack or Cheddar cheese, diced
⅓ cup olive or salad oil
3 tablespoons fresh lemon juice
3 tablespoons chopped fresh coriander or parsley
Salt, pepper to taste
Crisp lettuce leaves, washed and dried
2 hard-cooked eggs, shelled and quartered

Combine chick-peas, onions, and cheese in a large bowl. Mix oil, lemon juice, coriander or parsley, salt, and pepper; pour over salad; mix well. Refrigerate 1 hour or longer to blend flavors. Serve on lettuce leaves and garnish with egg quarters. Serves 4 to 6.

Korean Kimchee

A staple Korean vegetable salad, or relish, called *kimchee* is made in many variations with winter vegetables and seasonings. Each is highly seasoned with garlic, onions, and hot peppers. An excellent source of vitamins, *kimchee* is generally made in large quantities and stored in huge jars to last throughout the winter. There are also summer varieties of *kimchee* that are used immediately. This recipe is for a simplified version.

4 cups chopped washed celery or (Chinese) cabbage
Salt
12 scallions, cleaned and sliced, with some tops
2 to 4 garlic cloves, crushed
2 teaspoons minced ginger root
1 to 2 teaspoons sugar
1 teaspoon minced or ground red peppers

Put cabbage in a medium bowl or crock and sprinkle with 2 to 3 tablespoons salt. Allow to stand 30 minutes. Wash and dry. Mix with remaining ingredients and 1 to 2 tablespoons salt. Put in an earthenware or glass jar and cover with water. Let stand several days at room temperature and drain well before serving. Serves 8 to 10.

Maine Jerusalem Artichoke Salad

The Jerusalem artichoke, a native North American vegetable, was a favorite on Colonial tables, but it has since been practically forgotten. This is unfortunate since Jerusalem artichokes are starch-free, low in calories, and nutritious. Raw Jerusalem artichokes have qualities resembling water chestnuts and can be added to tossed salads and greens, or served with vinaigrette or creamy salad dressings. This salad goes well with pork dishes.

2 pounds Jerusalem artichokes
1 medium-sized onion, peeled and chopped
1 or 2 garlic cloves, crushed
⅓ cup olive or salad oil
3 tablespoons cider vinegar

3 tablespoons chopped fresh parsley
Salt, pepper to taste
1 large tomato, peeled and cut into wedges

Wash Jerusalem artichokes; peel and slice thinly. If not used at once, leave in cold water with some lemon juice added to prevent discoloration. Wipe dry and combine in a serving dish with remaining ingredients, except tomatoes. Refrigerate 1 hour or longer to blend flavors. Serve garnished with tomato wedges. Serves 6.

Israeli Carrot-Watercress Salad

Israelis are very fond of salads featuring raw or cooked carrots, which are combined with fruits, other vegetables, and greens, and seasoned with herbs or piquant flavorings. Serve with corned beef, veal, or tongue.

1 bunch watercress
3 cups thinly sliced raw carrots
½ cup sliced scallions, with some tops
3 tablespoons olive or salad oil
Juice of 1 large lemon
Salt, pepper to taste
2 tablespoons drained capers
2 hard-cooked eggs, shelled and cut into quarters

Wash watercress well to remove all dirt. Remove leaves from stems and discard any wilted leaves. Dry leaves and refrigerate. When ready to serve, put watercress in a bowl or on a plate. Arrange carrots and scallions over watercress. Combine oil, lemon juice, salt, and pepper; pour over salad. Sprinkle top with capers and garnish with egg quarters. Serves 4 to 6.

Turkish Cauliflower Salad

In Turkey, vegetable markets in winter display attractive and nutritious large cauliflowers that are usually snowy-white but may be green or even purple in color. Serve this salad with shish kebab, roast lamb or grilled chops.

1 whole cauliflower
Salt
1 tablespoon fresh lemon juice
1 large green pepper, cleaned and chopped
12 pitted black olives, cut into halves
8 scallions, cleaned and sliced, with some tops
⅓ cup olive oil
2 tablespoons cider vinegar
½ teaspoon dried oregano or thyme
Salt, pepper to taste
3 tablespoons chopped fresh dill or parsley

Cut off base and tough outer leaves of cauliflower. Wash in cold running water, holding upside down. Heat 1 inch salted water in a large kettle; add lemon juice. Cook cauliflower, uncovered, 5 minutes. Cover and boil until just tender, about 20 minutes. Drain; cool; break into flowerets and place in a salad bowl. Add peppers, olives, and scallions. Combine oil, vinegar, oregano or thyme, salt, and pepper; add to vegetables. Toss. Serve sprinkled with dill or parsley. Serves 4 to 6.

Hungarian Pepper Salad

Hungarians are very fond of all kinds of peppers, both sweet and hot and of various colors. Their national spice is the world's best paprika, made with native red peppers. This is one of their many pepper dishes, and it can be made spicier with the addition of minced or ground red peppers, if desired. A good winter salad to serve with sausages or other meats.

4 large sweet red or green peppers
3 to 4 tablespoons salad oil
1 large onion, peeled and chopped
2 to 3 teaspoons paprika
2 tablespoons wine vinegar
½ cup sour cream
3 tablespoons chopped fresh dill or parsley
Salt, pepper to taste

Clean peppers and cut into strips. Sauté in heated oil in a medium skillet until just tender. Remove with a slotted spoon to a serving dish. Add onion to oil drippings and sauté until tender. Mix in paprika and cook 1 minute. Add to peppers. Stir in remaining ingredients and mix well. Allow to stand at room temperature to cool or refrigerate 1 hour before serving. Serves 4.

Peruvian Potato Salad

Peruvian cooks have utilized their native white potato to make innovative dishes, one of the best of which is this salad with a cottage cheese dressing and colorful garnishes. Serve with roast beef or steaks.

> *6 medium-sized potatoes, washed*
> *Salt*
> *1 large onion, peeled and chopped*
> *2 tablespoons olive or salad oil*
> *2 tablespoons chili powder*
> *1 cup small-curd cottage cheese*
> *¼ cup milk*
> *1 tablespoon fresh lemon juice*
> *Pepper to taste*
> *4 radishes, cleaned and sliced*
> *¼ cup chopped fresh parsley*
> *4 pitted black olives, halved*

Cook potatoes in their jackets in a little salted boiling water until tender, about 25 minutes. Drain; peel; cube; and place in a bowl. Meanwhile, sauté onion in heated oil in a medium skillet until tender. Add chili powder and cook 1 minute. Remove from heat and mix with cheese, milk, and lemon juice. Season with salt and pepper. Beat until smooth. Spoon over potatoes and garnish with radishes, parsley, and olives. Serves 6 to 8.

Egyptian Fool

Fool, or beans, are a staple food in Egypt and are eaten the year round. During the winter, this bean salad is served with roast lamb or grilled fish.

> *2 cups dried white beans, washed and picked over*
> *3 garlic cloves, crushed*
> *½ cup chopped onions*

½ cup olive oil
3 tablespoons fresh lemon juice
1 teaspoon cayenne
Salt, pepper to taste
½ cup chopped fresh coriander or parsley

Put beans in a large kettle and cover with water. Bring to a boil and cook briskly for 2 minutes. Remove from heat and let stand, covered, 1 hour. Bring again to a boil. Lower heat and cook slowly, covered, until beans are just tender, about 1 hour. Do not overcook. Add more water while cooking, if needed. Drain; cool; and turn into a large bowl. Add remaining ingredients and mix well. Serve at room temperature or refrigerate until ready to serve. Serves 6 to 8.

New England Parsnip Salad

The parsnip, a member of the carrot family, was a favorite early American vegetable, but it has not been very popular in recent years. It is still highly prized in New England during the winter. The sweet, nutty flavor has particular appeal, and parsnips make good winter salads to serve with roast meat or poultry.

1 small head leafy lettuce
2 cups shredded raw parsnips
½ cup chopped green pepper
1 cup grated or finely chopped raw carrots
1 apple, peeled, cored, and diced
2 tablespoons salad dressing or thick cream
3 tablespoons salad oil
1 tablespoon cider vinegar
Salt, pepper to taste

Wash lettuce; dry well; refrigerate. When ready to serve, combine parsnips, green pepper, carrots, and apple in a bowl. Mix together salad dressing or cream, oil, vinegar, salt, and pepper; add to vegetables; toss. Serve over lettuce leaves, if desired. Serves 4.

Welsh Leek Salad

The leek is not only a favorite food in Wales; it's also the national emblem and is featured in a number of traditional dishes. This salad is one of the best and may be served with grilled meat or fish.

> *12 medium-sized leeks*
> *Salt*
> *⅓ cup olive or salad oil*
> *3 tablespoons wine vinegar*
> *1 small onion, peeled and minced*
> *¼ cup chopped fresh parsley*
> *2 tablespoons chopped chives*
> *½ teaspoon dried chervil*
> *Pepper to taste*
> *2 hard-cooked eggs, shelled and chopped*

Cut green tops from leeks and trim roots. Wash well to remove all sand. Cook in a little salted boiling water, covered, until tender, about 12 minutes. Drain and cool. Combine remaining ingredients, except eggs, in a small saucepan. Bring to a boil and boil 2 minutes. Place leeks in a serving dish and pour oil-vinegar mixture over them. Top with chopped eggs. Serve at room temperature or refrigerate 1 hour before serving. Serves 4 to 6.

Provençal Hearts of Celery Salad

Raw celery is generally added to salads as a minor ingredient, but celery hearts assume a primary role in dishes such as this one. Serve with a hearty stew or casserole.

4 celery hearts
⅓ cup olive oil
2 tablespoons fresh lemon juice
½ teaspoon dried basil
Salt, pepper to taste
4 flat anchovy fillets, drained and chopped
3 tablespoons chopped fresh parsley
8 pitted black olives
1 large tomato, peeled and cut into wedges

Split each celery heart in half lengthwise. Cut out root and trim leaves, leaving only baby ones. Wash under running cold water to remove all dirt. Cut into 1½-inch pieces; wipe dry; place in a salad bowl. Combine oil, lemon juice, basil, salt, and pepper; pour over celery; mix well. Top with anchovy fillets and parsley. Garnish with olives and tomato wedges. Serves 4 to 6.

Czech Potato-Sauerkraut Salad

This hearty Czechoslovakian salad is served in winter with meat dishes made with pork or veal.

4 medium-sized potatoes, washed
Salt
2 cups drained sauerkraut
1 medium-sized onion, peeled and chopped

¼ cup salad oil
2 tablespoons cider vinegar
½ teaspoon caraway seeds
2 teaspoons sugar
Pepper to taste
1 large carrot, scraped and grated

Cook potatoes in their jackets in a little salted boiling water until tender, about 25 minutes. Peel and slice while still warm. Combine with sauerkraut and onion in a large bowl. Mix together oil, vinegar, caraway seeds, sugar, salt, and pepper. Add to vegetable mixture and mix well. Serve sprinkled with grated carrot. Serves 4 to 6.

Wyoming Bean Salad

American pioneer families moving westward relied heavily on dried beans to make well-seasoned winter salads. This is one of the best old-time recipes.

3 cups cold, cooked or canned kidney beans, drained
1 medium-sized onion, peeled and chopped
1 medium-sized green pepper, cleaned and chopped
1 cup diced, peeled cucumber
½ cup salad dressing
2 tablespoons cider vinegar
2 teaspoons Worcestershire sauce
Salt, pepper to taste
Crisp lettuce leaves, washed and dried
2 hard-cooked eggs, shelled and sliced

Combine beans, onion, green pepper, and cucumber in a large bowl. Mix together salad dressing, vinegar, Worcestershire sauce, salt, and pepper; add to bean mixture. Refrigerate 1 hour or longer to blend flavors. Serve on lettuce leaves, garnished with egg slices. Serves 4 to 6.

Lithuanian Mixed Vegetable Salad

Lithuanians are fond of winter salads made with vegetables and piquant flavorings, and served with game or poultry.

1 cup sliced cold, cooked carrots
1 cup diced cold, cooked beets
2 cups sliced cold, cooked potatoes
1 cup cold, cooked green peas
2 tablespoons minced dill pickles
1 cup sour cream
¼ teaspoon cayenne
Salt, pepper to taste
Crisp salad greens, washed and dried

Combine vegetables and pickles in a serving dish. Mix sour cream, cayenne, salt, and pepper; add to salad. Refrigerate 1 hour or longer to blend flavors. Serve over greens. Serves 4 to 6.

Austrian Red-White Coleslaw

A recipe for a European coleslaw to serve with schnitzels or other veal dishes.

2½ cups shredded green cabbage
1½ cups shredded red cabbage
2 tablespoons sugar
¼ cup salad dressing

¼ cup salad oil
2 to 3 tablespoons cider vinegar
¾ teaspoon celery seeds
Salt, pepper to taste

Combine green and red cabbages and sugar in a large bowl. Cover and refrigerate 1 hour. Combine remaining ingredients and add to cabbage. Refrigerate 2 hours or longer to blend flavors. Serves 4 to 6.

Southern Black-Eyed Pea Salad

The edible pea of a twining plant of the bean family is called cowpea but is better known as the black-eyed or goober pea. A great Southern favorite, the nutritious pea is made into a number of interesting dishes, including this inexpensive and flavorful salad. Serve with pork or game.

1 package (10 ounces) frozen black-eyed peas
1 cup shredded raw carrots
1 cup diced tomatoes
½ cup sliced scallions, with some tops
⅓ cup salad oil
3 tablespoons cider vinegar
1 teaspoon sugar
Several drops Tabasco sauce
Salt, pepper to taste

Cook peas according to package directions; drain; and cool. Combine peas, carrots, tomatoes, and scallions in a serving dish. Combine remaining ingredients and pour over salad; mix well. Serves 4.

German Beet Salad

Germans are partial to beet salads, which go well with their winter pork and game dishes.

1 medium-sized onion, peeled and chopped
½ cup vinegar
½ teaspoon caraway seeds
1 bay leaf
2 teaspoons sugar
Salt, pepper to taste
2 cups sliced cooked or canned beets, drained
1 tablespoon grated fresh or prepared horseradish

Combine onion, vinegar, caraway seeds, bay leaf, sugar, salt, and pepper in a small saucepan. Bring to a boil. Lower heat and cook slowly 5 minutes. Remove and discard bay leaf. Add to beets and refrigerate at least 24 hours. Serve garnished with horseradish. Serves 4.

Vermont Cabbage Salad

An old-time winter salad that is excellent with meat loaf or roasts.

3 cups shredded green cabbage
1 cup heavy cream
3 tablespoons fresh lemon juice
1 teaspoon sugar

2 tablespoons grated onion
1 tablespoon prepared horseradish
Several drops Tabasco sauce
Salt to taste

Put cabbage in refrigerator to become crisp. Just before serving, whip cream until stiff. Put cabbage in a serving dish and carefully fold in whipped cream. Mix in remaining ingredients and serve at once. Serve 4 to 6.

Liechtenstein Corn-Bean Salad

An appealing salad from the tiny European principality of Liechtenstein. It is a good winter dish to accompany any kind of meat or poultry.

1 cup cooked fresh or canned corn, drained
2 cups cooked or canned kidney beans, drained
1 cup diced, peeled cucumber
1 medium-sized onion, peeled and diced
2 medium-sized tomatoes, peeled and chopped
3 tablespoons olive or salad oil
1 tablespoon cider vinegar
2 tablespoons minced fresh parsley
Salt, pepper to taste
Crisp lettuce leaves, washed and dried

Combine all ingredients, except lettuce, in a medium bowl and refrigerate 2 to 3 hours to blend flavors. To serve, place lettuce leaves in a bowl and top with salad. Serves 4 to 6.

Near Eastern Beet-Yogurt Salad

Near Easterners make an interesting variety of winter salads with beets, which are grown in several varieties and colors. These piquant-flavored dishes are generally served with poultry or lamb.

2 cups sliced cooked or canned beets, drained
2 tablespoons wine vinegar
2 teaspoons prepared horseradish
1 teaspoon sugar
½ cup plain yogurt
Salt, pepper to taste

Combine ingredients and refrigerate 1 hour or longer to blend flavors. Serves 4.

New Jersey Mixed Pepper Salad

This easy-to-prepare salad, or relish, is a good winter accompaniment for meat and can be kept in the refrigerator to be used as needed.

2 cups finely chopped green peppers
2 cups finely chopped sweet red peppers
1 medium-sized onion, peeled and chopped
½ cup sugar
1 teaspoon salt
½ cup cider vinegar

Combine peppers, onion, sugar, and salt in a bowl or large jar. Bring vinegar to a boil and pour over pepper mixture. Let stand 2 to 3 hours before serving. The salad, tightly covered, will keep in the refrigerator about 1 week. Serves 6 to 8.

English Brussels Sprouts Salad

This unusual salad is a good accompaniment for roast beef or game.

> 3 cups cold, cooked Brussels sprouts
> 1 medium-sized red onion, peeled and thinly sliced
> 1 cup diced celery
> ¼ cup sour cream
> 2 tablespoons fresh lemon juice
> 2 tablespoons drained capers
> ½ teaspoon dried basil
> Salt, pepper to taste
> Crisp lettuce leaves, washed and dried

Combine Brussels sprouts, onion, and celery in a bowl. Mix remaining ingredients, except lettuce, and add to vegetables. To serve, place lettuce leaves in a serving dish and top with salad. Serves 6.

Cheese-Vegetable Salad

Serve with hot dogs or hamburgers.

> 1 cup cold, cooked green peas
> 1 cup diced, cold, cooked beets
> 1 medium-sized carrot, scraped and grated
> 1 cup chopped celery

1 small onion, peeled and minced
About ½ cup mayonnaise or salad dressing
1 cup shredded American cheese
Salt, pepper to taste
Crisp lettuce leaves, washed and dried

Combine vegetables in a bowl. Add mayonnaise, enough to bind ingredients. Fold in cheese. Season with salt and pepper. To serve place lettuce leaves in a serving dish and top with salad. Serves 4 to 6.

Swedish Cabbage Salad

Serve with fish or poultry.

2 cups each of coarsely shredded red and green cabbage,
washed, dried, and chilled
2 red apples, unpeeled, cored, and sliced
3 medium-sized celery stalks, cleaned and chopped
⅓ cup sour cream
2 tablespoons orange juice
1 teaspoon sugar
Salt, pepper to taste

Combine cabbage, apples, and celery in a medium bowl. Mix remaining ingredients and add to cabbage mixture. Mix well. Serve at once or refrigerate 1 hour or longer to blend flavors. Serves 4 to 6.

Fruit

and Molded Salads

Fruit and molded salads are attractive specialties that have been created primarily by American cooks. They're great favorites for entertaining.

While fruit salads are not held in high esteem by many gastronomes and are not favored by Europeans, especially the French, they are enjoyed in many countries, particularly those of the subtropics and tropics, where a great variety of fruit abounds.

During the early 1900s, American housewives began creating fanciful salads with canned, dried, and fresh fruits. Especially popular for these salads were apples, apricots, bananas, berries, cherries, melons, peaches, pears, pineapples, plums, oranges, and grapefruit. The ingredients also included such additions as nuts, raisins, celery, marshmallows, coconut, cream and cottage cheese, and sweet flavorings or dressings.

Citrus fruits add color contrast and a subtle flavor to salads made with seafood, mixed greens, and onions, but should be used sparingly so as not to overpower the other foods.

Middle Easterners and Africans have long enjoyed salads made with melons, apricots, figs, dates, peaches, avocados, and pomegranates—the latter also as a popular salad garnish.

In the Caribbean islands, where over seventy-five varieties of fruit are grown, the salads feature such colorful and interesting ingredients as the guava, mango, papaya, ugli, sapodilla, soursop, star apple, pineapple, and avocado.

Southeast Asians have good mixed fruit salads. One from the Philippines is made with pineapple, bananas, mangos, guavas, or other fruits, and strips of fresh coconut combined with a sweet cream dressing.

In many lands, fruit salads are served in hollowed-out fruit shells or boats made with halved pineapples, avocados, guavas, or bananas.

Lime and lemon juice give a marvelous uplift to many fruit salads, as the citrus juice brings out flavors and livens the fruit. Fruit salads may also be attractively garnished with grated coconut, mint leaves, chopped nuts, or other colorful foods.

European molded salads were first made with jellied broths or bouillon and encased poultry, meat, seafood, and vegetables. These types of salad were also prepared and served by American settlers.

Since the late 1800s, when commerical powdered gelatin was developed, molded salads of infinite variety, prepared with a wide selection of foods, especially fruits, have been commonplace on American tables.

Gelatin, a protein substance, is dissolved in hot liquid and becomes jellylike when it cools. The word comes from the Latin *gelare,* to freeze.

Molded salads have a gelatin base that is easy to make with packaged plain gelatin powder or prepared fruit or vegetable gelatins that have a distinctive flavor. Although making them is not difficult, the procedure requires careful attention if you want the result to be perfect.

The gelatin is first sprinkled over a cold liquid to soften and then is dissolved in a hot liquid such as water, bouillon, vegetable, tomato, orange, or lemon juice. Fresh or frozen pineapple juice (or the fruit itself) must be boiled 2 minutes before adding to gelatin mixtures; fresh pineapple contains an enzyme that destroys the gelling power of the mixture.

The dissolved gelatin base is chilled until slightly thickened or the consistency of unbeaten egg white before adding solids such as fruits, vegetables, seafoods or meats, or whipped cream or beaten egg whites. Because the mixture should not become too stiff, it is best to stir it occasionally to check its consistency.

For the final chilling, allow at least 3 hours for the mixture to become firm. Some may require chilling for several hours or overnight.

To unmold the salad, dip the mold into warm water, making sure no water comes over the edge. Loosen around the edges with a paring knife. Put a plate over the top of the mold and reverse the mold quickly. Hold the mold and the plate with your hands and shake them back and forth, if necessary, to loosen the gelatin salad. Carefully lift the mold. Repeat the process if the dish doesn't unmold the first time.

There are attractive salad molds in many sizes and shapes— ring, shell, pineapple, fish, and so on. Ordinary bowls, loaf pans, rectangular pans, and square dishes may also be used. Individual molds also come in a variety of shapes; even custard cups will serve the purpose.

When unmolded, the salads may be served whole or cut into portions. They may be placed alone on a serving dish or on a bed of greens. Sometimes creamy sauces or dressings are served with the salads, or they may be garnished with mayonnaise, sour cream, or other dressings.

Gelatin salads must be served cold, preferably on chilled dishes. The salads must not be allowed to come into contact with hot foods; heat melts gelatin. It's best to serve them separately on individual plates.

Molded salads are excellent for entertaining, especially in summer, as well as for family meals. They can be prepared beforehand and, taken fresh from the refrigerator, are attractive and delicate, whether served as first courses, entrées, or side dishes. They are also especially suitable for luncheons and buffets.

Here, now, is a selection of tasty fruit and molded salad recipes, primarily American in origin. They begin with three novelty or decorative salads that are typical of those created by cooks for children's parties or ladies' luncheons. Never mind if some purists consider that sort of thing beneath them.

Novelty Fruit Salads

CANDLE: Place a whole slice of canned pineapple on a lettuce leaf. Stick half a banana upright in the center of the pineapple. Top the banana with a red cherry. Garnish with yellow salad dressing to represent tallow running down the sides of a lighted candle.

BUTTERFLY SALAD: Cut a slice of pineapple in half. Place the curved edges opposite each other, with a date between them to represent the body of the butterfly. Use thin strips of lettuce for the antennae. Place sliced stuffed olives, bits of nuts, and drops of salad dressing on the pineapple "wings."

SUNBONNET SUE: Arrange 5 halves of cooked or canned pears or peaches, round sides up, over 5 curly lettuce leaves. The leaf curls up around the fruit and forms the sunbonnet. Place 2 whole cloves in each pear or peach half to form the eyes, 2 each blanched almonds for the ears, and slip thin slices of canned pimiento into cuts made for nose and mouth. The expressions may be varied. Put 1 tablespoon salad dressing around outside of fruit, to represent golden locks, and arrange a bow of red pimiento under the chin of Sunbonnet Sue.

Thai Orange Salad

This fruit salad from Thailand is not only unusual but has a fascinating name, *Ma Ho,* or galloping horses. It can be made with fresh pineapple as well as oranges.

> 2 garlic cloves, crushed
> ½ cup minced onions
> 2 tablespoons peanut or salad oil
> ½ cup minced or ground raw pork
> 2 tablespoons tamarind or lemon juice
> 2 teaspoons sugar
> Pepper to taste
> 3 tablespoons finely chopped peanuts
> 6 thick navel orange slices
> 2 shredded red chilis
> ⅓ cup chopped fresh coriander or parsley

Sauté garlic and onions in oil in a medium skillet until tender. Add pork, tamarind or lemon juice, sugar, and pepper; cook about 15 minutes, or until pork is done. Remove from heat; add peanuts and cool. To serve, place a spoonful of the pork-peanut mixture over each orange slice and garnish the tops with chilis and coriander or parsley. Serves 6.

Virgin Island Mango-Papaya Salad

This delectable salad is made with two highly prized subtropical fruits, the mango and the papaya. Mangoes grow in various shapes, may be green, yellow, or red, and have juicy, yellowish-red flesh with a flavor resembling a combination of apricot, peach, and pineapple. The unripe and somewhat hard mango is used to make chutneys and preserves. To be eaten raw or used in salads, the mango should be fully ripe. The papaya, also called papaw or paw-paw, has a yellow-orange rind and is often likened to a melon. It is best eaten raw, particularly with a little freshly squeezed lime or lemon juice to point up the fruit's subtle flavor. When cut in half and hollowed, the shell may be filled with a seafood salad or mixed fresh fruit.

1 large papaya, peeled, seeded, and cubed
1 large ripe mango, peeled and cubed
3 tablespoons salad oil
2 tablespoons fresh orange juice
1 tablespoon fresh lemon juice
Salad greens, washed and dried
2 tablespoons grated coconut

Place fruit cubes in a bowl. Combine oil, orange and lemon juices; pour over fruit; mix well. To serve, place greens in a serving dish. Top with fruit mixture and spinkle with coconut. Serves 4.

Swedish Smorgasbord Fruit Salad

This colorful salad is served with cold meats and other dishes at the traditional Swedish *smorgasbord*. It can be made with other kinds of fresh fruit as well as the ones in this recipe.

2 navel oranges, peeled and chopped
2 red apples, cored and chopped
2 pears, peeled, cored, and diced
1 cup white grapes, cut in halves and seeded

¼ cup orange juice
½ cup mayonnaise
About ½ cup sour cream
½ cup chopped walnuts

Combine fruit and orange juice in a serving dish. Mix mayonnaise and sour cream; spoon over fruit mixture. Sprinkle with nuts. Serves 4 to 6.

Middle Eastern Fruit Salad with Minted Yogurt Dressing

Middle Eastern cooks have created colorful salads with their luscious fresh and dried fruits. Mint is a favorite garnish for many of them.

2 navel oranges, peeled, broken into sections, and white
*   membranes removed*
2 cups diced, peeled peaches
1 cup diced, peeled watermelon or cantaloupe
1 cup diced, peeled apricots
1 cup chopped dates
½ cup golden raisins
1 cup plain yogurt
2 tablespoons orange juice
2 tablespoons chopped fresh mint

Combine fruits, dates, and raisins in a serving dish. Mix yogurt and orange juice; spoon over salad. Serve garnished with mint. Serves 4 to 6.

Holiday Molded Cranberry Salad

A good and colorful salad for Thanksgiving or Christmas, featuring the native American cranberry.

> *2 envelopes unflavored gelatin*
> *¼ cup cold orange juice*
> *2 cans (1 pound each) whole-berry cranberry sauce*
> *½ cup sugar*
> *1 cup diced, peeled apples*
> *1 cup chopped walnuts*
> *½ cup diced celery*
> *Lettuce leaves, washed and dried*

Soften gelatin in orange juice in a medium saucepan. Add cranberries and sugar; cook 5 minutes. Remove from heat; add apples, walnuts, and celery. Turn into a 6-cup mold and refrigerate several hours until firm. Unmold and serve over lettuce leaves on a large plate. Serves 6 to 8.

Swiss Apple-Cheese Salad

A marvelous salad to serve at a family or children's luncheon.

> *4 unpeeled, cored red apples, diced*
> *2 tablespoons fresh lemon juice*
> *1 cup diced celery*
> *1 cup shredded Swiss cheese*
> *About 1 cup mayonnaise*
> *1 tablespoon sharp prepared mustard*

Salt, pepper to taste
Lettuce leaves, washed and dried
½ cup chopped filberts or walnuts

Put apples in a serving dish. Sprinkle with lemon juice. Add celery and cheese. Mix mayonnaise and mustard. Season with salt and pepper. Add to apple mixture. Refrigerate 1 hour to blend flavors. Serve in lettuce cups sprinkled with nuts. Serves 4.

Arabian Orange Salad

A good salad to serve with skewered or grilled lamb or beef.

3 navel oranges, peeled and sliced
2 medium-sized onions, peeled and sliced
3 tablespoons salad oil
1 tablespoon fresh lemon juice
Dash of cayenne
Salt, pepper to taste
6 pitted black or green olives

Arrange orange slices in a serving dish. Top with onion slices. Combine remaining ingredients, except olives, and pour over salad. Serve garnished with olives. Serves 6.

West Indies Melon Salad

A mouth-watering summer luncheon salad.

3 cups mixed melon balls
2 navel oranges, peeled, sectioned, and white membranes
  removed

1 quart bite-size salad greens, washed, dried, and chilled
¼ cup salad oil
2 tablespoons fresh lime or lemon juice
1 teaspoon sugar
½ teaspoon ground ginger
Dash of salt

Put melon balls, oranges, and salad greens in a bowl; toss. Combine remaining ingredients and pour over salad; toss. Serve at once. Serves 6.

Louisiana Bird-of-Paradise Salad

A colorful salad to serve with cold, cooked ham or poultry.

1 package (3 ounces) orange gelatin
1 cup hot orange juice
1 can (16 ounces) sliced beets
¼ teaspoon Tabasco sauce
Salt to taste
1 navel orange, peeled, sliced, and white membranes
   removed

Dissolve orange gelatin in hot orange juice in a medium bowl. Add liquid from beets, Tabasco sauce, and salt. Arrange beets and oranges in alternate layers in a rectangle mold; pour gelatin mixture over them. Refrigerate several hours until firm. Unmold on a chilled plate and serve garnished with sour cream or mayonnaise, if desired. Serves 4 to 6.

Russian Fruit Salad with Sour Cream

A mixed fruit salad that is enhanced with the addition of grated orange rind.

1 head chicory, washed, dried, torn into bite-size pieces,
*   and chilled*
4 fresh peaches, peeled and sliced
4 fresh plums, washed and sliced
1 banana, peeled and sliced
2 cups cut-up melon
1 cup sour cream
3 tablespoons fresh lemon juice
1 teaspoon sugar
1 teaspoon grated orange rind

Put chicory and fruits in a salad bowl or serving dish; toss. Combine remaining ingredients and serve with salad. Serves 4 to 6.

Basic Tomato Aspic Salad

A very popular basic salad that has two excellent variations—one with ham and one with shrimp.

1 envelope unflavored gelatin
2½ cups tomato juice
½ teaspoon dried basil
1 small bay leaf
1 tablespoon cider vinegar
½ to 1 teaspoon sugar

Salt, pepper to taste
1 cup diced celery
¼ cup minced onion

Soften gelatin in ½ cup cold tomato juice in a medium bowl. Heat 2 cups tomato juice, basil, bay leaf, vinegar, sugar, salt, and pepper in a small saucepan; simmer, uncovered, 5 minutes. Remove from heat and strain. Pour over softened gelatin and stir until dissolved. Chill until partially set. Fold in celery and onion. Turn into a 4-cup mold or individual molds. Refrigerate several hours until firm. Unmold and serve plain or on lettuce leaves, garnished with mayonnaise or sour cream, if desired. Serves 4 to 6.

Ham Aspic Salad

1 recipe basic tomato aspic (above)
2 tablespoons prepared horseradish
2 cups minced cold, cooked ham

When making tomato aspic, omit celery and reduce amount of minced onion to 2 tablespoons. When aspic has begun to set, fold in onion, horseradish, and ham. Chill until firm.

Shrimp Aspic Salad

Add 1 cup shelled cooked or canned small or medium shrimp with celery and onion to recipe for basic tomato aspic (above). Chill until firm.

English Molded Turkey Salad

A good salad to make with leftover cooked turkey. Serve as a buffet specialty or for luncheon.

> *1 envelope unflavored gelatin*
> *¼ cup cold chicken broth or water*
> *½ cup boiling chicken broth or water*
> *1 tablespoon fresh lemon juice*
> *1 teaspoon salt*
> *1 tablespoon Worcestershire sauce*
> *1½ cups diced cold, cooked white meat of turkey*
> *½ cup diced celery*
> *½ cup diced green pepper*
> *½ cup mayonnaise*
> *½ cup sour cream*
> *Few drops Tabasco sauce*

Soften gelatin in chicken broth or water in a medium bowl. Add boiling broth or water, lemon juice, salt, and Worcestershire sauce; stir to dissolve. Chill until partially set. Fold in remaining ingredients and turn into a 4-cup mold. Refrigerate several hours until firm. Unmold on a chilled plate over lettuce leaves, if desired. Serves 4 to 6.

Israeli Orange-Onion Salad

The Israelis prepare a number of interesting salads with their luscious fruits, such as oranges and avocados. This one is especially yummy. The appealing visual harmony of oranges and red onions is a pleasant bonus.

1 quart bite-size romaine, washed, dried, and chilled
2 large navel oranges, peeled and sliced crosswise
1 large red onion, peeled, sliced, and separated into rings
4 to 5 tablespoons salad oil
2 to 3 tablespoons fresh lemon juice
¼ teaspoon sugar
Salt, pepper to taste
Fresh mint leaves (optional)

Put romaine in a salad bowl. Top with orange slices and onion rings. Combine oil, lemon juice, sugar, salt, and pepper; pour over salad and toss. Garnish with mint, if desired. Serves 4 to 6.

Luncheon Avocado-Yogurt Mold

A colorful and nutritious salad for a summer luncheon.

1 package (3 ounces) lime or lemon gelatin
1 cup boiling water
1 medium-sized ripe avocado
2 tablespoons fresh lemon juice
Salt to taste
1 cup plain yogurt
¾ cup small-curd cottage cheese
1 large orange, peeled, sectioned, and diced
⅓ cup chopped blanched almonds

Put gelatin in a medium bowl; add water; stir until dissolved. Cool and chill until partially set. Peel avocado and remove pit. Put avocado flesh in a bowl and mash or whirl in a blender with lemon juice and salt. Fold avocado mixture and remaining ingredients into gelatin; turn into a 6-cup mold. Chill several hours until firm. When ready to serve, unmold on a chilled large plate. Serves 6.

New Zealand Banana Salad

In New Zealand this salad, or a variation of it, is often served for summer afternoon tea.

> 3 bananas, peeled and sliced in half lengthwise
> Watercress or leafy lettuce, washed and dried
> 2 navel oranges, peeled, sectioned, and membranes
>   removed
> ¼ cup fresh lemon juice
> ¼ cup sugar
> 1 cup heavy cream, whipped
> ½ cup chopped walnuts

For each serving, place half a banana over watercress or lettuce on a small plate. Put orange sections around it. Combine lemon juice, sugar, and cream; spoon over fruit; sprinkle with nuts. Serves 6.

Molded Orange-Carrot Salad

One of America's most popular molded salads, which began appearing regularly on luncheon, church social, and holiday tables during the early 1900s, is a glimmering, orange-colored specialty that has been titled sunshine, sunset, golden glow, and some other descriptive names. It's made with plain gelatin or lemon or orange-flavored gelatin or Jell-O and contains such foods as grated raw carrots, orange or other juices, orange segments, crushed pineapple, and sometimes apricots. This is one of the many variations of the salad.

1 envelope plain gelatin
½ cut cold orange juice
¾ cup hot canned pineapple juice
¼ cup cider vinegar
¼ cup sugar
¼ teaspoon salt
1 cup drained, crushed canned pineapple
½ cup diced orange sections with skins and seeds removed
½ cup shredded raw carrots

Sprinkle gelatin over orange juice in a medium bowl. Add hot pineapple juice; stir to dissolve. Add vinegar, sugar, and salt. Refrigerate until partially set. Fold in remaining ingredients and turn into a 4-cup mold. Refrigerate several hours until firm. Unmold onto a chilled plate. Serves 6 to 8.

German Jellied Ham Salad

A good summer luncheon or supper main-dish salad.

1 envelope plain gelatin
¼ cup cold water
1½ cups hot bouillon
2 tablespoons cider vinegar
2 cups finely chopped cooked ham
¼ cup chopped pickles
½ cup minced celery

¼ cup minced green pepper
½ cup sour cream
1 teaspoon dry mustard
Salt, pepper to taste

Soften gelatin in cold water in a medium bowl. Add hot bouillon and vinegar; stir to dissolve. Cool and refrigerate until partially set. Fold in remaining ingredients and turn into a mold or loaf pan. Chill several hours until firm. Unmold onto a chilled plate over lettuce leaves, if desired. Cut into slices to serve. Serves 6.

Low-Calorie Tomato-Cottage Cheese Mold

1 envelope unflavored gelatin
1¾ cups tomato juice
2 tablespoons fresh lemon juice
2 teaspoons Worcestershire sauce
½ teaspoon dried basil
Few drops Tabasco sauce
Salt, pepper to taste
1 cup small-curd cottage cheese
½ cup grated raw carrots
Salad greens, washed and dried

Soften gelatin in ¼ cup cold tomato juice in a medium bowl. Heat remaining 1½ cups tomato juice, lemon juice, Worcestershire sauce, basil, Tabasco sauce, salt, and pepper, uncovered, for 5 minutes. Pour over gelatin and stir to dissolve. Refrigerate until partially set. Fold in cottage cheese and carrots. Turn into a 4-cup mold, chill several hours until firm. Serve on salad greens. Serves 4 to 6.

American Apple Salads

American cooks have created countless recipes for salads using our bountiful supply of delicious eating apples. The fruit is combined with such foods as cheese, raisins, nuts, dates, olives, onions, cucumber, celery, cabbage, carrots, avocados, pears, pineapple, grapes, macaroni, ham, turkey, chicken, seafood, and meats, among others, and bound with a diverse selection of dressings. Apples are also used to make colorful molded salads. There are even some salads made with stuffed cooked apples. Given below are two apple salad recipes.

Waldorf Salad

This famous salad was invented by "Oscar of the Waldorf," Oscar M. Tschirky, maitre d'hotel at that famous New York hotel, during the early 1900s. The original recipe was a simple combination of equal parts of raw apples and celery moistened with mayonnaise and served on lettuce leaves. Later a number of other ingredients, notably chopped walnuts, were added to the original version. This combination is now the best known.

4 red eating apples, unpeeled, cored, and chopped
2 tablespoons fresh lemon juice
2 cups chopped celery
½ cup chopped walnuts
About 1 cup mayonnaise
Lettuce leaves, washed and dried

Combine ingredients, except lettuce, and mix well. Spoon over lettuce and serve at once. Serves 4 to 6.

Jellied Apple-Nut Salad

1 package (3 ounces) lemon gelatin
1 cup boiling water
¾ cup cold apple juice
1 tablespoon fresh lemon juice
Salt to taste
1½ cups chopped, peeled apples
½ cup diced celery
¼ cup chopped pecans

Dissolve gelatin in boiling water in a medium bowl. Add apple and lemon juices and salt. Chill until partially set. Fold in remaining ingredients and turn into a mold. Chill several hours until firm. Unmold onto a chilled plate. Serves 6.

Swedish Salmon Salad

A good salad for a buffet or summer luncheon.

1 envelope plain gelatin
¼ cup cold water
½ cup boiling water
2 tablespoons fresh lemon juice
1 cup mayonnaise
½ teaspoon dried dillweed
Salt, pepper to taste
2 cups flaked, boned, fresh-cooked or canned salmon
½ cup diced celery
1 cup cold, cooked green peas

Soften gelatin in cold water in a medium bowl. Add boiling water and lemon juice; stir to dissolve. Add mayonnaise, dillweed, salt, and pepper; beat until smooth. Chill until partially set. Fold in remaining ingredients and turn into a 5- or 6-cup mold. Chill several hours until firm. Unmold onto a chilled plate over salad greens, if desired. Serves 4 to 6.

Tomato Salad Ring

This is an attractive salad for a luncheon or buffet, and it can be filled with potato salad or a mixture of herb-flavored sliced cucumbers and sour cream, if desired.

2 envelopes unflavored gelatin
4 cups tomato juice
1 medium-sized stalk celery
2 lemon slices
2 small bay leaves
Salt, pepper to taste
3 tablespoons vinegar
1 cup finely chopped celery
⅓ cup finely chopped green pepper

Soften gelatin in 1 cup cold tomato juice in a medium bowl. Combine remaining 3 cups tomato juice, celery, lemon slices, bay leaves, salt, and pepper in a medium saucepan and simmer, uncovered, 5 minutes; strain. Add hot tomato liquid to gelatin and stir to dissolve. Chill until partially set. Stir in celery and green pepper. Turn into a 5½- or 6-cup mold. Chill several hours until firm. Unmold onto a chilled platter. Serves 6 to 8.

Indonesian Mixed Fruit Salad

This traditional dish, called *rudjak*, is a holiday specialty that is eaten in Indonesia both as a salad and as a dessert. Some of the seasonings in this recipe are substitutes for native ingredients that are not generally available in America.

>*½ teaspoon chili powder*
>*2 tablespoons brown sugar*
>*3 tablespoons fresh lemon juice*
>*2 teaspoons anchovy paste*
>*3 tablespoons salad oil*
>*Pepper to taste*
>*4 cups diced mixed fresh fruit (pineapple, mangoes, oranges, grapefruit)*
>*1 medium-sized cucumber, peeled, seeded, and diced*

Combine first six ingredients to blend thoroughly. Put fruit and cucumber in a bowl; add dressing. Refrigerate 1 hour to blend flavors. Serves 4 to 6.

Perfection Salad

In 1905, a Pennsylvania housewife won third prize in a Knox Gelatin contest with a recipe called Perfection Salad. It's been a great American favorite ever since. Over the years it has appeared in many cookbooks in many variations. This version is adapted from the original recipe.

>*1 tablespoon unflavored gelatin*
>*¼ cup cold water*
>*1 cup boiling water*

¼ cup sugar
½ teaspoon salt
1 tablespoon fresh lemon juice
¼ cup vinegar
½ cup finely chopped cabbage
3 tablespoons finely chopped pimiento

Soften gelatin in cold water in a medium bowl. Add boiling water; stir to dissolve. Mix in sugar, salt, lemon juice, and vinegar. Chill until partially set. Fold in remaining ingredients and turn into a 4-cup mold or 4 individual molds. Chill several hours until firm. Unmold onto a chilled plate over salad greens, if desired. Serve alone or with mayonnaise. Serves 4.

California Avocado-Citrus Salad

A scrumptious salad to serve with cold, cooked chicken or turkey.

1 cup sour cream
½ cup diced pitted dates
2 tablespoons orange juice
Dash of nutmeg
Endive or other greens, washed and dried
3 medium-sized ripe avocados, peeled and sliced
2 grapefruit, peeled and broken into sections, membranes
  removed
2 oranges, peeled and broken into sections, membranes
  removed

Combine sour cream, dates, orange juice, and nutmeg; refrigerate. When ready to serve, place greens in a serving dish or salad bowl. Arrange fruit over them. Serve with the sour cream–date mixture. Serves 6 to 8.

Moroccan Orange-Radish Salad

Moroccans are fond of colorful salads made with sliced or sectioned oranges and sliced or shredded radishes that are enhanced with orange-flower water.

Romaine leaves, washed, dried, and chilled
4 navel oranges, peeled and sliced crosswise
12 radishes, cleaned and sliced or shredded
⅓ cup olive or salad oil
2 tablespoons fresh lemon juice
1 teaspoon sugar
1 tablespoon orange-flower water (optional)
Salt, pepper to taste

Arrange a bed of romaine leaves in a serving dish. Top with oranges and radishes. Combine remaining ingredients and serve with salad or pour over it. Serves 4 to 6.

Old-Time Molded Egg Salad

A great salad for a summer outdoor meal.

1 envelope unflavored gelatin
¼ cup cold water
2 tablespoons fresh lemon juice
1 cup mayonnaise
½ cup chopped celery

2 tablespoons chopped green pepper
2 tablespoons pickle relish
2 tablespoons chopped onion
4 hard-cooked eggs, shelled and sliced
Salt, pepper to taste
Endive or salad greens, washed and dried
2 medium-sized tomatoes, peeled and cut into wedges

Soften gelatin in cold water and lemon juice in a small saucepan or top of a double boiler. Heat over simmering water until dissolved. Cool to lukewarm; combine with mayonnaise in a medium bowl. Beat until smooth; chill until mixture thickens slightly. Carefully fold in celery, pepper, relish, onion, and eggs. Season with salt and pepper. Turn into a 4 cup-mold. Chill several hours until firm. When ready to serve, place endive or greens on a serving dish and unmold egg salad over them. Serve garnished with tomato wedges. Serves 4 to 6.

Washington Pear Salad

American cooks have created a large number of luscious salads that feature or include pears. The pears may be sliced and combined with fruits and/or seafood in mixed salads; cut in half and stuffed with cream cheese and nuts, herb-flavored jelly, chutney, Roquefort cheese balls, or Camembert; used in making colorful molded salads and fanciful delights for children; or sliced and served on lettuce and topped with salad dressing. This salad is from the state of Washington, where many of our best pears are grown.

4 large fresh pears
Lettuce leaves, washed, dried, and chilled
2 tablespoons fresh lemon juice

1 package (3 ounces) cream cheese, softened
½ cup minced green peppers
½ cup chopped walnuts

Peel pears and cut in half lengthwise. Remove cores. Place 2 pear halves, cored side up, over lettuce leaves on each of 4 small plates. Sprinkle with lemon juice. Combine cream cheese and green peppers and fill pear centers with mixture. Sprinkle with nuts. Serve with mayonnaise or salad dressing, if desired. Serves 4.

Summer Fruit Salad with Cottage Cheese

Weight-watchers will like this colorful salad for luncheon or supper. Substitite plain yogurt for the salad oil, if desired.

2 small cantaloupes
1 pound cottage cheese
2 cups seedless white grapes
2 cups cherry tomatoes, stemmed and washed
⅓ cup salad oil
2 tablespoons fresh lemon juice
2 tablespoons honey
2 tablespoons chopped fresh mint leaves

Cut cantaloupes into thick, crosswise slices; remove rind and seeds; place on a platter. Put spoonfuls of cottage cheese in the centers of the cantaloupe slices. Top and surround with grapes and tomatoes. Combine oil, lemon juice, and honey. Serve with the salad. Garnish salad with the mint. Serves 8.

Manitoba Jellied Cucumber Salad

The Canadian province of Manitoba is noted for its excellent cucumbers, which are used to make interesting salads such as this one.

1 package (3 ounces) lime gelatin
¾ cup hot water
½ cup cold water
2 tablespoons fresh lemon juice
1 cup sour cream
2 tablespoons minced chives
½ teaspoon dried dillweed
1 cup diced, peeled cucumbers
Salt, pepper to taste
Watercress leaves, washed and dried

Dissolve gelatin in hot water in a medium bowl. Stir in cold water and lemon juice. Add sour cream, chives, and dillweed; beat until smooth. Chill until mixture thickens slightly. Fold in cucumbers; season with salt and pepper. Turn into a 4-cup mold and chill several hours until firm. When ready to serve, unmold onto a chilled plate and garnish with watercress. Serves 4 to 6.

Orange-Raspberry Molded Salad

This is a colorful layered salad that's perfect for a buffet or holiday meal.

1 can (11 ounces) mandarin orange segments
1 package (3 ounces) orange gelatin
2 cups boiling water

½ cup chopped celery
½ cup small-curd cottage cheese
1 cup sour cream or plain yogurt
1 package (10 ounces) frozen raspberries, thawed
1 package (3 ounces) raspberry gelatin

Drain orange segments, reserving ½ cup orange syrup. Put orange gelatin in a medium bowl; add 1 cup boiling water; stir to dissolve. Add reserved orange syrup; mix well. Chill until partially set. Fold in orange segments, celery, cottage cheese, and ½ cup sour cream or yogurt. Turn into a 7-cup mold; chill until almost set.

Meanwhile, drain raspberries, reserving ½ cup syrup. Put raspberry gelatin into a bowl and pour 1 cup boiling water over it. Stir to dissolve; add raspberry syrup; chill until mixture thickens slightly. Add raspberries and remaining ½ cup sour cream or yogurt. Spoon over orange layer and chill several hours until firm. Serves 8 to 10.

West African Fruit Salad with Honey Dressing

Luscious fresh subtropical and tropical fruits are grown in West Africa in great variety. Cooks use them to make colorful salads that are served as side dishes with entrées or as desserts. This one is typical of the many variations.

2 cups sliced bananas
2 cups diced pineapple
2 cups diced guavas
½ cup honey
3 tablespoons fresh lime or lemon juice
2 teaspoons finely chopped ginger root

Combine fruits in a serving dish. Mix remaining ingredients and pour over salad. Serves 4 to 6.

Marvelous Mushroom Aspic

This is a good basic salad to serve as a first course or side dish.

½ pound fresh mushrooms
¼ cup water
2 tablespoons fresh lemon juice
1 envelope plain gelatin
½ cup cold beef bouillon
1½ cups boiling beef bouillon
3 tablespoons dry sherry
½ teaspoon dried basil
2 teaspoon dried parsley
Salt, pepper to taste

Wash mushrooms quickly under running water or wipe with wet paper toweling to remove all dirt. Cut off any tough stem ends and chop. Put in a small saucepan with water and lemon juice. Cook 2 minutes. Remove from heat and cool. Soften gelatin in cold beef bouillon in a medium bowl. Add boiling bouillon and stir to dissolve. Mix in remaining ingredients. Chill until partially set. Add mushrooms and mix well. Turn into a 4-cup mold and chill several hours until firm. Serve over salad greens, if desired. Serves 4 to 6.

Frances Colgan's Seafood Mold

This attractive seafood mold is served by my friend, Frances Colgan, as a pre-dinner first course or as a luncheon specialty.

4 *envelopes unflavored gelatin*
2 *cups cold water*
2 *cups sour cream*
2 *cups salad dressing, preferably homemade*
2 *teaspoons dried dillweed*
1 *teaspoon fennel seed*
1 *teaspoon or more salt*
⅓ *cup fresh lemon juice*
2 *teaspoons Worcestershire sauce*
1 *teaspoon minced onion*
¼ *teaspoon Tabasco sauce*
1½ *cups finely chopped celery*
½ *cup finely chopped green pepper*
¼ *cup diced canned pimiento*
3 *packages (8 to 10 ounces) tiny cooked and deveined*
    shrimp, thawed and drained
1 *can (6½ ounces) tuna, drained and flaked*
1 *can (6½ ounces) crabmeat, drained and flaked*

Sprinkle gelatin over water in a small saucepan. Put over low heat for about 3 minutes and stir constantly until gelatin dissolves. Remove from heat and cool. Combine sour cream, salad dressing, seasonings, and chopped vegetables in a large bowl and mix well. Fold in cooled gelatin and seafood. Turn into 20 individual molds or an 8-cup ring mold. Refrigerate until firm. Unmold on small plates or on one large plate over lettuce leaves, if desired. Serves 20 as a first course or 12 as a luncheon entrée.

Note: Mrs. Colgan fills the center of the ring mold with peeled cherry tomatoes previously marinated in an oil-vinegar dressing.

Frosted Pineapple-Lime Salad Mold

Another favorite salad recipe of Frances Colgan's. She serves this specialty for luncheons.

1 cup boiling water
2 packages (3 ounces each) lime gelatin
1 cup canned pineapple juice
2 packages (8 ounces each) softened cream cheese
½ cup mayonnaise, preferably homemade
2 cups diced celery
1 can (20 ounces) crushed, unsweetened pineapple,
*   drained*

Pour boiling water over gelatin in a large bowl; stir to dissolve. Add pineapple juice; mix well. Add cream cheese; whip with rotary or electric beater to blend. Stir in mayonnaise, celery, and pineapple; mix well. Turn into an 8-cup ring mold and chill several hours until firm. Unmold onto a chilled large plate over lettuce leaves, if desired. Serves about 12.
Note: Line the mold with maraschino cherry halves before adding salad, if desired.

Party Salads

Many of the salad recipes in this book are great for entertaining; those in this chapter have been chosen to display the versatility of party salads.

Attractive and delectable salads are excellent for company meals because they are unusual, can often be prepared beforehand, and are convenient to serve. These salads are good for luncheons, buffets, dinners, suppers, or late evening gatherings.

As you learned in the introduction, composed or grand salads were featured attractions for fashionable suppers in Europe during the late 1800s. The recipe for Alexandre Dumas' celebrated party salad appeared in his well-known *Dictionary of Cuisine* and is still interesting to read.

First I put the ingredients into the salad bowl, then overturn them onto a platter. Into the empty bowl I put one hard-boiled egg yolk for each two persons—six for a dozen guests. These I mash with oil to form a paste, to which I add chervil, crushed tuna, macerated anchovies, Maille mustard, a large spoonful of soya, chopped gherkins, and the chopped white of the eggs. I thin this mixture by stirring in the finest vinegar obtainable. Finally I put the salad back into the bowl, and my servant tosses it. On the tossed salad I sprinkle a pinch of paprika, which is the Hungarian red pepper.

Other party salads are generally made with a greater variety of ingredients than Dumas used. Like the grand "sallets" of the past, each should be artfully garnished and presented as attractively as possible in a large bowl, on a handsome platter, or in a pretty serving dish.

The French definition of a salad is *une réunion des choses confusement assemblées,* a reunion of things confusingly assembled. While the party salads in this section are not necessarily put together in a state of confusion, they are made with marvelous reunion of ingredients and are great fun to prepare and serve.

Tarpon Springs Greek Salad

Tarpon Springs, a small, colorful community northwest of Tampa, Florida, on the Gulf of Mexico, is nationally known for its Greek culture, sponge divers, traditions, and food. The Springs' most famous restaurant is Louis Pappas' Riverside Café, which features Grecian specialties and a marvelous salad masterpiece fashioned as carefully as a mosaic with a galaxy of local ingredients. Here is Pappas' recipe for the salad. It is an excellent luncheon or buffet specialty.

Louis Pappas' Famous Greek Salad

1 large head lettuce
3 cups potato salad (recipe below)
12 roka leaves (Greek vegetable) or 12 sprigs watercress
2 tomatoes, cut into 6 wedges each
1 peeled cucumber, cut lengthwise into 8 fingers
1 avocado, peeled and cut into wedges
4 portions of Feta cheese
1 green pepper, cut into 8 rings
4 slices canned cooked beets
4 peeled, cooked shrimp
4 anchovy fillets
12 black olives (Greek-style preferred)
12 medium hot Salonika peppers (bought in bottles)
4 fancy-cut radishes
4 whole green onions
½ cup white vinegar
¼ cup each of olive and salad oil blended
Oregano

Potato Salad:

6 boiling potatoes
2 medium-sized onions or 4 green onions
¼ cup finely chopped parsley
½ cup thinly sliced green onion
½ cup salad dressing
Salt

Line a large platter with the outside lettuce leaves; place 3 cups of the potato salad in a mound in the center of the platter. Cover with the remaining lettuce, which has been shredded. Arrange the *roka* or watercress on top of this. Place the tomato wedges around the outer edge of the salad with a few on top, and place the cucumber wedges in between the tomatoes, making a solid base of the salad. Place the avocado slices around the outside. Slices of Feta cheese should be arranged on the top of the salad, with the green pepper slices over all. On the very top, place the sliced beets with a shrimp on each beet slice and an anchovy fillet on the shrimp. The olives, peppers, radishes, and green onions can be arranged as desired. The entire salad is then sprinkled with the vinegar (more may be used) and then with the blended oil. Sprinkle the oregano over all and serve at once. Garlic-toasted Greek bread is served with this salad, and Louis Pappas called this a "Salad for 4 persons."

POTATO SALAD: Boil the potatoes in the jackets for about 30 minutes or until tender but not soft when tested. Drain, cool, and peel the potatoes, and when cold, slice into a bowl. Cut onions and peppers into thin slices, and chop the parsley. Add to the potatoes and sprinkle lightly with salt. Fold in the salad dressing, using more if necessary to hold salad together lightly.

Turkey-Mushroom Salad

A distinguished salad for a company luncheon.

2 cups sliced, cleaned fresh mushrooms
2 cups diced, cooked white meat of turkey
1 cup diced, peeled, and seeded cucumber
⅓ cup olive or salad oil
2 tablespoons wine vinegar
Salt, pepper to taste
1 cup cold, cooked green peas

½ *cup sour cream*
1 *tablespoon chopped fresh dill or 1 teaspoon dried*
   dillweed
Crisp lettuce leaves, washed and dried
¼ *cup toasted, blanched almond slivers*

Put mushrooms, turkey, and cucumber in a medium bowl. Add oil, vinegar, salt, and pepper. Allow to marinate, mixing ingredients occasionally, for 1 hour. When ready to serve, add peas, sour cream, and dill. Spoon over lettuce leaves and sprinkle with almonds. Serves 4.

Russian Salad Olivier

This familiar chicken and vegetable salad, created by and named for a French chef in the service of Tsar Nicholas II, is a handsome creation that can be made with various meats, poultry, game, and vegetables, which are bound with a flavorful sauce. Piled high as a pyramid or shaped into a mound, the salad is elaborately garnished and most attractive. It is a good buffet specialty.

2 *cups diced cold, cooked white meat of chicken*
1 *cup diced cold, cooked carrots*
1 *cup cold, cooked green peas*
2 *cups diced cold, peeled, cooked potatoes*
⅓ *cup minced dill pickles*
6 *scallions, cleaned and sliced*
½ *cup mayonnaise*
About ½ *cup sour cream*
2 *tablespoons drained capers*
3 *tablespoons chopped fresh dill or 1 teaspoon dried*
   dillweed
Salt, pepper to taste

Crisp lettuce leaves, washed and dried
Garnishes: Cubes of cold, cooked lobster; shelled and
  cleaned, cooked, medium-sized shrimp; hard-cooked
  egg wedges; tomato slices; pitted black olives

Combine chicken, vegetables, pickles, and scallions in a medium-sized bowl. Mix mayonnaise, sour cream, capers, dill, salt, and pepper; add to chicken mixture. Refrigerate 1 hour or longer to blend flavors. To serve, arrange lettuce leaves on a serving dish. Top with salad, shaping as a pyramid or mound. Decorate top and sides and surround with garnishes. Serves 6.

Eastern Shore Crabmeat Salad

This is always a popular luncheon favorite.

1 pound backfin crabmeat
¾ cup finely chopped celery
⅓ cup mayonnaise or salad dressing
2 tablespoons fresh lemon juice
1 teaspoon drained capers (optional)
Salt, pepper to taste.

Remove any cartilage from crabmeat. Put celery in a medium bowl. Add remaining ingredients; mix well. Fold in crabmeat and mix gently but thoroughly. Refrigerate until ready to serve. Serves 4.

Celery Victor

This well-known salad, created by a San Francisco chef at the Saint Francis Hotel, is unusually attractive. It is a good salad to serve at a buffet or for a summer luncheon.

4 celery hearts
1½ cups chicken broth
1 bouquet garni (1 bay leaf, 2 parsley sprigs, ¼ teaspoon
    dried thyme, tied together in cheesecloth)
Salt, pepper to taste
⅓ cup olive or salad oil
2 to 3 tablespoons fresh lemon juice
2 hard-cooked eggs, shelled and sliced

Split each celery heart in half, lengthwise. Cut out root and
trim leaves, leaving only baby ones. Wash celery to remove all
dirt. Arrange in a shallow, flameproof dish or skillet in which the
celery can lie flat. Cover with chicken broth. Add *bouquet garni;*
season with salt and pepper. Bring to a boil. Reduce heat and
cook slowly, covered, until just tender, about 12 minutes. Cool in
broth. Drain celery and arrange on a platter. Combine oil and
lemon juice; season with salt and pepper; pour over salad.
Garnish with egg and tomato slices. Sprinkle with anchovy fillets
and parsley. Serves 4.

Caribbean Shrimp-Pineapple Salad

A prize salad for a weekend luncheon.

3 cans (4½ ounces each) shrimp
1 large fresh pineapple
2 cups diced oranges or grapefruit, white membranes
    removed
1 medium-sized avocado, peeled and cubed
4 tablespoons fresh lime or lemon juice
⅓ cup grated coconut
½ cup salad oil

2 *teaspoons honey*
Few drops Tabasco sauce (optional)
Salt, pepper to taste

Drain and clean shrimp. Chill. With a sharp knife, cut fruit and crown of pineapple in half, lengthwise. Cut away the hard, fibrous core, leaving on the crown. Loosen fruit from shell. (A grapefruit knife or any thin, sharp knife, preferably curved, is best.) Remove fruit from shells and cut into small chunks. Combine with shrimp, oranges or grapefruit, avocado, and 1 tablespoon lime or lemon juice. Spoon into pineapple shells and garnish with coconut. Combine remaining 3 tablespoons lime or lemon juice, oil, honey, Tabasco sauce, salt, and pepper, and serve with the salad. Serves 6.

Norwegian West Coast Seafood Salad

A Scandinavian salad for a Sunday luncheon.

1 garlic clove, halved
Meat from a whole lobster, cleaned and cubed
1 cup cold, shelled, and cleaned small shrimp
1 cup cold, cleaned, cooked clams
1 cup chopped celery
1 cup cold, cooked green peas
1 cup sliced fresh or canned mushrooms
About 1½ cups mayonnaise or salad dressing
2 tablespoons minced onion
3 tablespoons chopped fresh dill
Salt, pepper to taste

Rub salad bowl with garlic and discard. Put seafood, celery, peas, and mushrooms in the bowl, arranging the ingredients attractively. Combine remaining ingredients and serve with salad. Garnish with sliced hard-cooked eggs and tomato wedges, if desired. Serves 4.

Oregon Wild Rice–Salmon Salad

A special salad for a late evening supper.

> 2 cans (1 pound each) salmon
> 1 cup sliced scallions, with some tops
> 2 cups chopped, peeled cucumber
> 4 cups cooked wild rice
> 1 cup mayonnaise
> 1 cup sour cream
> 3 tablespoons fresh lemon juice
> 1 teaspoon dried dillweed
> Salt, pepper to taste
> 1 head leafy lettuce, washed, dried, and chilled
> 4 hard-cooked eggs, shelled and quartered
> 2 large tomatoes, peeled and cut into wedges

Drain salmon; remove skin; break into chunks. Combine with scallions, cucumber, and wild rice in a large bowl. Mix mayonnaise, sour cream, lemon juice, dillweed, salt, and pepper. Add to salmon mixture. Arrange lettuce leaves in a large bowl or on a platter. Top with salad. Garnish with eggs and tomatoes. Serves 8.

Charleston Shrimp-Rice Salad

An acclaimed salad for a ladies' luncheon.

3 cups cold, shelled, cooked, medium-sized shrimp
3 cups cold, cooked rice
¾ cup chopped celery
¾ cup diced green pepper
About ¾ cup French dressing
Few drops Tabasco sauce
Crisp lettuce leaves, washed and dried
1 large tomato, peeled and cut into wedges
1 medium-sized cucumber, washed, scored, and sliced

Combine first six ingredients in a bowl; mix well. Refrigerate 1 hour to blend flavors. Serve over lettuce leaves garnished with tomato wedges and cucumber slices. Serves 6.

Indonesian Vegetable Salad With Peanut-Butter Sauce

This favorite Indonesian salad, called *gado gado,* is an attractive and unusual dish to serve at a buffet.

2 cups cut-up cold cooked green beans
2 cups sliced cold, cooked carrots
2 cups sliced cold, boiled potatoes
2 cups shredded green cabbage or lettuce
2 large tomatoes, peeled and sliced
2 medium-sized cucumbers, peeled and sliced
⅔ cup peanut butter

2 garlic cloves, crushed
1 to 1½ teaspoons cayenne
1 teaspoon sugar
2 cups milk

Arrange vegetables attractively on a platter. Refrigerate. Heat peanut butter in a small saucepan until runny. Add remaining ingredients and cook over low heat, stirring, until smooth. Cool. Serve with vegetables. Serves 12.

Shrimp-Grapefruit Salad

A satisfying salad for a weekend brunch.

4 cups cold, shelled, cooked shrimp
2 cups coarsely chopped grapefruit sections
½ cup diced celery
¼ cup minced green onions
1 cup mayonnaise
2 tablespoons fresh lemon juice
2 teaspoons curry powder
Crisp lettuce leaves, washed and dried
½ cup almond slivers

Combine first four ingredients in a bowl. Mix mayonnaise, lemon juice, and curry powder. Add to shrimp mixture and mix well. Refrigerate 1 hour to blend flavors. Serve on lettuce leaves, garnished with almonds. Serves 6.

Finnish Crayfish Salad

Finns are devotees of crayfish, which are caught during a short early summer season. Restaurants feature them as specialties to be eaten in the shell. A truly delicious food, they're also ingredients in this flavorful weekend supper salad.

> *2 small heads leafy lettuce, washed, dried, and chilled*
> *3 cups diced, cleaned, cooked crayfish meat*
> *3 hard-boiled eggs, shelled and sliced*
> *½ cup olive or salad oil*
> *3 tablespoons wine vinegar*
> *1 teaspoon sugar*
> *½ teaspoon dry mustard*
> *3 tablespoons chopped fresh dill*
> *Salt, white pepper to taste*

Shred lettuce, leaving some leaves to use as a lining for the salad bowl. When ready to serve, line a salad bowl with lettuce leaves. Arrange shredded lettuce, crayfish, and egg slices in layers over the lettuce leaves. Combine remaining ingredients and serve with the salad. Serves 4 to 6.

Smoked Turkey Salad

A delectable salad for a late evening supper or Sunday luncheon.

> *2 cups diced smoked turkey*
> *3 cups diced cold, cooked potatoes*
> *3 cups diced cold, cooked or canned beets*
> *2 cups diced or shredded Swiss or American cheese*
> *1 medium-sized sweet red pepper or pimiento, chopped*
> *2 cups chopped romaine*
> *About 1¼ cups French dressing*
> *1 tablespoon chopped chives*

Combine all ingredients, except dressing and chives, in a salad bowl. Serve with dressing and garnished with chives. Serves 8.

English Vegetable Salad Platter

An attractive salad for a buffet or dinner party.

1 whole cauliflower, cooked, drained, and chilled
1 head leafy lettuce, washed, dried, and chilled
2 packages (10 ounces each) frozen green asparagus
    spears, cooked, drained, and chilled
2 cups sliced cold, cooked carrots
2 cups sliced cold, boiled potatoes
2 cups cooked fresh or canned mushroom buttons
2 medium-sized cucumbers, scored and thinly sliced
2 large tomatoes, peeled and sliced
1 pimiento, cut into strips
3 tablespoons chopped fresh dill
About 2 cups French dressing

Place whole cauliflower over lettuce leaves in center of a large round or oval platter. Surround with asparagus, carrots, and potatoes. Arrange mushrooms, cucumbers, and tomatoes around them. Garnish top of cauliflower with pimiento strips. Sprinkle vegetables with dill. Serve with dressing. Serves 8 to 10.

Argentine Meat-Vegetable Salad

A solid salad entrée for a dinner or late evening party.

3 cups diced cold, cooked potatoes
3 cups cold, cooked green peas
3 cups cut-up cold, cooked green beans

3 cups cold, cooked whole-kernel corn
3 cups canned kidney beans, drained
1½ cups olive or salad oil
1 cup wine vinegar
2 teaspoons dry mustard
½ teaspoon cayenne
½ cup chopped fresh coriander or parsley
1½ teaspoons dried oregano
Salt, pepper to taste
12 crisp lettuce leaves, washed and dried
3 pounds thinly sliced cold, cooked meats (beef, ham, pork, salami, or other sausage)
1 pound thinly sliced cold, cooked chicken or turkey
4 hard-cooked eggs, shelled and cut into wedges
½ pound cheese (yellow or white), cubed
4 medium-sized tomatoes, peeled and sliced.

Combine first five ingredients in a large bowl. Mix next seven ingredients and add to vegetables. Mix well and allow to marinate 24 hours or longer. When ready to serve, remove vegetables from marinade with a slotted spoon. Spoon into 12 lettuce leaf "cups." Arrange vegetable "cups," cold meats, and chicken or turkey attractively on a large platter. Place remaining ingredients between or around them. Serves 12.

Salmon-Filled Avocados

A sensational salad for summer luncheons.

2 cans (1 pound each) salmon
1 cup minced celery
⅓ cup diced green pepper
¼ cup sliced scallions, with some tops
½ teaspoon dried dillweed

Salt, pepper to taste
1 tablespoon fresh lemon juice
3 large avocados, halved, peeled, and pitted
Romaine leaves
2 large tomatoes, peeled and cut into wedges

Drain, flake, and clean salmon. Combine with celery, green pepper, scallions, dillweed, salt, pepper, and lemon juice. Place avocado halves, pitted side up, over romaine leaves. Mound salmon mixture into avocado halves. Serve garnished with tomato wedges. Serves 6.

Genoese Cappon Magro

One of the world's most elaborate dishes is often awarded the title "queen of salads" by the Genoese. *Cappon magro,* a large fish-and-vegetable combination, is eaten by Catholics on fast days. It is a work of architecture that is very difficult to make in the home and is therefore most often served in restaurants.

The salad is constructed in the shape of a pyramid in a number of differently colored layers over a base of ship's biscuits or stale bread that has first been soaked in olive oil and wine vinegar. Seafoods such as lobster, shrimp or prawns, scallops, white fish, and sea bass are combined with individually cooked and cut-up potatoes, green beans, beets, cauliflower, and artichokes, as well as chopped celery, mushrooms, and green and black olives. The salad is coated with a thick sauce made from pounded capers, anchovies, parsley, garlic, fennel, and breadcrumbs mixed with olive oil and with vinegar or lemon juice. Finally, the pyramid is garnished with crayfish or prawns, olives, hard-cooked egg quarters, and anchovies.

Italian Antipasto Salad Platter

A good salad for an informal dinner or supper.

> *6 cups cold, cooked dried white beans (navy or pea)*
> *1 cup diced green pepper*
> *1 cup diced sweet red pepper or pimento*
> *1 cup diced onions*
> *½ cup chopped fresh parsley*
> *1 teaspoon dried oregano*
> *Salt, pepper to taste*
> *1 cup olive oil*
> *½ cup wine vinegar*
> *1 cup black olives*
> *1 cup stuffed green olives*
> *2 jars marinated artichoke hearts, drained*
> *4 hard-cooked eggs, shelled and cut into wedges*
> *24 thin salami slices, rolled into cornucopias*
> *3 cans (6½ or 7 ounces each) tuna fish, drained and*
> *   flaked*
> *2 cups pickled mushrooms*
> *3 cups cherry tomatoes, washed and stemmed*

Combine first six ingredients in a large bowl. Season with salt and pepper. Add oil and vinegar. Mix well. Refrigerate 24 hours to blend flavors. To serve, spoon bean mixture into center of an extra-large platter. Surround with remaining ingredients, arranging them attractively. Serves 12 to 14.

Macaroni-Tuna Salad

An inexpensive salad anyone can serve confidently for a brunch, luncheon, or supper.

3 cups elbow or shell macaroni
⅔ cup French dressing
3 cups diced, peeled cucumber
3 cups diced celery
1½ cups diced onion
6 cups flaked tuna fish
3 cups mayonnaise
½ cup prepared mustard
Salt, pepper to taste
3 hard-cooked eggs, shelled and sliced
3 medium-sized tomatoes, peeled and sliced
1 large green pepper, cleaned and cut into strips

Cook macaroni until just tender according to package directions. Drain and turn into a large bowl. Stir in French dressing. Refrigerate 1 hour. Combine with cucumber, celery, onion, tuna, mayonnaise, mustard, salt, and pepper. Spoon onto a large platter and garnish with eggs, tomatoes, and green peppers. Serves 12.

Lobster Salads

Salads made with lobster are treasured fare in many countries and are especially good for small luncheons and dinners.

Cooked lobster meat is so delectable that it can be simply and elegantly served on lettuce leaves with a topping of plain or lemon-flavored mayonnaise and a garnish of tomato wedges and hard-cooked egg slices.

The lobster may also be combined with shrimp, diced celery, quartered artichoke hearts, cold, cooked asparagus spears, sliced cold white meat of chicken, or fresh fruit.

Given below are two recipes for lobster salad. One is for an easy-to-prepare salad. The other is an old-time American favorite that's an elegant presentation suitable for a formal occasion.

Lobster Salad

1 pound cooked lobster meat
⅓ cup homemade mayonnaise
1 tablespoon fresh lemon juice
Salt, pepper to taste (optional)
Boston or Bibb lettuce leaves, washed and dried
2 medium-sized tomatoes, peeled and cut into wedges

Cut lobster meat into ½-inch pieces. Add mayonnaise, lemon juice, and, if desired, salt and pepper. Serve on lettuce leaves garnished with tomato wedges. Serves 4 to 6.

Mrs. Rorer's Lobster Salad

2 lobsters (weighing 4 or 5 pounds)
The tender leaves from 2 heads of lettuce
½ pint of mayonnaise

Boil the lobsters. When cold, take out the meat, being careful not to break the body or tail shells, and rejecting the stomach, the black vein running along the back of the tail, and the spongy fingers on the outside of the body. Cut the meat into dice with a silver knife, and stand it in a cold place until wanted. Make the mayonnaise. Clean the two tail shells, and one back, in cold water, and with scissors, remove the thin shell from the under side of the tail. Wash and dry the lettuce leaves, put them around the salad dish in two or three layers. Join the shells together in the form of a boat, the body shell in the centre, place them in the salad dish. Mix the mayonnaise and lobster together, put it into this boat. If there is any coral, mash it fine and sprinkle it over the whole. Garnish with a chain of the whites of hard-boiled eggs cut into slices and linked together. Serve immediately.

Russian Ham Salad Platter

A pleasing salad for an informal dinner or buffet.

3 cups diced cooked ham
3 cups diced cold, boiled potatoes
2 cups cooked green peas
½ cup minced scallions, with some tops
6 gherkins, diced
1 cup chopped celery
About 1½ cups mayonnaise
3 tablespoons prepared sharp mustard
Salt, pepper to taste
Crisp lettuce leaves
16 stuffed hard-cooked egg halves
16 hollowed cherry tomatoes filled with chive-flavored mayonnaise
16 one-inch thick cucumber rounds topped with dill-flavored sour cream
8 large mushroom caps filled with anchovy-flavored cream cheese

Combine first eight ingredients in a large bowl. Season with salt and pepper. Refrigerate 1 hour or longer to blend flavors. When ready to serve, spoon salad over lettuce leaves in center of a large round or oval platter. Surround with remaining ingredients. Serves 8.

Exotic Salads

Here are some little-known salads that are curious, odd, unusual, and exotic. All of them will add interest to your table.

Of course, one really can't define an exotic salad. The foods or methods of preparation that are commonplace in the Orient may be unusual in the United States, and vice versa. Even in America a salad well known in the Southwest may be considered strange in New England.

The salads labeled here as exotic are made with foods that aren't commonly associated with salads. Some were favorites on the tables of our forefathers but have been largely forgotten by moderns. Others are prepared with rare or expensive foods that must be considered luxurious, if not exotic.

The derivation of these exotic salads is fascinating. There are recipes, for example, for salads made with fish roe, squid, whelks, winkles, eels, smoked and pickled fish, snails, horse meat, rabbit, bear meat, opossum, and turtle meat. The Chinese have a favorite salad utilizing strips of dried jellyfish, cucumbers, and carrots that are seasoned with sesame oil and soy sauce.

In tropical climates, salads are made with native fruits such as the akee, sapodilla, mangosteen, custard apple, cherimoya, lychee (or litchi nut), passion fruit, and a variety of bananas.

Orientals often prefer salads made with many kinds of seaweed, and freshwater vegetable roots and flowers. A particular favorite is the pierced lotus root, called the Oriental or sacred lotus.

There are hundreds of unusual but edible wild and cultivated greens and plants that may be used in salads. In the American Southwest, the petals of some varieties of the yucca, or Indian banana, are added to salads. A fleshly-stemmed perennial herb called samphire, which grows along rocky costs, is a favorite salad ingredient in some areas of Northern Europe.

Salads may be prepared with agar-agar, also called Chinese, Japanese, or vegetable gelatin. It's derived from a type of seaweed and is used not only by Orientals but by vegetarians as a replacement for the ordinary gelatin that's made from animal protein. It comes in the form of flakes, granules, or bars, and must be soaked in liquid before using.

Since the Middle Ages, flowers have added distinctive flavor and decor to salads. Some Europeans and Americans still are fond of adding blossoms of the rose, violet, geranium, chrysanthemum, marigold, or nasturtium to salads.

The rose lends itself to fruit salads. In Thailand, however, a colorful rose salad is made with a number of other ingredients, including chicken or meat. A rose champagne mold served on mint leaves makes a beautiful and delectable salad.

Flower blossoms for salad should be unsprayed and are best gathered just as the morning dew is evaporating. They may be wrapped loosely in damp paper toweling and stored in the refrigerator until they are used.

Needless to say, a few of these salads will not be to everyone's taste. Indeed, some will tempt only the most venturesome palates. If you want to enhance an unusual menu, however, you'll certainly find this selection valuable.

American Arrowhead Salad

The native American arrowhead, also called arrowleaf, wapato, and duck potato, is an ancient vegetable that has long been used by the Indians as a potato substitute. The plant, which grows along streams and swamps and around ponds, has leaves that are shaped like an arrowhead. A related species grows in Europe and Asia. The raw bluish-gray or yellowish tubers have an unpleasant taste, but the cooked pale-yellow or buff-colored flesh has an appealing, nutty flavor somewhat like that of a water chestnut. The tubers are cooked like potatoes, in a small amount of salted boiling water, or may be roasted.

*4 cups cubed or sliced warm, peeled, and cooked
   arrowhead tubers
1 onion, peeled and chopped
1 cup diced green pepper
¼ cup salad oil
2 to 3 tablespoons cider vinegar
Salt, pepper to taste
3 tablespoons chopped fresh parsley
2 hard-cooked eggs, shelled and cut into wedges*

Combine arrowhead, onion, and green pepper in a medium bowl. Mix oil, vinegar, salt, and pepper; pour over salad and mix well. Allow to stand at room temperature 1 hour or longer to blend flavors. Serve sprinkled with parsley and garnished with egg wedges. Serves 4.

Brazilian Hearts of Palm Salad

Heart of palm, the stripped white heart, core, or "bud" of a young palm or palmetto tree, is a popular food in Florida, the West Indies, and South America. It is also called palm cabbage because of its resemblance to a small cabbage, and in Florida by the unflattering name of swamp cabbage. The hearts have a bland and delicate flavor and taste something like chestnuts. They may be boiled as a vegetable or eaten raw in salads. Raw hearts of palm have an appealingly crisp and mild flavor reminiscent of asparagus. Canned hearts do not have the crispness but retain the delicacy. Fresh hearts of palm are available in areas where they are grown. Elsewhere they are sold in cans in specialty food stores and some supermarkets.

> 1 can (14 ounces) hearts of palm, drained and cut into
>   ¼-inch slices
> 1 medium-sized ripe avocado, peeled and diced
> 1 small head leafy lettuce, washed, dried, torn into bite-
>   size pieces, and chilled
> ⅓ cup olive oil
> 2 to 3 tablespoons fresh lemon juice
> ½ teaspoon dried basil
> Salt, pepper to taste
> 1 large tomato, peeled and cut into wedges

Combine hearts of palm, avocado, and lettuce in a salad bowl. Mix oil, lemon juice, basil, salt, and pepper; pour over salad; toss. Serve at once garnished with tomatoes. Serves 4 to 6.

Italian Cardoon Salad

The cardoon, a thistlelike plant related to the globe àrtichoke but similar in appearance to a large bunch of celery, is whitish-green with a delicate and slightly bitter taste. It has a tough skin and outer stalks that must be removed before cooking, as only the inner stalks are edible. The smaller plants are preferable for salads. Cardoon must be blanched or precooked, and, once cut, it should be rubbed with lemon juice or put in acidulated water to prevent discoloring.

> *2 bunches cardoons*
> *Salt*
> *½ pound fresh mushrooms, cleaned and sliced*
> *⅓ cup olive oil*
> *3 to 4 tablespoons fresh lemon juice*
> *½ teaspoon dried oregano*
> *Salt, pepper to taste*
> *2 medium-sized tomatoes, peeled and cut into wedges*
> *2 hard-cooked eggs, shelled and quartered*

Remove tough outer and wilted stalks of cardoons, Remove all leaves and strings from inner stalks and cut into 3-inch pieces. Trim hearts and cut into pieces. Drop at once into cold water with a little vinegar or lemon juice added. Cook in boiling salted water, covered, until just tender. Drain and cool. Combine with mushrooms in a serving dish. Sprinkle with oil, lemon juice, oregano, salt, and pepper. Serve garnished with tomatoes and eggs. Serves 4 to 6.

Chrysanthemum Salad

This recipe has appeared in several old publications, but its origin is unknown.

> *1 can or jar (8½ ounces) artichoke hearts, drained*
> *1 pound shelled, cooked medium-sized shrimp*
> *3 cubed, peeled, cold, boiled potatoes*
> *4 hard-cooked eggs, shelled and sliced*
> *2 tablespoons capers*
> *8 chrysanthemums, washed and dried*
> *⅓ cup saffron-flavored French dressing*

Combine first five ingredients in a medium bowl. Chop 4 chrysanthemums and add to artichoke mixture. Add dressing; mix well. Serve topped with 4 whole chrysanthemums. Serves 4.

Belgian Hop Sprout Salad

Hop sprouts, called in French *jets de houblon,* and in German *Hopfensprossen,* are the edible flowers of a perennial herb important to the brewing of ale and beer. The young shoots are cut in spring from the hop vines and are considered great delicacies in Belgium, France, and Germany. They are boiled and served with butter and cream, with sauces, or cold as a salad. Many cooks point out that the hops may be prepared in the same way as asparagus and are especially good with lemon-flavored mayonnaise, hollandaise, or a vinaigrette sauce. In one good salad the hops are combined with chopped, cooked ham, hard-cooked eggs, and tomatoes, bound with mayonnaise, and served on watercress. In Europe and some areas of America, the hop sprouts are available for only a few weeks in spring. To cook, boil in a little salted water with a few drops of lemon juice until tender; drain and cool. Serve as suggested above.

English Yorkshire Salad

This salad is unusual because it is possibly the only one that is served with a molasses-flavored dressing. Yorkshire dishes are hearty and imaginative, and many of them include a rich, dark molasses.

> *2 small heads leafy lettuce, washed, dried, torn into bite-*
> *size pieces, and chilled*
> *½ cup sliced scallions, with some tops*
> *About ⅓ cup vinegar*
> *3 to 4 tablespoons molasses*
> *Salt, pepper to taste*

Combine lettuce and scallions in a salad bowl. Combine vinegar, molasses, salt, and pepper; pour over salad; toss. Serve at once. Serves 4.

Jamaican Breadfruit Salad

Breadfruit, a prickly, large, round, green fruit with yellowish-white flesh, is a staple food in Africa, the West Indies, South America, and the South Pacific. When baked or toasted, the flesh has the texture of bread. The fruit comes in many varieties, is rich in vitamins, and has a high carbohydrate value. It is not edible until cooked, and is eaten and served like potatoes or as a starchy vegetable. Breadfruit is available fresh and canned in some specialty food stores.

> *2 cups diced, cooked or canned breadfruit*
> *1 medium-sized onion, peeled and chopped*
> *½ cup chopped celery*
> *½ cup chopped green pepper*
> *½ cup mayonnaise*
> *2 to 3 teaspoons prepared mustard*
> *1 tablespoon vinegar*
> *Salt, pepper to taste*
> *Crisp lettuce leaves, washed and dried*
> *1 canned pimiento, cut into strips*
> *2 hard-cooked eggs, shelled and cut into wedges*

Combine breadfruit, onion, celery, and green pepper in a medium bowl. Mix mayonnaise, mustard, vinegar, salt, and pepper; add to breadfruit mixture. Serve over lettuce leaves, garnished with pimiento strips and egg wedges. Serves 4.

American Oyster Salads

When the first settlers came to America from Europe, they were impressed with the great abundance, large size, and excellence of the oysters. These shellfish became a commonplace food on Colonial tables.

Beginning in the early part of the nineteenth century, a craze for oysters developed across the country; they were shipped inland regularly to be enjoyed there as well as in coastal areas. The supply was plentiful then, and prices were low. Oysters were *de rigueur* for any important home or restaurant meal, and they appeared on menus in innovative dishes, including oyster salads.

The many interesting nineteenth-century recipes for oyster salads include oyster aspic; watercress topped with steamed oysters, French dressing, and garnishes of minced celery, capers, and crisp bacon curls; and shredded lettuce topped with pickled oysters, a layer of mayonnaise, and garnishes of lobster coral, capers, cooked beets, gherkins, hard-cooked eggs, pickled oyster crabs, and young peppergrass.

In recent years, oysters have become luxury fare, and oyster salads have been neglected. They may still be prepared, however, and are delectable.

Here are two recipes for oyster salads. The first is modern, and the second from an 1892 cookbook entitled *600 Selected Recipes*.

Oyster Salad

1 pint oysters
1 tablespoon butter or margarine
½ cup mayonnaise
1 tablespoon fresh lemon juice
1½ teaspoons prepared horseradish
Few drops Tabasco sauce
Salt, pepper to taste
Crisp lettuce leaves, washed and dried

Cook oysters in their liquor and the butter until edges begin to curl. Cool; cut into bite-size pieces; chill. Combine remaining ingredients, except lettuce leaves, and chill. Serve oysters on lettuce leaves, topped with the mayonnaise dressing. Serves 4.

Juliet Corson's Oyster Salad

2 quarts oysters
6 raw egg yolks
½ cup butter
½ cup sugar
½ cup vinegar
¼ cup made mustard, prepared with vinegar
1 level tablespoon salt
1 level tablespoon pepper

Carefully remove all particles of shell from the oysters, and strain their liquor; put the oysters and liquor together in a saucepan, and place them over a fire to boil; mix in another saucepan the yolks of eggs, butter, sugar, vinegar, mustard, salt, and pepper; stir the ingredients together over the fire until the egg yolks begin to thicken; then at once remove them from the fire, and continue to stir them for two minutes; when the oysters begin to boil take them up and drain off the liquor; thoroughly wash and dry four heads of lettuce, and tear them in small pieces; or use instead of the lettuce as much tender celery, carefully cleaned and chopped, as will equal the oysters in quantity; when the oysters are cold chop them a little, but do not cut them in very small bits; add to them the dressing made above (a cream dressing) and the lettuce or celery. The salad should be used soon after it is made.

Miami Stone Crab Salad

The highly esteemed stone crab, found in rocky places along the coasts of Florida and Cuba, has a delectable, sweet white meat that comes from the crab's two large, bulbous claws. The shell material turns bright orange with shiny black tips when cooked. The crabmeat is served cold with tart mayonnaise, made with lime juice instead of vinegar, and is also used to make excellent salads. Stone crabs, sold in a number of Eastern fish markets, are simply cooked in salted boiling water until tender.

2 cups cooked stone-crab meat
¼ cup chopped celery
¼ cup sliced stuffed olives
¼ cup chopped onion
¼ cup chopped green pepper
About ½ cup mayonnaise
1 tablespoon fresh lime or lemon juice
Salt, pepper to taste

Combine ingredients in a medium bowl and mix well. Refrigerate 2 hours to blend flavors. Serve alone or on romaine leaves. Serves 4.

British Sea Kale Salad

Several kinds of sea kale, a nutritious herb of the mustard family, are gathered along the coast of Britain and are highly prized for salads. The tender young curly grayish-green or blue-green leaves are sold either bleached or unbleached. When washed and dried, the kale may be simply tossed with a vinaigrette dressing, or it may be combined with chopped chives and tarragon leaves and a mustard-flavored oil-vinegar dressing.

Hawaiian Kumquat Salad

A small, yellowish-orange citrus fruit called the kumquat, originally from China and Japan but now cultivated in the United States, has an appealing, tart, juicy flesh and sweet, edible skin. When fully ripe, it may be eaten raw. To cook, remove stems and leaves, wash, and boil in water about 5 minutes. The fruit is also sold preserved in thick syrup and may be eaten whole or in slices. The colorful "golden orange" may be added to fruit-flavored gelatin salads, or it may be cooked, split, stuffed with cream cheese and nuts, and served on lettuce leaves with a salad dressing or orange-flavored mayonnaise. The kumquat is also a good addition to mixed fruit salads.

4 ripe or preserved kumquats, sliced
2 cups chopped fresh or canned pineapple
1 cup halved orange sections, peeled and membranes removed
½ cup mayonnaise
2 tablespoons pineapple or orange juice
¼ teaspoon ground ginger
Dash of salt
Crisp lettuce leaves, washed and dried
2 tablespoons chopped macadamia nuts or almond slivers

Combine kumquats, pineapple, and oranges in a medium bowl. Mix mayonnaise, pineapple or orange juice, ginger, and salt. Just before serving, add to fruits. Serve in lettuce cups and sprinkle with nuts. Serves 4.

Puerto Rican Chayote Salad

The ancient chayote (pronounced *shy-o-tee*), a member of the squash family and actually a fruit, although prepared and served as a vegetable, is highly prized in African, West Indian, and South American cuisines. It has a green or white pear shape and firm, rather crisp flesh. If the skin is not tough, it does not have to be peeled. Because the chayote has a bland flavor, it is generally well seasoned. It is particularly good when cooked and marinated in a dressing, with or without other fruits and vegetables, to be served as an appetizer or salad. Also known as vegetable pear and christophine, the chayote is available in some supermarkets and specialty food stores.

> *4 medium-sized chayotes*
> *Salt*
> *1 medium-sized onion, peeled and minced*
> *1 medium-sized ripe avocado, peeled and cubed*
> *2 small hot red peppers, seeded and chopped*
> *¼ cup olive or salad oil*
> *2 to 3 tablespoons fresh lime or lemon juice*
> *1 tablespoon wine vinegar*
> *½ teaspoon dried oregano*
> *Salt, pepper to taste*
> *Garnishes: 1 large tomato, peeled and cut into wedges; 3*
> *   tablespoons chopped fresh coriander or parsley*

Scrub chayote well and cut into cubes, discarding any seeds. Steam in a small amount of salted water until tender, about 12 minutes. Drain and cool. Combine with onion, avocado, and red peppers. Mix remaining ingredients, except garnishes, and pour over salad; mix well. Serve with garnishes. Serves 4 to 6.

Mexican Cactus Leaf Salad

Mexico's most characteristic salad, *ensalada de nopalitos*, is made with the tender, fleshy, flat, oval green leaves or paddles of the prickly pear cactus, which are called *nopales* or *nopalitos* when chopped. The leaves have an appealing, crisp, vegetablelike quality somewhat like that of green beans. They can be used alone or with other ingredients in salads. They are sometimes sold fresh, but more often are available canned or in jars as *nopalitos*.

To prepare fresh *nopales*, carefully remove the eyes with a sharp-pointed knife. Wash and cut into small cubes. Cook in a little salted water until tender, about 7 minutes. Drain well. Rinse in cold water.

> 2 cups chopped freshly cooked or canned nopalitos,
>   drained and rinsed
> 2 cups chopped tomatoes
> ½ cup chopped onion
> ½ teaspoon minced chili peppers
> 3 tablespoons olive or salad oil
> 1 tablespoon wine vinegar
> ½ teaspoon dried oregano
> Salt, pepper to taste
> 3 tablespoons chopped fresh coriander or parsley

Combine *nopalitos*, tomatoes, and onion in a medium bowl. Mix remaining ingredients, except coriander, and pour over salad; toss. Garnish with coriander or parsley. Serves 4 to 6.

Key West Conch Salad

Conch (pronounced *konk*) is delicious. It is taken from a beautiful amber-colored spiral shell with a highly polished pink, peach, and yellow, pearllike luster. Collectors hold the shells to the ear to hear the roar of the sea, and they use them as decorative pieces. The conch is native to the West Indies and also inhabits the waters of the Florida Keys and the Bahamas. Conch meat is fried or used to make fritters, chowders, and salads. Because conch has a tendency to be tough, it is usually tenderized by pounding with a mallet before using.

> *2 cups minced or ground raw conch*
> *Juice of 2 limes or lemons*
> *1 medium-sized onion, peeled and minced*
> *½ cup minced green peppers*
> *1 large tomato, peeled and chopped*
> *½ cup chopped celery*
> *¼ teaspoon minced red pepper (optional)*
> *3 to 4 tablespoons salad oil*
> *2 tablespoons wine vinegar*
> *Salt, pepper to taste*

Put conch in a medium bowl. Add lime or lemon juice and let stand 1 hour. Drain. Combine conch with onion, green pepper, tomato, celery, and red pepper. Mix oil, vinegar, salt, and pepper; add to salad. It may be served alone, on salad greens, or in avocado halves. Serves 4.

Italian Radicchio Salad

Radicchio is an interesting salad green with an appealing flavor. It grows only in the Veneto region of northeastern Italy and is highly prized by the cooks of that area. A form of chicory or curly endive, *radicchio* comes in two varieties. *Rosso*, light red or rose and white veins, is grown in the environs of Treviso. The other, named *Castelfranco* for its place of origin, has leaves sprinkled with bright colors; it is both blander and sweeter. In late fall and winter, the markets of the Veneto region are bright with these colorful greens, which are as beautiful as they are tasty. An Italian poet called *radicchio* "a flower to eat." Although some cooks combine the two varieties in salads, purists insist that each be prepared and served separately. They are usually dressed with an olive oil–vinegar dressing.

Polynesian Raw-Fish Salad

Throughout Polynesia a characteristic salad is made with raw fish that's "cooked" in lime or lemon juice and flavored with piquant seasonings. It is similar to the more familiar *seviche* of Latin American countries. There are probably as many variations of the dish as there are islands. The salads go by different names, include different varieties of fish, and are formulated differently. This recipe is from Tahiti.

> *1 pound fresh or frozen white-fleshed fish fillets (cod,*
> *flounder, halibut, or haddock)*
> *Juice of 2 or 3 limes or lemons*
> *½ cup coconut milk (recipe below)*
> *1 cup chopped onions*
> *1 tablespoon minced hot peppers*

Salt to taste
Garnishes: 2 medium-sized tomatoes, peeled and cut into
   wedges, and 1 cup sliced cucumbers

Cut fish into 1½-inch cubes. Put in a medium bowl and cover
with lime or lemon juice. Allow to stand at least 4 hours, stirring
fish occasionally. When the color of the fish has turned opaque,
indicating that it is "cooked," drain to remove all liquid. Put in a
serving dish and add coconut milk, onions, peppers, and salt.
Refrigerate at least 1 hour to blend flavors. Serve garnished with
tomatoes and cucumbers. Serves 4.

Coconut Milk: Put ½ cup freshly grated or packaged or frozen
unsweetened coconut and ½ cup hot water in a bowl and leave
at room temperature 1 hour. Strain liquid from the coconut,
discarding the coconut. Use the "milk" as directed in the recipe.
For a thicker milk, use less liquid.

Florida Dasheen Salad

An ancient plant grown in the tropics for its nutritious, large,
starchy tubers is known in many lands as taro. Now it is
cultivated in Florida, where it is called dasheen. The tuber has a
brown fibrous skin and flesh that becomes cream-colored and
mealy when cooked. It is reminiscent of the white potato but has
a pleasant, nutlike flavor and a somewhat moister consistency.
The dasheen doesn't take as long to cook as the potato does, but
it's used in many of the same ways. It's also called the Chinese
potato.

4 cups diced, cooked, peeled dasheen
1 medium-sized onion, peeled and chopped
1 cup diced celery

½ cup chopped sweet red pepper or pimiento
½ teaspoon celery seeds
About ½ cup mayonnaise
Salt, pepper to taste
3 tablespoons chopped fresh coriander or parsley

Combine the first five ingredients in a medium bowl. Add enough mayonnaise to bind ingredients. Season with salt and pepper. Serve garnished with coriander or parsley. Serves 4.

Belgian Endive Salad

One of Europe's most highly prized salad ingredients is Belgian endive, also called witloof (white leaf) and Brussels chicory (or *chicorée*). Its growth is as curious as its name, and its discovery was accidental. In 1845, a gardener in Brussels, experimenting to improve chicory roots, found that a group of them, left in a cellar for several days, had begun to sprout firm white leaves. Further testing led to the development of white-leaved heads. Over the years the pampered production of endive in especially prepared underground "growing houses" became an important Belgian industry. Endive does not thrive as well anywhere else. Raw, the slightly bitter leaves are great favorites for salad. This is an elegant salad to serve as a first course or side dish for a special dinner party.

1 bunch watercress
4 heads endive, washed
⅓ cup olive or salad oil
2 tablespoons tarragon or wine vinegar
Salt, pepper to taste
2 tablespoons minced chives or scallions

Wash watercress well and cut off leaves, discarding any wilted leaves and stems. Cut endive heads in half, lengthwise, and cut out cores. Break into bite-size pieces. Crisp watercress and endive in ice water for 5 minutes. Drain and wipe dry. Put in a salad bowl or serving dish. Add remaining ingredients and toss. Serve at once. Serves 4.

Mrs. Rorer's Shad Roe Salad

This unusual recipe is from Mrs. Rorer's *Philadelphia Cookbook,* published in 1886. She also has interesting recipes for salads made with sweetbreads and oyster crabs.

1 set shad roes
Salt
1 cup mayonnaise

Wash one set of shad roes, put them in a saucepan, cover them with boiling water, add a teaspoonful of salt, put the lid on the saucepan and simmer gently twenty minutes. When done, lift them carefully from the water and stand away until perfectly cold. Make a half-pint of mayonnaise and let stand it away also. When ready to serve, remove the skin from the outside of the shad roe and cut them into thin slices. Put one slice of onion in the centre of the salad dish, arrange around it crisp salad leaves, heap the shad roe in the centre, pour over it the mayonnaise, and it is ready to serve.

Irish Cockle and Mussel Salad

In the nineteenth century, great quantities of cockles and mussels were available at street stalls in Ireland's fair city— Dublin. The cries of "cockles and mussels alive, alive, O!" are still heard at convivial gatherings everywhere when the hour gets late. Then someone is sure to sing "Sweet Molly Malone." Both cockles and mussels are mollusks that are found along Northern European coasts. Cockles, however, are smaller and recognizable by their "cockleshells." Sometimes called "oysters of the poor," and related to the oyster, cockles and mussels may be eaten raw, but they are often steamed before eating or being used in salads.

> *2 dozen cockles*
> *2 dozen mussels*
> *Salt*
> *1 cup salad dressing or mayonnaise*
> *1 tablespoon vinegar*
> *¼ teaspoon dry mustard*
> *2 tablespoons chopped chives*
> *Salt, pepper to taste*
> *Watercress or salad greens, washed and dried*
> *2 hard-cooked eggs, shelled and cut into wedges*

Scrub cockles and mussels and rinse in cold water to remove all dirt. Put about 1½ inch of water in a kettle; add salt and bring to a boil. Add cockles and mussels; cover and steam about 3 minutes, or until shells begin to open. Remove and drain. Take cockles from shells. Take mussels from shells and remove beards. Cool. Combine salad dressing or mayonnaise, vinegar, mustard, chives, salt, and pepper. Arrange cockles and mussels on a bed of watercress or greens. Top with dressing and garnish with egg wedges. Serves 4.

Mexican Jicama Salad

Jicama (pronounced hee-kah-mah) is a brownish root vegetable that somewhat resembles a rutabaga. It has a white, crisp flesh something like that of a potato, but it tastes like a fresh water chestnut. Generally quite large, the vegetable usually is sold whole, but also cut in half or quarters, in Latin American and Oriental markets. It is also called yam bean. In Mexico, jicama is eaten raw with chili powder and lemon juice as a popular street snack. It combines well with other vegetables and fruits in salads. Jicama is also a popular substitute for water chestnuts.

> *2 cups peeled and chopped raw jicama*
> *1 medium-sized onion, peeled and chopped*
> *1 medium-sized green pepper, cleaned and chopped*
> *2 medium-sized tomatoes, peeled and sliced*
> *⅓ cup olive oil*
> *2 to 3 tablespoons fresh lemon juice*
> *½ teaspoon dried oregano*
> *Salt, pepper to taste*

Put jicama and vegetables in a salad bowl. Combine remaining ingredients and pour over salad. Mix and serve at once. Serves 4 to 6.

Down-East Fiddlehead Salad

In northern New England and neighboring Canadian areas, tender, green, fuzzy, and curled fern shoots, or sprouts, called fiddleheads (and also known as fern fronds, ostrich ferns and cinnamon ferns), have long been treasured delicacies. Found growing on the shores of streams, they are picked just as they're pushing up through the ground in spring. They're best when they're young and tender. Many years ago, the greens provided welcome relief from the monotonous winter diet of root vegetables. Today they're still sought after as spring fare.

Fresh fiddleheads are available in the locales where they're grown, but canned or frozen fiddleheads may be purchased in other parts of the country.

Fresh fiddleheads must be thoroughly washed and then steamed for a few minutes in a small amount of water. Cold, cooked fresh or frozen or canned fiddleheads may be mixed with any favorite salad dressing, such as mustard-flavored mayonnaise or chive-flavored sour cream.

West Indies Guava Salad

Guava, a small, thin-skinned, oval or round, yellow or red tropical American fruit has an aromatic, sweetish, juicy white or pink flesh with an appealing, spicy taste. It comes in many varieties and has a high vitamin content. The fruit is usually prepared in jams, jellies, or preserves, but the fresh fruit may be eaten raw and used in salads.

2 fresh guavas
2 cups cut-up watermelon or cantaloupe
2 cups diced fresh or canned pineapple
¼ cup mayonnaise
¼ cup whipped heavy cream
1 tablespoon melted guava jelly
1 tablespoon fresh lime juice
¼ cup grated coconut

Wash guavas and remove stem ends. Skin and slice. Combine with other fruit in a serving dish. Mix remaining ingredients, except coconut, and spoon over salad. Sprinkle with coconut. Serves 4 to 6.

Note: Guava shells are available in cans. When drained and sliced, they may be used in salads.

Hawaiian Bok Choy Salad

Bok choy, one of the best and most widely used Chinese vegetables, is commonly called Chinese cabbage or chard. The name, however, means "white cabbage." The vegetable has long, thick white stalks and large, dark-green leaves with white veins. *Bok choy* has a very pleasant flavor, is crisp, and should be used promptly. Although generally cooked, it may be used raw in salads. The vegetable is sold fresh by the bunch in Oriental or specialty food stores and in some supermarkets.

> *6 cups chopped fresh bok choy*
> *1 cup chopped celery*
> *1 medium-sized green pepper, cleaned and chopped*
> *½ cup sliced bamboo shoots*
> *1 cup diced fresh or canned pineapple*
> *About ⅓ cup salad oil*
> *2 tablespoons vinegar*
> *1 tablespoon soy sauce*
> *1 or 2 garlic cloves, crushed*
> *Pepper to taste*

Put *bok choy,* celery, pepper, bamboo shoots, and pineapple in a salad bowl. Combine remaining ingredients and pour over salad; toss. Serve at once. Serves 4 to 6.

Delmonico's Frog's Leg Salad

There aren't many recipes for salads made with frog's legs, and it's not certain if those that do exist are American or French creations. In *Food Favorites of St. Augustine* by Joan Adams Wickham, a recipe for Frog Salad combines the meat of boiled large frogs, or legs of small frogs, with lettuce leaves or celery, watercress, parsley, or sweet basil. It's served with a mild mayonnaise or French dressing and a garnish of hard-cooked eggs or crayfish.

The following recipe for the *Salade de Grenouilles* that was served at New York's famous Delmonico's Restaurant in the late nineteenth century is more elaborate.

Have one pound of very white medium-sized frogs, cooked in a little mushroom broth, and seasoned with salt, pepper, butter, and lemon juice; when cold cut the meats into three-eighths of an inch squares, and put them in a vessel with cooked artichoke bottoms, potatoes and hard-boiled eggs, all cut the same size as the frogs; season with salt, pepper, oil and vinegar, and marinate for fifteen to twenty minutes. Drain the salad on a sieve, return it to the vessel, and dress it with a consistent mayonnaise, finished with mustard and chopped tarragon; arrange it in a salad bowl, smoothing the top to a dome. Split some lobster claws in two, season and form into a rosette in the center of the salad; decorate around with truffles and gherkins, having a lettuce heart exactly in the middle.

Caribbean Codfish Salad

There are a number of interesting Caribbean salads made with a favorite staple, salted dried codfish. They may include sliced or cubed boiled potatoes, cooked carrots or green beans, raw vegetables, and piquant seasonings. Some salads are garnished or topped with red onion rings and/or avocado wedges. This is a typical codfish salad.

> *1 pound salted dried codfish*
> *1 medium-sized onion, peeled and chopped*
> *1 medium-sized green pepper, cleaned and chopped*
> *2 medium-sized tomatoes, peeled and chopped*
> *1 or 2 garlic cloves, crushed*
> *1/3 cup salad oil*
> *3 tablespoons wine vinegar*
> *Dash of cayenne or ¼ teaspoon ground red pepper*
> *Salt, pepper to taste*
> *3 tablespoons chopped fresh coriander or parsley*

Put codfish in a medium bowl. Cover with cold water and let soak at least 4 hours. Drain thoroughly. Remove any skin and bones and shred or cut into bite-size pieces. Combine with remaining ingredients, except coriander, in a serving dish. Refrigerate or leave at room temperature 2 hours to blend flavors. Serve garnished with coriander or parsley. Serves 4 to 6.

European White Asparagus Salad

In Belgium, France, and Germany one of the most treasured foods is tender, thick, pearl-white asparagus, grown underground and carefully harvested by hand each spring. In season only a short time, it is prized as the "king of vegetables" and is carefully cooked to preserve both nutrients and appearance. When purchased, asparagus must be carefully peeled from just below the tip to the base. Then it's boiled and served warm, or it may be left to cool and be served cold. As a salad, it may be served with a vinaigrette, hollandaise, maltaise (orange-flavored hollandaise), mousselline (hollandaise enriched with cream), or herb-flavored sour cream dressing. Fresh white asparagus is available in season in some American locales. Canned white asparagus can be purchased in specialty food stores. The following salad may be prepared with white or green asparagus.

> *1½ pounds fresh white or green asparagus*
> *Salt*
> *1 cup mayonnaise, preferably homemade*
> *2 hard-cooked eggs, shelled and chopped*
> *2 tablespoons chopped chives*
> *2 tablespoons chopped fresh parsley*
> *Pepper to taste*
> *Crisp lettuce leaves, washed and dried*
> *1 large tomato, peeled and cut into wedges*

Wash asparagus well to remove all sand. Peel and remove any woody parts of stems. Arrange stalks in a large skillet or wide-bottomed pan. Add ½ inch boiling water and season lightly with salt. Cover and bring quickly to a boil. Reduce heat to medium or low and cook about 10 minutes, or until stalks are just tender. Lift from pan and drain. Put whole or cut-up stalks in a serving dish. Cool and chill. Combine mayonnaise, eggs, chives, and parsley. Season with salt and pepper. To serve, place cold asparagus over lettuce leaves. Top with the mayonnaise dressing and garnish with tomatoes. Serves 4.

Shaker String Bean–Nasturtium Salad

The fresh leaves, buds, and colorful orange, yellow, and red flowers of the nasturtium are pleasant additions to salads and were frequently used by the innovative Shakers to add color and a crisp flavor to a number of salads. The buds or pods may be pickled and used like capers or added to vinegars for flavoring. This salad is from an old Shaker recipe collection.

2 cups cooked string beans
2 cups shredded lettuce
2 scallions, cleaned and minced
2 sprigs summer savory
6 nasturtium leaves
12 nasturtium pods
Salt, pepper to taste
About ⅓ cup salad dressing or vinaigrette

Combine string beans and lettuce in a salad bowl. Sprinkle with remaining ingredients, except dressing. Serve with dressing. Serves 4.

German Bouquet Salad

Another colorful salad that includes nasturtiums. This recipe is from a German friend.

4 tablespoons olive oil
3 tablespoons white wine vinegar
Pinch of sugar
Little shake of pepper
Watercress
Nasturtium leaves, very young and tender
Nasturtium flowers, various shades
Hard-cooked eggs, sliced

Mix the oil, vinegar, sugar, and pepper in the bottom of a large bowl; then fill the bowl with alternate layers of watercress and small nasturtium leaves around the edge of the bowl, then a ring of variegated nasturtium flowers, then a ring of thin slices of hard-cooked egg, each slice overlapping the last. In the center of the bowl, place a tuft of flowers. Serve with rich mayonnaise. This salad is best with delicate cold ham or thinly sliced sausage.

Truffle Salads

An intriguing number of exotic salads have been prepared with truffles, the mysterious fungi that grow underground, primarily in the Périgord region of France and the Piedmont district of Italy.

Although they have been known for over two thousand years, the origin of truffles remains an enigma. Why and how they grow has never been ascertained. It's still necessary to use specially trained pigs or dogs to locate truffles and root them from the ground.

"Black diamonds," as they are often called, are prized for their rarity, appealing flavor, and remarkably penetrating aroma, which can overpower other foods. Truffles vary in size and are usually black, dark brown, or "white" (actually cream-colored). There are also pink and light-purple truffles.

One of the most famous truffle salads, *Salade Rossini*, was created by the great Italian composer. The words of a letter by Rossini attest to his pride in the dish:

"What is going to interest you much more than my opera is the discovery I have just made of a new salad for which I hasten to send you the recipe.

"Take Provence oil, English mustard, French vinegar, a little lemon juice, pepper and salt, whisk and mix together. Then throw in a few truffles, which you have taken care to cut in tiny pieces. The truffles give to this seasoning a kind of nimbus to plunge the gourmand into an ecstasy."

In Italy, an exceptional salad is made with white truffles and the highly prized soft, creamy fontina cheese—one food that can stand up to the powerful truffle flavor—and a mustard-flavored cream dressing.

The Viennese have a black-and-white salad made with truffles and potatoes. There is also one made with truffles boiled in Madeira wine, which are combined with celery root, and a well-seasoned oil-vinegar dressing. Even more unusual is a salad of truffles and boiled potatoes marinated in champagne and combined with mussels, chives, and parsley.

No truffle salad could be more exotic than the one prepared by an actress friend of Alexandre Dumas and described by him as *Mademoiselle George's Salade de Truffes*:

Then they went into a dining-room where a luxuriously appointed table was already laid. In the very center stood a huge gold and silver bowl filled to overflowing with five or six pounds of truffles, whose priceless scent perfumed the air and assailed their nostrils as they entered the room.

The mistress of the house then began to peel the truffles, using a silver knife reserved solely for that purpose. She seasoned them with milk of almonds, wine, champagne or liqueur as the mood seized her. Then followed *pâtés*, aspics or chicken and various cold dishes that one of the guests, under Mademoiselle George's instructions, would fetch, all prepared, from a table in the pantry. To wind up this love-feast, Dumas was generally asked to prepare a salad "in his own style," the famous *Salade à la Dumas* [See the final recipe in the Side-Dish Salads Chapter] for which he was to give us the recipe in writing.

Chinese Snow Pea–Mushroom Salad

Delicate snow peas, also called Chinese or edible pea pods and sugar peas, have an appealing bright-green color. They've a crisp, firm texture, but are so tender that the entire vegetable, both pea and pod, is eaten. The ends and strings, if any, must be removed, and the peas should be used as promptly as possible to retain their freshness. Originally grown only in the Orient, snow peas are now cultivated in the United States and are sold fresh in many specialty food stores and some supermarkets. Frozen snow peas are generally available, but they lack the crisp texture and sweet flavor of the fresh peas. This colorful salad was created by a Chinese-American cook; the dish is not served in China.

> *1 pound fresh snow peas*
> *Salt*
> *½ pound fresh mushrooms*
> *¾ cup sliced scallions, with some tops*
> *½ cup sliced canned water chestnuts or bamboo shoots*
> *¼ cup salad oil*
> *1½ tablespoons vinegar*
> *2 teaspoons soy sauce*
> *1 or 2 garlic cloves, crushed*
> *Pepper to taste*

Remove ends and strings, if any, from snow peas. Drop into boiling salted water to cover. Cook 2 to 3 minutes. Do not overcook. The peas should be crisp. Drain and cool. Combine with mushroons, scallions, and water chestnuts in a medium bowl. Mix remaining ingredients; pour over salad. Serve at once. Serves 4 to 6.

Note: Frozen snow peas may be substituted for fresh peas. Cook according to package directions.

New Zealand Kiwi Fruit Salad

Kiwi fruit, also known as Chinese gooseberry, is the same size and shape as a lime; it has a fuzzy brown skin and soft, brilliant green flesh with a flavor something like watermelon with a dash of strawberry. This exotic subtropical fruit was discovered in China, but now New Zealand grows and exports it. Kiwi fruit is ripe for eating when it is soft to the touch. Simply rub off the hairs, cut the fruit in half, and eat the attractive flesh and tiny black seeds with a spoon. You may also peel and slice kiwi fruit and use it to make desserts, salads, or garnishes. This fruit is extremely rich in vitamin C.

The following salad from New Zealand is called Kiwi Fruit Jewel Salad.

> *3 cups fresh pineapple chunks*
> *2 medium-sized bananas, peeled and sliced*
> *2 navel oranges, peeled, separated into segments, and*
> *   membranes removed*
> *Juice of 2 lemons*
> *1 cup sliced fresh strawberries*
> *3 kiwi fruit, cleaned and sliced*
> *1 tablespoon honey*

Put pineapple, bananas, and oranges in a bowl. Squeeze lemon juice over them. Add strawberries and kiwi fruit, and mix well. Boil honey with ¾ cup water; cool; pour over salad; mix well. Refrigerate 1 hour to blend flavors. Serves 6 to 8.

Oriental Bitter Melon Salad

The balsam pear, commonly known as bitter melon, is a small, green, tapered vegetable that resembles the cucumber in size and shape but has a warted or wrinkled green surface. It grows in tropical climates and is highly prized by African and Asian cooks. As the name suggests, it has a distinctive bitter taste that is also refreshingly cool. The vegetable, available fresh and/or canned in Oriental and specialty food stores, doesn't have to be peeled, but it has a white, spongy center portion that must be removed before cooking or eating.

> *1 medium-sized bitter melon, about ¾ pound, washed*
> *Salt*
> *1 medium-sized cucumber, peeled and sliced*
> *½ cup sliced scallions, with some tops*
> *½ cup sliced white or red radishes*
> *⅓ cup salad oil*
> *2 to 3 tablespoons white vinegar*
> *2 teaspoons soy sauce*
> *Salt, pepper to taste*

Cut off and discard ends of the bitter melon. Split in half lengthwise and cut out and discard the white center portion of each slice. Cut into slices about ¼ inch thick. Put in a bowl and sprinkle with salt. Let stand about 15 minutes. Squeeze to completely remove all liquid. Wash and dry. Combine with cucumber, scallions, and radishes. Add remaining ingredients and refrigerate until ready to serve. Serves 4.

Note: If canned bitter melon is used, merely drain, slice, and combine with other ingredients.

Salad Dressings

No aspect of good salad-making is more important than the dressing. It should be prepared only with the finest ingredients and varied to suit the individual salad.

Ever since the ancients invented simple salad dressings of oil, lemon juice or vinegar, and seasonings, cooks around the world have been devising hundreds of variations.

All dressings descend from that original inspiration. Even now we've but three "mother" or basic salad dressings—oil and lemon juice or vinegar, mayonnaise dressings, and cooked dressings, each of which, however, is subject to infinite variation.

Americans, in particular, have created a wide selection of dressings. Most notable is the ubiquitous French dressing, based on the original oil and lemon juice or vinegar combination. It can be formulated and flavored with a diverse selection of ingredients ranging from anchovies to watercress, earning for these recipes such fanciful names as surprise, festive, supreme, glorious, crystal, royal, and glistening.

Despite the popularity and availability of bottled or commercial salad dressings, those that are made in the home can be best and cost less. Making dressings from scratch is easy, and each can be seasoned according to personal taste.

Because the preparation of dressings is so important, basic data is provided in the introduction. Remember that a dressing also adds character to a salad and should be chosen to complement the ingredients—flavorful with bland foods, and vice versa. Consider the dishes on the menu; an overseasoned dressing could intrude upon a subtly flavored entrée or dessert.

In most cases, the dressing should be added to the salad just before it is served. It should be used sparingly and judiciously. Add only enough to coat the greens; too much dressing will wilt them. You may make an exception to that rule when the dressing is to be used to marinate the ingredients.

Given below is one of the most famous salad recipes, together with others for classic and lesser-known dressings.

Sydney Smith's Receipt for Salad Dressing

Two boiled potatoes, strained through a kitchen sieve,
Softness and smoothness to the salad give;
Of mordant mustard take a single spoon—
Distrust the condiment that bites too soon;
Yet deem it not, thou man of taste, a fault,
To add a double quantity of salt.
Four times the spoon with oil of Lucca crown,
And twice with vinegar procured from town;
True taste requires it, and your poet begs
The pounded yellow of two well-boiled eggs.
Let onions' atoms lurk within the bowl,
And, scarce suspected, animate the whole;

And lastly, in the flavored compound toss
A magic spoonful of anchovy sauce.
Oh, great and glorious! oh, herbaceous meat!
'Twould tempt the dying anchorite to eat.
Back to the world he'd turn his weary soul,
And plunge his fingers in the salad bowl.

French Vinaigrette Dressing

The classic French dressing for salads is a simple and versatile vinaigrette made with oil, vinegar, salt, and pepper—usually olive oil, wine vinegar, and freshly ground pepper. The proportion of oil to vinegar can vary according to taste, but usually it is three or four parts oil to one part vinegar. It may be made in advance, but many cooks prefer to prepare it just before using. It requires only a good beating or mixing, but because the oil and vinegar separate, the dressing should be shaken or beaten just before it is used. Other ingredients such as garlic, shallots, mustard, or herbs are sometimes added if they complement the salad you've made. Here's a basic recipe that can be varied as desired.

> *1 cup olive oil (or combination of olive and good salad oil)*
> *⅓ cup vinegar (wine, cider, or herb-flavored or fresh lemon juice)*
> *1 teaspoon salt*
> *¼ teaspoon freshly ground pepper*

Combine ingredients in a screw-top jar, shaker, or bowl. Shake or mix to blend thoroughly. Refrigerate or use at once. In any event, shake or mix just before serving. Makes 1⅓ cups.

To VARY: Add 1 garlic clove, crushed; 1 shallot, minced; ½ teaspoon dry mustard; or 2 teaspoons fresh or ½ teaspoon dried dill, tarragon, basil, oregano, thyme, or other herbs. Add herbs just before using.

Basic French Dressing

America's most popular salad dressing is the so-called French dressing, made commercially in many varieties that are generally creamy in consistency, well flavored with mustard, paprika, or cayenne, and orange-red in color. Some include onions, horse-radish, garlic, catsup, chili sauce, Worcestershire sauce, cheeses, spices, herbs, and other ingredients. The name is a misnomer since the dressing is not French in origin; nor is it used in France. The dressing is widely used in the United States on mixed green, vegetable, fruit, and main-dish salads. The homemade variety is best. This is a basic recipe.

> *1 cup olive or salad oil or combination of both*
> *⅓ cup vinegar (cider, wine, or flavored)*
> *½ teaspoon dry mustard*
> *½ teaspoon paprika*
> *1 teaspoon sugar*
> *1 teaspoon salt*
> *⅛ teaspoon pepper*

Combine ingredients in a screw-top jar or shaker and shake well. Refrigerate until ready to use. Shake again before using. Make 1⅓ cups.

The dressing may be varied by adding to 1 cup of the basic French dressing any of the following:

ANCHOVY: 2 tablespoons anchovy paste and 1 tablespoon minced onion.

CAPER: ⅓ cup minced, drained capers.

CHEESE: ½ cup crumbled Roquefort, blue, or Gorgonzola cheese or cottage cheese with 1 tablespoon chopped chives.

CHIFFONADE: 1 chopped hard-cooked egg, 1 tablespoon each minced green pepper and pimiento, 1 tablespoon minced onion, and 1 tablespoon chopped fresh parsley.

CREAMY: 1 package (3 ounces) cream cheese and 1 tablespoon minced onions.

GARLIC: 1 clove garlic, crushed.

HERB: 2 tablespoons chopped fresh herbs or 1½ teaspoons dried herbs.

ITALIAN: ¼ cup grated Parmesan cheese, ½ teaspoon dried oregano, ¼ teaspoon dried basil.

LEMON: Substitute lemon juice for vinegar.

MUSTARD: 2 teaspoons prepared sharp mustard and 1 crushed garlic clove.

Old-fashioned Boiled Dressing

Boiled or cooked salad dressing is an American creation that is made of a combination starch and custard base. It has an acid flavor. Originally, the dressing was a tangy simple mixture that was used primarily with potato salads and coleslaws. Over the years, American cooks have created a number of variations of the dressing that are used with many kinds of salad. The basic recipe is:

2 tablespoons all-purpose flour
1 tablespoon sugar
½ teaspoon dry mustard
1 teaspoon salt or to taste
Dash of cayenne
1 cup milk
1 egg or 2 egg yolks, slightly beaten
3 to 4 tablespoons cider vinegar or fresh lemon juice

Combine flour, sugar, mustard, salt, and cayenne in top of a double boiler; mix well. Gradually add milk and cook over simmering water, stirring constantly, until slightly thickened and smooth. Add some of the hot mixture to beaten egg or egg yolks; add to remaining hot mixture and cook over simmering water until thickened, about 3 minutes. Remove from heat and stir in vinegar or lemon juice. Chill before serving. Makes 1¼ cups.

The recipe above may be varied by adding to 1¼ cups of the dressing:
¼ cup cottage cheese and 1 tablespoon minced scallions
or 1 cup whipped cream
or 1 to 2 tablespoons horseradish before cooling
or ½ cup chopped, peeled, and seeded cucumbers
or 2 chopped hard-cooked eggs and 1 tablespoon chopped chives
or 1 cup sour cream and 1 tablespoon chopped fresh dill
or ¼ cup minced onion, 3 tablespoons chili sauce, and 1 tablespoon chopped gherkin.

Basic Sour Cream Dressing

Sour cream is an excellent ingredient for making salad dressings. It may be combined with chopped herbs such as dill, mint, or chives; Roquefort or blue cheese; chopped olives; grated fresh or prepared horseradish; chopped onions or scallions; chopped nuts; chopped cucumbers, celery, or green peppers; or mixed with yogurt, mayonnaise, or French dressing. The basic recipe may be used with mixed green, molded, or vegetable salads.

1 cup sour cream
2 tablespoons fresh lemon juice or vinegar
1 tablespoon sugar (optional)
½ teaspoon paprika
2 teaspoons prepared sharp mustard
Salt, pepper to taste

Combine ingredients and mix well. Refrigerate until ready to use. Makes about 1 cup.

Whipped Cream Dressing

Whipped cream dressing and its variations are excellent for fruit salads, molded salads, and some vegetable salads.

½ cup heavy cream
1 to 2 tablespoons fresh lemon juice
Salt to taste or ¼ teaspoon
Dash white pepper

Whip cream until partially stiff. Add lemon juice, salt, and pepper, and continue whipping until stiff. Serve at once. Makes about 1 cup.

This recipe may be varied by adding to 1 cup of the basic dressing any of the following:

ANCHOVY: 3 minced anchovies and 1 teaspoon grated lemon rind.

CUCUMBER: ½ cup diced, peeled cucumbers and ¼ teaspoon dried dillweed.

FRUIT: ¼ cup crushed pineapple or berries.

HORSERADISH: Omit lemon juice and add 2 tablespoons grated fresh horseradish.

Mayonnaise

This classic French cold sauce, used throughout the Western world, is one of the most popular salad dressings. It has many variations and is the base for other sauces and dressings.

The origin of the word *mayonnaise* is not certain. Some authorities claim it derived from *moyeu,* the old French word for egg yolk, or from the French verb *manier,* to stir. Others maintain that it was a name given to the sauce by the Duke of Richelieu after he won the battle of Mahon on the Mediterranean island of Minorca in 1757.

Commercial mayonnaise is widely available in American stores, and it can be used either plain or with lemon juice, olive oil, sour cream, or yogurt added.

Mayonnaise is a smooth emulsion of egg yolks in either olive or salad oil, to which either vinegar or lemon juice and seasonings are added. Either egg yolks or whole eggs may be used. The latter makes a thinner mayonnaise.

Although many people believe it is difficult to make home-made mayonnaise, the technique is well worth mastering. The result is much better than the commercial product.

The trick in preparation is that the egg yolk or egg must absorb the oil to make the emulsion. To do this, add the oil a drop at a time at first. Otherwise, a separation may occur with the oil floating over the egg. If this does happen, the dressing may be beaten into another egg yolk until an emulsion forms. Then proceed with the original recipe.

Making your first homemade mayonnaise will take a little time. The oftener you practice, the less time it will take. Mayonnaise is easy to make in an electric blender, but it is usually not quite as good or as rich as that prepared by hand.

These are two basic mayonnaise recipes and some delightful variations.

Homemade Mayonnaise

1 egg yolk
½ teaspoon salt
¼ teaspoon dry mustard
1 to 2 tablespoons vinegar or fresh lemon juice
1 cup olive or salad oil or combination of both

Combine egg yolk, salt, mustard, and 1 teaspoon vinegar or lemon juice in a metal bowl and beat with a wire whisk until thickened. Then, drop by drop, add oil, beating constantly, and making certain that each drop is absorbed, until ⅓, or perhaps ½, of the oil is emulsified with egg yolk. Then add remaining oil in a steady stream, beating steadily. Add remaining vinegar or lemon juice and beat well until light-colored and smooth. Refrigerate until ready to use. Makes about 1½ cups.

Blender Mayonnaise

1 egg
2 tablespoons vinegar or lemon juice
½ teaspoon salt or salt to taste

¼ to ½ teaspoon dry mustard
1 cup olive or salad oil or combination of both

Put egg, vinegar, salt, mustard, and ½ cup oil in blender container. Cover and blend 5 seconds until smooth. Without stopping, pour remaining oil in a steady stream through opening in blender top. Blend a few seconds longer, until thick and smooth. Makes 1¼ cups.

To 1 cup homemade or commercial mayonnaise, add any of the following.

ANCHOVY: 2 tablespoons anchovy paste and 1 crushed garlic clove.

CAPER: ⅓ cup capers.

CREAM: 1 cup whipped cream and 1 tablespoon grated lemon or orange rind.

CUCUMBER: 1 cup diced, peeled, and seeded cucumber and ½ teaspoon dried dillweed.

CURRY: 1 to 3 teaspoons curry powder and ¼ teaspoon paprika, which should be cooked briefly in a little oil before adding to mayonnaise.

GREEN: 1 tablespoon each chopped parsley, chives, and spinach or watercress.

HORSERADISH: 2 tablespoons prepared or freshly grated horse-radish.

MUSTARD: 2 tablespoons or more of prepared sharp mustard.

RÉMOULADE: 1 tablespoon chopped gherkins, 2 teaspoons sharp mustard, 1 tablespoon chopped, drained capers, 1 teaspoon chopped fresh parsley, ½ teaspoon chopped tarragon, and ½ teaspoon anchovy paste.

RUSSIAN: ⅓ cup chili sauce, 1 teaspoon grated onion, 1 table-spoon fresh lemon juice, and 2 teaspoons Worcestershire sauce. Optional additions: 2 tablespoons chopped sweet pickles or sliced stuffed olives, or 1 tablespoon grated horseradish.

THOUSAND ISLAND DRESSING: ¼ cup chili sauce, 1 tablespoon minced green pepper, 2 tablespoons chopped red pepper or pimiento, and 2 tablespoons chopped stuffed olives.

TARRAGON: 1 tablespoon tarragon vinegar and 2 teaspoons lemon juice.

West Indies Avocado Dressing

An exciting dressing for mixed green or fruit salads.

1 medium-sized avocado, peeled and mashed
2 tablespoons fresh lemon juice
1 cup mayonnaise
¼ cup chopped scallions
¼ cup chopped green pepper
Few drops Tabasco sauce
Salt, pepper to taste

Combine all ingredients and refrigerate at least 1 hour to blend flavors. Makes 2½ to 3 cups.

African Peanut-Butter Dressing

A yummy dressing for mixed green and vegetable salads. The kids are sure to love it.

⅓ cup smooth peanut butter
½ cup peanut or salad oil
Juice or 1 lemon
1 or 2 garlic cloves, crushed
⅛ to ¼ teaspoon ground red pepper
Salt, pepper to taste

Combine ingredients and mix well. Makes about 1 cup.

Oriental Seasame-Soy Dressing

A dressing that's just right for fresh spinach and other greens, sliced white radishes, or cucumbers.

½ cup peanut or salad oil
3 tablespoons rice or white wine vinegar
1 to 2 tablespoons soy sauce
1 teaspoon sugar
2 tablespoons sesame seeds, toasted
¼ cup sliced scallions, with some tops (optional)
Pepper to taste

Combine ingredients and mix well. Makes about 1 cup.

English Egg Dressing

A noble dressing for mixed green salads.

1 cup olive or salad oil
⅓ cup vinegar or lemon juice
½ teaspoon dry mustard
Dash of cayenne
Salt, pepper to taste
2 hard-cooked eggs, shelled and chopped
¼ cup chopped fresh parsley

Combine ingredients and mix well. Makes about 2 cups.

Arabian Sesame Dressing

A dressing with the flavor of the East for romaine or other lettuces.

½ cup tahini
½ cup olive oil
¼ cup fresh lemon juice
2 garlic cloves, crushed
Dash of cayenne
Salt, pepper to taste
¼ cup chopped fresh parsley

Combine ingredients, except parsley, and mix well, preferably in an electric blender. When well mixed, stir in parsley. Makes about 1½ cups.

Note: For a thinner dressing, add more lemon juice or a little water.

Albanian Mint Dressing

A perfect dressing for fruit, cottage cheese, mixed green, cucumber, or tomato salads.

> ½ cup chopped fresh mint leaves
> 2 teaspoons sugar
> 2 tablespoons fresh lemon juice
> Salt, pepper to taste
> 1 cup plain yogurt

Crush mint leaves in a small bowl. Mix with sugar, lemon juice, salt, and pepper. Fold in yogurt. Refrigerate 1 hour or longer to blend flavors. Make about 1¼ cups.

Old-fashioned Milk Dressing

Just right for coleslaws.

> ⅔ cup sweetened condensed milk
> ¼ cup salad oil
> 2 tablespoons cider vinegar
> ½ teaspoon dry mustard
> Salt, pepper to taste

Put ingredients in a screw-top jar and shake vigorously to combine well. Refrigerate until ready to use. Shake before using. Makes about 1 cup.

Low-Calorie Tomato Dressing

For cottage cheese, vegetables, and mixed green salads, this dressing won't trouble the conscience of the calorie-conscious.

1 cup tomato juice
2 tablespoons grated onion
2 tablespoons fresh lemon juice
1 teaspoon Worcestershire sauce
½ teaspoon dried basil
Salt, pepper to taste

Combine ingredients and mix well. Refrigerate until ready to use. Makes about 1¼ cups.

German Caper Dressing

A splendid dressing for fish, raw and cooked vegetable salads.

1½ cups sour cream
2 hard-cooked eggs, shelled and chopped
2 teaspoons prepared sharp mustard
1 tablespoon capers, drained
Salt, pepper to taste

Combine ingredients and mix well. Refrigerate 1 hour or longer to blend flavors. Makes about 2 cups.

Turkish Yogurt Dressing

A delightful dressing for fish, poultry, or vegetable salads.

1½ cups plain yogurt
⅓ cup olive or salad oil
3 tablespoons vinegar or lemon juice
½ cup finely chopped, peeled, seeded cucumbers
2 tablespoons minced onion
2 tablespoons chopped fresh dill, mint, or parsley
Salt, pepper to taste

Combine ingredients and mix well. Refrigerate 1 hour or longer to blend flavors. Makes about 2½ cups.

Dilled Buttermilk Dressing

A really good dressing for cottage cheese, tomato, cucumber, or mixed green salads

1 cup buttermilk
3 tablespoons fresh lemon juice
2 tablespoon minced onion
¼ teaspoon dry mustard
½ teaspoon dried dillweed

Combine ingredients and mix well. Refrigerate 1 hour or longer to blend flavors. Makes 1¼ cups.

Caribbean Citrus Dressing

A dressing that's a taste of sunshine for fruit and mixed green salads.

1 cup crushed pineapple
½ cup orange juice
2 tablespoons fresh lime or lemon juice
¾ cup salad oil
Pinch of cayenne
2 tablespoons chopped fresh mint

Combine ingredients and mix well. Refrigerate 1 hour or longer to blend flavors. Makes about 2 cups.

Russian Sour Cream Dressing

An imperial dressing for seafood, poultry, or vegetable salads.

2 hard-cooked eggs, shelled
1 cup sour cream
2 tablespoons vinegar or lemon juice
1 tablespoon drained capers
2 gherkins, minced
Salt, pepper to taste

Sieve egg yolks and blend with sour cream. Chop egg whites and add, with other ingredients, to sour cream mixture. Refrigerate 1 hour or longer to blend flavors. Makes about 2 cups.

Roquefort Cheese Dressing

A luscious dressing for mixed green salads.

½ cup crumbled Roquefort or blue cheese
1 cup sour cream
2 tablespoons red wine vinegar
Cayenne, salt, pepper to taste

Combine ingredients and mix well. Refrigerate 1 hour or longer to blend flavors. Makes about 1½ cups.

Balkan Tomato-Yogurt Dressing

A superior dressing for romaine or other salad greens.

1 medium-sized onion, peeled and chopped
2 medium-sized tomatoes, peeled and chopped
2 garlic cloves, crushed
2 cups plain yogurt or sour cream
½ cup olive or salad oil
¼ cup vinegar
¼ cup chopped fresh parsley
Salt, pepper to taste

Combine ingredients and mix well. Refrigerate 1 hour or longer to blend flavors. Makes about 4 cups.

Curried Dressing Indienne

A dressing for fruit salads, fit for a maharaja.

1 cup mayonnaise
2 tablespoons fresh lemon juice
2 tablespoons curry powder
¼ cup chutney
¼ cup chopped nuts

Combine ingredients and mix well. Refrigerate 1 hour or longer to blend flavors. Makes about 1⅔ cups.

Chinese Sweet-Sour Dressing

Eat like a mandarin with this dressing for raw vegetable salads.

½ cup rice or white wine vinegar
3 tablespoons sesame or salad oil
2 tablespoons soy sauce
1 or 2 tablespoons sugar
½ teaspoon dry mustard
Pepper to taste

Combine ingredients and mix well. Makes about 1 cup.

Peanut-Butter Fruit Dressing

An unforgettable dressing for fruit salads.

½ cup peanut butter
½ cup orange juice
½ cup pineapple juice
3 tablespoons fresh lemon juice
2 tablespoons honey
Salt, pepper to taste

Blend peanut butter with juices until smooth. Add honey, salt and pepper, and mix well. Makes 1⅔ cups.

Bulgarian Walnut Dressing

A dressing you'll serve again and again with raw vegetables.

2 slices white bread, crusts removed
1 cup chopped walnuts
2 garlic cloves, crushed
1 cup olive or salad oil
3 tablespoons lemon juice or vinegar
Dash of cayenne
Salt, pepper to taste

Soak bread in water and squeeze it out. Pound nuts in a mortar with bread and garlic. Slowly mix in oil, beating until thick and smooth. Add remaining ingredients and mix well. Makes about 2½ cups.
Note: Whirl in an electric blender, if desired.

Watercress Dressing

½ *cup chopped fresh watercress leaves, washed and*
  dried
½ *cup sour cream*
2 *tablespoons wine vinegar*
Few drops Tabasco sauce
Salt, pepper to taste

Combine ingredients to mix well. Serve at once or shortly after preparing. Makes 1 cup.

Irish Egg-Sour Cream Dressing

Serve with lettuce, greens, raw cabbage, or cooked beets.

2 *hard-cooked eggs, shelled and chopped*
2 *teaspoons sugar*
1 *teaspoon dry mustard*
1 *tablespoon vinegar*
1 *cup sour cream*
2 *tablespoons chopped fresh dill or parsley*

Combine ingredients and mix well. Refrigerate 1 hour or longer to blend flavors. Makes about 2 cups.

Low-Calorie Cottage Cheese Dressing

A flavorful dressing especially recommended for cooked vegetable and fruit salads.

>   *1 cup cream-style cottage cheese*
>   *½ cup plain yogurt*
>   *2 teaspoons Worcestershire sauce*
>   *Few drops Tabasco sauce*
>   *Salt, pepper to taste*
>   *⅓ cup minced onion*
>   *⅓ cup minced green pepper*

Beat together the first four ingredients. Season with salt and pepper. Mix in remaining ingredients. Refrigerate 1 hour or longer to blend flavors. Makes about 2 cups.

Hungarian Sour Cream Dressing

An excellent dressing for mixed green, vegetable, or fish salads.

>   *1 cup sour cream*
>   *2 tablespoons sliced scallions, with some tops*
>   *2 tablespoons vinegar*
>   *2 tablespoons chopped fresh dill or ½ teaspoon dried*
>   *dillweed*
>   *1 teaspoon sugar*
>   *Salt, pepper to taste*

Combine ingredients and refrigerate 1 hour or longer to blend flavors. Makes about 1¼ cups.

Danish Blue Cheese Dressing

A zesty dressing to serve on lettuce wedges or mixed green salads.

1 cup salad oil
¼ cup wine vinegar or lemon juice
1 teaspoon sugar
½ teaspoon dry mustard
Dash of cayenne
Salt, pepper to taste
⅓ cup crumbled blue cheese

Combine ingredients in a screw-top jar; mix well. Refrigerate 1 hour or longer to blend flavors. Shake before serving. Makes about 1¼ cups.

Shaker Herb Salad Dressing

Especially good for mixed green, vegetable and potato salads.

1 cup salad oil
¼ cup tarragon or other herb vinegar
1 tablespoon minced shallots or scallions
2 tablespoons minced fresh parsley
½ teaspoon dry mustard
Salt, pepper to taste

Combine ingredients in a screw-top jar and mix well. Shake before serving. Makes about 1¼ cups.

Austrian Horseradish Cream Dressing

A marvelous dressing for meat, fish or shellfish salads.

1 cup heavy cream
1 tablespoon fresh lemon juice
2 tablespoons wine vinegar
¼ cup grated fresh horseradish
¼ teaspoon prepared sharp mustard
Salt, pepper to taste

Whip cream until stiff; gradually add lemon juice and vinegar. Fold in remaining ingredients. Serve at once. Makes about 2¼ cups.

Central American Avocado Dressing

This colorful and delicious dressing will enhance mixed green, vegetable or fruit salads.

1 medium-sized ripe avocado
¼ cup minced onions
3 tablespoons minced canned green chili peppers
¼ teaspoon dried oregano
¼ cup salad oil
2 tablespoons fresh lime or lemon juice
Salt, pepper to taste

Peel avocado; remove pit; mash to a pulp with a fork or electric mixer. Add remaining ingredients and blend well. Makes about 1½ cups.

American Tomato Soup Dressing

This is an old-time favorite made with condensed tomato soup. A good dressing for raw or cooked vegetable salads.

1 can (10½ ounces) condensed tomato soup
½ cup salad oil
¼ cup cider vinegar
1 teaspoon dry mustard
½ teaspoon paprika
1 tablespoon sugar
Salt, pepper to taste

Combine ingredients and mix well. Makes about 2¼ cups.

Note: Optional ingredients for this salad dressing include 1 tablespoon minced onion, 1 crushed garlic clove, 2 teaspoons Worcestershire sauce, 1 teaspoon dried herbs, or ½ teaspoon curry powder.

Spanish Herbed Anchovy Dressing

An innovative dressing for pasta, vegetable, or seafood salads.

1 small onion, peeled and minced
2 garlic cloves, minced or crushed
12 flat anchovies, with their oil
¼ teaspoon dried basil, thyme, and oregano
⅓ cup wine vinegar
⅔ cup olive oil
1 teaspoon Worcestershire sauce
Salt, pepper to taste

Put onion, garlic, anchovies and their oil, and herbs in a mortar or bowl and mash with a pestle or wooden spoon. Add remaining ingredients and mix with a fork. Taste before adding salt as anchovies will make the dressing salty. Makes about 1¼ cups.

Pennsylvanian Dutch Hot Salad Dressing

An old-time favorite dressing for coleslaw, mixed green, and cooked vegetable salads.

> *6 thin slices bacon, chopped*
> *1 cup water*
> *2 tablespoons vinegar*
> *2 tablespoons sugar*
> *2 eggs*
> *1 teaspoon all-purpose flour*
> *Salt, pepper to taste*

Fry bacon in a medium skillet until crisp. Remove bacon and drain on paper toweling. Spoon out some of bacon grease leaving 3 tablespoons grease in skillet. Combine remaining ingredients and add to heated grease. Cook over low heat, stirring, until thickened and smooth. Add to salad and sprinkle with bacon. Makes about 1½ cups.

Index